The Kinds of Things

The Kinds of Things

A Theory of Personal Identity Based on Transcendental Argument

FREDERICK C. DOEPKE

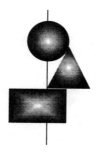

OPEN COURT
Chicago and La Salle, Illinois

Open Court Trade and Academic Books is a division of Carus Publishing Company.

© 1996 by Carus Publishing Company

First printing 1996

Printed and bound in the United States of America.

Library of Congress Cataloging-in-Publication Data

Doepke, Frederick C.
    The kinds of things : a theory of personal identity based on
transcendental argument / Frederick C Doepke.
        p.   cm.
    Includes bibliographical references (p.   ) and index.
    ISBN 0–8126–9319–1 (alk. paper). — ISBN 0–8126–9320–5 (pbk. :
alk. paper).
    1. Self (Philosophy)   2. Identity (Psychology)   3. Identity.
4. Transcendental logic.   5. Kant, Immanuel, 1724–1804.   6. Hume,
David, 1711–1776.   I. Title.
    BD450.D63   1996
    126—dc20
                                                                    96-9228
                                                                        CIP

To my parents,
Frederick and Marjorie

Contents

Preface

The main purpose of this book is to provide an account of our identity. It is especially concerned to decide between what John Rawls has called the Humean and the Kantian conceptions of the self. This difference is associated with different ethical orientations. The Kantian view takes seriously our identity over time, just as Kantian ethics takes seriously our responsibility for the things we have done in the past. Derek Parfit has defended the Humean view. This book defends the Kantian one.

I have titled the book "The Kinds of Things" to call attention to its devotion to more general metaphysical issues. Since an account of our identity will apply the concept of identity to ourselves, it is better supported by a theory of how to re-identify things of other kinds as well. A number of books on the subject have already been written on the same conviction. This book differs from most of them in its resolve not to rely on the metaphysics of ordinary thought. We commonly think of the things around us, and ourselves, as objects which persist undiminished through relatively long stretches of time. Hume, however, like Heraclitus and Buddha, denied this degree of permanence; and Hume's attitude towards persistence is reflected in his view of the self. Since the Humean is not wedded to our common metaphysics, we cannot hope to settle our main issue by a "descriptive" metaphysics which is content merely to lay bare how we ordinarily think of ourselves and other things.

To avoid begging the question against the Humean, we must not merely rely upon, but must defend, the metaphysics of persistence in which the Kantian view finds its home. As I explain in the first chapter, we cannot, therefore, resort to the orthodox "method of cases," which hopes to gather and systematize our linguistic intuitions concerning identity; these are bound only to reflect, and not to support, our common metaphysics. My alternative is to follow a roughly Kantian strategy.

Arguments are called "transcendental" insofar as they resemble those for which Kant is famous. As I understand them, such arguments attempt to show consequences of premises which are, in some relevant way, unavoidable. It is controversial whether they are effective against traditional forms of skepticism. But that is immaterial to me, since I put them to a different use. Since we are concerned to justify a view of what we are, the idea that can justify our views forms for us a non-arbitrary starting point. To the best of my knowledge, this book is unique in offering a theory of personal identity based on transcendental argument. The virtue of this approach, I believe, is that it offers a level of justification which is deep enough to refute alternative metaphysical outlooks such as the Humean adopts.

I do not assume, without argument, that the metaphysical question of our identity is practically important. In Chapter 3 I argue that we cannot avoid having intentions and desires which are expressed by I-thoughts; in Chapter 2 I argue that such thoughts belong to only one thing. Together these chapters show that it is not trivial to think that persons who are distinct from me cannot really carry out my decisions or fulfill desires involving myself. The boundaries of our existence circumscribe the reach of our will and limit our hopes for the future. This shows something of the importance of our death.

The transcendental arguments unfold in stages. In Chapter 4, I argue in favor of the reality of persistence by showing that "continuants," which genuinely persist through time, are epistemically primary. Having seen in Chapter 2 that individuation terminates in self-awareness, we see that we are among these epistemically primary things, so that whatever principle of identity applies to these things will apply to us. Chapter 5 exploits and develops Ross Harrison's account of judgment to show that we are justified in applying the concept of identity to these first things in order to apply rules which enable us to confirm our empirical judgments. Chapter 6 explains how our Kantian epistemology leads to an Aristotelian metaphysics: the identity of each of our primary things is determined by how it tends to contribute to its own future. Although Chapter 6 also explains how this conception is far from vacuous in settling questions of identity, it is not clear enough to determine in a specific case whether a certain tendency of this kind is truly determinative of identity. The next two chapters develop a theory for answering this question for our primary things in general. Chapter 7 presents a conceptual framework for thinking of substantial change and accordingly of the "constitution" relation which obtains between a thing and its "matter." Chapter 8 applies to this the previous results so that we are able to tell in many cases whether a change is truly substantial or is merely an alteration, and so whether a property is possessed essentially or accidentally. In Chapter 9 this more general account of how to determine questions of identity is applied to the question of personal identity. By taking seriously questions of justification we find strong support for the view of Kant and common sense that in normal human life even changes in deeply held affections and ideals do not erode the basis of our identity. Since it is not as if we "die a bit" through these changes, anticipating them should not diminish our hopes or our sense of responsibility.

Over the years in which I have worked on this project I have benefited especially from conversations, in person or in writing, with Charles Chihara, Timothy Gould, (the late) Paul Grice, Richard Haynes, Mark Hinchliff, Charles Jarrett, Richard Mendelsohn, (the late) George Myro, Stephen Schiffer, Peter Simons, Barry Smith, Barry Stroud, Stephen Tighe, David Warner, and David Wiggins. I was aided by release from some of my teachings duties, from time to time, by Larry Johnson and by Stephen Benson. And I was encouraged and indulged by Denise Doepke, and by my children, Eric and Drake. My warmest thanks to you all.

1

Introduction:
What Are We?

What are we? It is true that we are members of a certain biological species and that we can reason and think and feel. But to say what we are, in the sense in which we will understand the notion, is not merely to describe us. It is to indicate the conditions under which it would be the very same individual who is being described.[1] I came from a certain fertilized egg: but was that egg *me*? When my cerebrum dies, so that I can no longer think, could *I* still be there? If after the death of my body a person just like me is created, perhaps by God or advanced scientists, would that person really be *me*? If I were to suffer complete

---

1. Although the conception of what we are as being a matter of our identity is a familiar one in metaphysics, it can be argued that this conception might be artificially restricted. The traditional conception of what something is, or what is essential to a thing, is that it provides a fundamental basis from which the other properties of a thing can be explained. Such a basis would explain, among other things, the identity of the thing in question, but it may be possible that a conception which is adequate to explain its identity would be inadequate to explain some of its other properties. One thing that seems to constitute a special problem for the idea that a thing's identity is what it is to be that thing is the fact that the identity of the thing might well be describable in terms which are inadequate to explain the subjectivity of the mind. On this problem, see Nagel 1986, especially pages 51–53. Since Nagel holds that there are subjective phenomena (such as the experiences associated with the sonar systems of bats) which we could never understand, his view appears to have the extraordinary consequence that we could never really fathom "what are," in the traditional sense, the creatures (such as the bats) in whom these phenomena occur.

As Wiggins explains (in Wiggins 1980), the question of what *x* is contrasts with the

and irreparable amnesia and afterwards a person in my body were to develop, with a different personality and character, would *that* person be me? And if not, can we say, without any sense of strain, that I can survive radical *changes* in personality and character?

These are examples of the question of "personal identity." Although I first put the question in the plural, by asking what "we" are, it is best put in the first person singular. One reason for this is that we want to be open to the fact that there might be different answers for different groups of people. It might turn out, for example, that members of different species or sexes have different "identity conditions," even if there is some generic account which covers them all. There is another reason for favoring the first person formulation, however, which brings out the special difficulty of the whole problem. In the case of anything other than myself it is at least doubtful that I can really succeed in picking it out from its environment without a general conception of its identity conditions. When thinking of "this dog," for example, I cannot be agnostic about such issues as whether it is the sort of thing which persists beyond this moment or simultaneously exists in other places. For how would my thought in such a case be distinct from a thought about a momentary event occurring in the same place or a universal such as the canine species? But I can think of myself in the first person (expressible by "I," "me," "my," and so forth) merely by noticing that I am currently in certain states. I know now, for example, that I am seeing a computer, sitting up and deciding to strike the keys. These facts describe me in the present circumstances. But it is not at all clear how they dictate in which other circumstances I have existed or will exist. It is for this reason that philosophers say that we can

---

question of what x is like, and this distinction harks back to Aristotle's distinction between secondary substances (species and genera), which Aristotle said "reveal" the thing in question, and other properties, such as its qualities and quantities, which otherwise characterize it (see Aristotle 1941a). It is very important, as I emphasize throughout this chapter, not to confuse the question of what we are in this sense with the question, which is of course of great interest in its own right, of what is involved in being a person, in the sense of having such psychological and moral properties as being rational, self-aware, and free. The relation between these two questions is explored throughout this book, especially in the first three chapters and the last. I believe that those philosophers who think that they can "read off" a metaphysics of personal identity from their psychological and moral convictions about what is involved in being a person fail to distinguish these questions properly, or fail to offer an adequate defense of how their view of the metaphysics of persons, so derived, is to fit into an overall metaphysics.

think of ourselves (in the first person) "without a criterion." The whole issue is to justify the choice of one "criterion" over another, one account of the conditions under which it would be *me* in those (described) circumstances other than the present.

To describe me as I am in all of my (possible) circumstances is to say what is "essential" to me. This contrasts with an "accidental" description which indicates only how I am in certain circumstances. I now know that I am seeing the computer, sitting up and striking the keys and I think of these states as "accidents" of mine, since I think that I enjoy an existence outside the present circumstances, in which I do not have these states. To ask for my identity conditions is to ask for something even more informative than a statement of what is essential to me. It is *necessary* for something to be me that it possess my essential properties; it is both necessary and *sufficient* for something to be me that it satisfy my identity conditions. In wondering what a thing is metaphysicians are particularly interested in the identity conditions of the thing in question, since these provide an especially informative conception of that thing.[2]

No doubt the most compelling reason for why I think that I exist outside the present circumstances is that I have memories of past events involving myself. It seems, in fact, rather obvious that I have a good deal of knowledge about my identity, since I actually remember myself as having been involved in a certain stream of circumstances leading up to the present and of such a nature as to point to a certain kind of possible future. And when I think of what gives this stream its characteristic direction through time it seems equally obvious that this is due to its association with a certain biological entity which I call "my body." What has struck philosophers who are interested in the question of personal identity is that these different sorts of considerations seem not to be necessarily connected. They have observed, at least in imagined cases, a conflict between "psychological" and "physical" criteria of identity. This conflict is illustrated in the questions with which we began. The fertilized egg from which I came seems to be my own body in its first stage, but since I have no memory or mental life

2. In equating essential properties with necessary ones I am following current usage. The search for identity conditions is thus the search for what Aristotle would call the essence (the what it is to be) of the thing.

3

at this stage it is not clear that it is really me. The same problem presents itself after the death of my cerebrum and after complete and irreparable amnesia. Again we seem to have the same body but owing to the break in psychology not obviously the same person. And it is this realization which opens up the possibility that when a person has changed a great deal mentally it may be somewhat trivial to insist upon personal identity even when there is plainly the same biological organism present. On the other hand, the case of replicating a person's body down to the finest detail seems to present a case in which mentality can be preserved in a different body; a psychological criterion suggests that the person has merely switched bodies, whereas a physical criterion suggests that a mentally similar but distinct person has been created.

Accounts of personal identity which favor the psychological are called "Lockean," owing to John Locke's insistence that the issue is decided by "sameness of consciousness" alone.[3] If the present mayor of Queenborough were to have the memories of Socrates, then, according to Locke, he would be "the same person," though not the same man. Locke had an argument for this view: "since consciousness always accompanies thinking, and 'tis that, that makes every one to be, what he calls *self*; and thereby distinguishes himself from all other thinking things, in this alone consists *personal identity*, i.e., sameness of a rational Being: And as far as this consciousness can be extended backwards to any past Action or Thought, so far reaches the Identity of that *person*..."[4] Locke is famous for employing the strategy of trying to see how to apply an idea correctly by tracing it to its source, which, for him, would have to reside either in sensation or in reflection upon one's own mind. To see how to apply the concept of the self, or the related concept of being the same self, we should accordingly try to see where we "get" the idea. Now Locke's claim is that we get the idea primarily through the fact that when we exercise the power of reflection we are directly aware of present states of consciousness, and the self is just that which possesses these and is so aware of them. We see in the fact that our present states of consciousness are each known directly how to apply the concept of the self, and since we

---

3. Locke 1975, pp. 335–36.
4. Ibid., p. 39.

apply them all to the same self, we see most clearly how to apply the concept of the same self. But then we see also that in memory we are presented with past experiences in the same, direct way; and since we are supposed to learn how to apply an idea like that of the identity of the self by seeing where we "get" it, and we "get" this one by ascribing directly known mental states to one thing, the conclusion is that our identity into the past is known precisely by how far this same kind of direct, introspective awareness will reach. For Locke, therefore, we may say that the concept of the self already contains certain identity conditions. The problem of personal identity is that of saying what are the identity conditions of that thing of which I think when I ascribe certain properties to it by having I-thoughts, the sort of thoughts which I have when I understand my own use of first person pronouns ("I," "me," "mine," and so forth). Locke's solution holds that this mode of thinking of something carries with it the implication that the thing satisfies certain identity conditions, specifically (and not surprisingly), ones that are stated in mental terms.

Although it is difficult to believe that my memories provide no evidence of my identity at other times, the flaw in Locke's argument was realized by Kant, who observed that consciousness could be passed along a series of subjects as motion is transferred from one billiard ball to another.[5] It is just such a possibility that philosophers envisage today in the destruction of a person's body and its perfect replication. The replica would seem to remember the past life of the original just as the mayor of Queenborough would seem to remember the life of Socrates. To say that the replica would be a distinct person, however, may appear to beg the question against Locke. But suppose now that the first body is not destroyed and the second is created like a shadow of the first. Now it does not look as if the first person has switched bodies since the first body is still around. And yet from the first-person point of view of the second person it will seem as if he is the first person just as surely as it does to the first person at the later time. This shows that the concept of the self contains at most apparent conditions of identity and that these appearances can be deceiving.

It may seem that Locke himself anticipated Kant, since he allowed

---

5. Kant 1968, A 362–66 (especially the footnote).

that consciousness could be preserved even through a switch of think-ing substances.[6] It seems clear to me, however, that what Locke is say-ing is that even in such a case there would be the same person even though there would not be the same thinking substance, so that in this sense of "thinking substance" we would not be thinking sub-stances, or we would be a different kind of one. What Kant envisages is a case in which it is *not* the same person—there is a series of numerically distinct persons—even though from the first person point of view of the second it seems as if this is not true. What Locke main-tains is the *sufficiency* of this point of view for determining personal identity: if the mayor seems to remember Socrates's life then he really does so, since it really was *he* living back then (even though there was not the same biological entity).[7] Locke's account is extreme in favor-ing a psychological criterion to the complete exclusion of the physi-cal. It is, however, of the utmost importance to Kant to disagree with Locke on precisely this issue. For Locke's account represents a form of just that "transcendent metaphysics" which Kant had been at pains to refute as unknowable. Understanding Kant's point will help us to see something important about how to answer the question of our identity.

Although there are aspects of Kant's position which are notoriously obscure, we can focus usefully on certain claims that are clear and, I believe, correct. For convenience of expression let us call "self-awareness" that special kind of awareness of oneself that one has with I-thoughts. And let us follow Locke in calling a "person"

---

6. Locke 1975, p 337. It does seem just this way to both Nagel and Parfit. See Nagel 1986, p. 33 and Parfit 1984, p. 223.

7. Against my interpretation it could be held (with much textual evidence) that personal "identity" is not, for Locke, a form of *numerical* identity: it would be instead a relation which can relate a thing to either itself or to a different thing by virtue of a psychological connection. Nagel seems to attribute such a position to Locke (Ibid.). If this were correct, virtually the entire literature which Locke's discussion has spawned would be mistaken in taking personal identity to be a form of numerical identity. Locke would also have clearly announced that the whole discussion is about the numerical identity of things of various kinds (e.g., God, plants, animals, and artifacts) and then, with no warning, would have introduced "personal identity" as another kind of rela-tion. Nor would any of his various examples allow us to discern that such a change of subject had occurred. Even if this is Locke's position, it is still crucially different from Kant's. For in a case in which consciousness is "passed" from one thing to another Locke would then *not* say that although there appears to the later person that there is one person there "really" are two persons. Our next chapter argues that, as Locke is standardly interpreted to think, personal identity is a form of numerical identity.

anyone capable of such awareness. Although this is not always how the term "person" is used, it is useful for us since our main question pertains to the identity of persons in this sense. Now, there is good reason for thinking that persons must be capable of having more than one I-thought and realize that they do. This is because the "I" applies to a subject of predication to which it must be possible to ascribe various predicates. Without realizing that various predicates can be applied to the same thing, the "I" would not be an informative part of the thoughts. And as Locke pointed out, sometimes the plurality of I-thoughts enables us to view our own identity through time, as when I both see a computer and remember hearing the phone ring; and sometimes they give us a view of our identity at the present moment, as when I both see and feel a pen. Even if I describe only my current subjective point of view, by thinking, for example, that I now seem to remember a phone ring, that I seem to see a computer, and that it feels to me that I am upright, so long as I am entertaining a plurality of I-thoughts I am committing myself to the identity of the subject of those thoughts. And as we have seen, it is necessary for self-awareness that one can have such a plurality of I-thoughts; hence, self-awareness requires that one can make at least implicitly the claim of personal identity. What Kant wants above all is to refute a form of skepticism in which one claims knowledge of one's current subjective state while denying knowledge of an objective world in which the subject exists, as one object among others. Although Kant is willing to allow that there might be an objective world other than the physical world of objects in space (the sort of world, for example, that God would know), he thinks it is evident that for us to know ourselves objectively is to know ourselves as physical objects. This means that I cannot know that I am the same subject who possesses the states which I ascribe to myself in self-awareness unless I acknowledge my existence as a physical object. I cannot, for example, take the stance of Descartes, early in his meditations, who claims to realize that he is the same thing which imagines and perceives and remembers merely from the fact that he is directly aware of the relevant I-thoughts, while remaining agnostic about the physical world. I take Kant's example of the billiard balls to show that the variety of I-thoughts necessary for self-awareness *could* belong to different subjects, different persons.

The point is not merely that Descartes has knowledge of his identity which is corrigible, but that he really has no such knowledge at all. The *mere* fact that I have various thoughts which seem all to be mine shows only the *appearance* of my identity; but I can know what my identity *really* is only if I have access to more, an additional perspective by which I can verify (or refute) this appearance.[8] Again, for us, this will only be if I can know myself as a physical being.

It is not difficult to see how the recourse to our physical status can help to establish the identity of the subject of various I-thoughts. Let us suppose again that I am agnostic about the physical world and think only that I seem to remember a phone ring, seem to see a computer and feel that I am upright. The challenge of Kant is to defend the implication that these are all states of the same thing, and without access to more than my subjective perspective I have no reason to think this. But now let us suppose that I am less cautious, as I usually am, and interpret these experiences as being veridical perceptions of the physical world. By thinking of myself as a certain physical object, spatially removed from a phone and a computer, and having a certain (upright) orientation, I do have reason to think of the experiences as belonging to the same person. My conception of myself as a certain physical object forms a kind of *theory* to which I can appeal to explain why these various states which I know from direct introspection *appear* to go together *really* do. Of course it might happen that some of my experiences are not veridical perceptions of the physical world in which I exist as one such object among others, but unless I presume that this is false in general, I cannot know of my identity.

It can easily seem that it is impossible that several of my I-thoughts belong to different subjects. Roderick Chisholm mentions approvingly a discussion of Brentano's supposed to show that there can be no such possibility, so that I have certain knowledge of my identity as the subject of such states.[9] Brentano imagines a person who is both seeing and hearing and is aware that he is. But if we suppose that there is one subject who is seeing and another who is hearing, where, Brentano

---

8. Nagel argues for such a possibility from Wittgenstein's view that even psychological concepts (such as that of the self) must have objective criteria of application (Nagel 1986, pp. 32-43).

9. Chisholm 1981, pp. 87-88.

asks, do we find the subject who perceives the simultaneity of the two perceptions? Finding absurd the idea that this subject could be either of the first two, Brentano rejects the possibility in question. Now let us consider how things are from the person's point of view when he reflects on his own mind and thinks that he is simultaneously seeing and hearing. It is important to realize that in this very thought the subject is really only ascribing one predicate to himself, that in which, as Brentano says, he realizes that he perceives the simultaneity of the two sensory experiences. It is difficult to see, however, how the two sensory experiences could themselves belong to different subjects. For surely, one is tempted to side with Brentano and say that the only way the subject can perceive the simultaneity of the two sensory experiences is by having it look and sound a certain way to him, and that is all that there *is* to having two sensory experiences. And so it seems that he cannot know that he is in one state (of perceiving the simultaneity) without also knowing that he is in two more. But if this is so, then he has some knowledge of which thing he is which he gets from the purely subjective point of view and Kant (as I have represented him) is wrong.

Let us grant what seems undeniable: that there is such a state of reflection in which one thinks that one is simultaneously seeing and hearing, and that to anyone in that state it will look and sound certain ways as well. Now ordinarily anyone who thinks he is in such a state will know much about himself other than that he is in this state. And if he must use such additional knowledge to realize that he is in several distinct states, then Brentano (and Chisholm) are wrong to think that he gets knowledge of his identity merely by realizing that he is in the state of reflection in question. I now see my computer and hear a hammer in the distance and I realize that my visual and auditory experiences are both occurring now. But I am able to think of these as distinct experiences because I know what it is like to have either without the other. When I use this knowledge to distinguish the experiences I ascribe other properties to myself, by thinking, for example, that I would hear that hammer even if I my eyes were closed. If I had no such additional knowledge, or no conscious access to it, I would have no basis for distinguishing aspects or elements of my total present experience. Kant makes just this point when he says that "each representation, in so far as it is contained in a single moment, can never be anything but absolute unity."[10] We can allow that Brentano's subject has knowledge of how it appears to him in the present moment, but if we deny him other knowledge of himself, the various aspects of his experience will blend into one gestalt for him. In realizing that he has this one gestalt-like property, the subject will have a genuine I-thought. This being so, there is a sense in which he knows "which" thing he is, since anyone knows of which thing he is thinking whenever he successfully ascribes a property to one thing. But he will know nothing substantive about his identity, nothing about the kind of thing he is. To dramatize the point, notice that, for all he knows, he could be a momentarily existing Cartesian soul or Spinoza's God, the whole of nature. After all, either could have such a property.[11] To know of my identity I must have knowledge of myself which rules out such alternatives. Since what appears to me now is by itself only a gestalt, what Kant calls "absolute unity," I cannot know of my identity from the way things appear in current introspection.

Although it has been obvious to students of Kant that he is aiming at skepticism about the external world, I want to make clear that his objection applies to Locke's account of personal identity. It must apply, since even though Locke was himself no such skeptic, his account of personal identity could easily be accepted by one. Descartes, for example, in his early meditations (before he discovers the external world through God's good graces), need not object to Locke's account. In fact he seems to subscribe to just such an idea since he takes the appearance of his identity in memory as showing his identity through time even while he supposes that he might be only a disembodied mind. What neither Locke nor Descartes sees is the sort of challenge raised by Kant's example, the possibility of the various I-thoughts in question belonging to different persons. If it were not for this possibility, if we could know our identity as they thought, then we could know that reality contains certain identifiable things without having to know them as members of the physical world. But it is just such knowledge

10. Kant 1968, A99.
11. Recall that Spinoza's God, though "really" impersonal, still possesses consciousness "under the aspect of duration," since it has modes, such as persons, which appear to be conscious.

that Kant denies in order to refute "transcendent metaphysics," the attempt to know what reality contains beyond that which comprises this physical world. That is, Kant denies transcendent metaphysics by arguing that it is impossible, that the only reality we can know is physical. But if the concept of self-awareness contained, as Locke thought, identity conditions of a certain kind, then we would *know* our identity by being self-aware *even* if we were merely disembodied minds. Notice that Kant does not rule out the possibility that we are such minds. His attack against the skeptic consists in linking two kinds of knowledge claims, in particular, the claim that we know our identity with the claim that we know ourselves as physical objects. Since Locke's account of personal identity permits the absence of this link, Kant must reject it.

I have discussed Kant's position at some length since I think it shows decisively why a tempting view of answering the question of our identity, one which in fact tempted Locke, is mistaken. Kant's own position on our question is obscured, however, by the lack of clarity interpreters find in the way he distinguishes appearance from reality. Karl Ameriks, for example, interprets Kant as skeptical about our ability to know our *real* identity since this would be to know ourselves as "things in themselves," not necessarily restricted to the physical world.[12] I want now to announce an assumption that is both anti-skeptical and empiricist (in a broad sense) and will very much guide the rest of this work. I will assume that we can know the conditions of our identity and I will assume that these are conditions of ourselves as physical beings, expressible, therefore, in empirically ascertainable terms. The second assumption follows from the first by the sort of consideration urged by Kant. Since the merely subjective point of view does not in itself reveal our identity we must have access to more than this perspective, which is, therefore, an objective perspective. And I follow Kant in thinking that it is evident that we achieve this perspective by conceiving of ourselves as physical objects, in space.

What, then, is there to say in favor of the substantive assumption that our identity is knowable by us? I have nothing really to say except that it allows us to go on. Our main question is that of our

---

12. Ameriks 1982, Ch. IV.

identity. When we ask any question, we assume that it can be answered, and to do this so as to resolve controversy we must supply reasons. So, in asking our question we assume that we can justify an account of our identity. Perhaps this is mistaken. But if it is, it would seem at this point to be due to a very general fact about reality and our inability to access it that would leave us knowing very little.

To see how substantive is our assumption of "empiricist" justification, notice that it already rules out the "Simple View" of our identity that is espoused today especially by Richard Swinburne and is traditionally associated with Descartes.[13] Swinburne emphasizes that there is a distinction between the evidence that we have for our identity and what determines our identity. He admits that all that we have in evidence of our identity are such matters as memory and bodily continuity, but to suppose that these determine our identity is to confuse what we use to *tell* if identity is present with what *makes* it present. His own view is "simple" in that it holds that what makes us identical with a person in other circumstances is simply our identity. He rejects what he calls the "empiricist" assumption that we are able to state what determines our identity in empirically ascertainable terms. To rebut this assumption he refers repeatedly to the *logical* possibility that our identity is not really as we think it is when we appeal to empirical data. Consider the imaginary case of personal "fission," conceived by analogy with the fission of amoeba. Suppose that the brain can be divided in two so that two psychologically indistinguishable persons result. The idea that neither is identical with the original is based on the fact that there would be no empirical way of telling which one is. According to the Simple View, this ignores the (logical) possibility that one of the latter persons still *is* the original.

It is remarkable how little metaphysics can be done by considerations of logical necessity and possibility alone. It seems logically possible, for example, that every one of "my" mental states really belongs to a different immaterial person. For how could reflection on what it is to be a mental state show that these very states I know in introspection are in the same subject? It also seems possible that to every belief there corresponds its own reality, so that people who seem to disagree

_____
13. Shoemaker 1984.

are really thinking of different worlds. So what if this would make reasoning about the truth of our beliefs impossible? Maybe reality is not accessible by reasoning. How does one deal with such logical possibilities, but by assuming an anti-skeptical attitude? Once we make this assumption we may look for necessities in metaphysics which are weaker than logical but stronger than physical. Lewis Carroll's example of the cat-less grin illustrates this level of "metaphysical" necessity. A state or aspect of a thing, such as the grin on a cat, cannot exist independently of the thing in which it "inheres." But the idea that it could is not self-contradictory; nor is it the business of physics to rule it out. Now, I admit that the Simple View might—logically—be true, just as I admit that there might—logically—be cat-less grins. By assuming that our identity is knowable, we hope to find what is *metaphysically* necessary about our identity.[14]

In light of our new assumption that we can know of our identity and the Kantian argument that this involves knowing ourselves as physical objects, it may seem that the question of our identity is answered. For it may seem obvious that the physical object by which I know of my identity is just my body. The problem with this idea is that the sense of "body" which is thus introduced is far too vague to answer the sorts of questions regarding our identity which are asked today. Is "this body" identical with the fertilized egg from which it grew? If the answer seem clear, it is because we are thinking of this body as "this biological entity." And while this may seem natural, it is not a conclusion which would be accepted by many who favor a psychological criterion. Although the Kantian lesson that we know our identity only by knowing ourselves as physical is surely important, to appreciate how unspecific it is, I will describe two views of our identity which both acknowledge this general point, but which differ in ways which will concern us a great deal in the following.

Derek Parfit has defended a Lockean view, in the broad sense that it favors a psychological criterion.[15] For him, personal identity is determined in large part by "psychological continuity," a relation that obtains by any series of "psychological connections," such as preserv-

14. This does not mean that we claim to establish our account with Cartesian certainty.

15. Parfit 1984, Part Three.

ing a belief or desire or carrying out an intention. A bodily consideration is made only by the stipulation that this relation not "branch." The need for this is due to the apparent fact that a person can be psychologically continuous with each of two future persons. The classic case of this involves personal fission, mentioned above, which is supposedly effected by carefully separating the two hemispheres of a person's brain, so that each carries on the mental life of the original person.[16] This enormously troubling case involves Kant's insight, in that from the point of view of each "offshoot," it will seem that he or she is identical with the original person. But obviously both of them cannot be the same person. What Parfit maintains is that we determine personal identity by determining psychological continuity and then consulting physical evidence to make sure that branching has not occurred.

David Wiggins represents the other extreme of favoring a physical criterion.[17] Simply put, he disagrees with Locke by saying that sameness of person is determined by sameness of "man." Even if the mayor of Queenborough did seem to remember all of Socrates's life, he would be a different person because he would be a different human being: a different biological entity. What Wiggins maintains in effect is that "my body," in the sense that is supposed to help me iden-

---

16. In Chapter 3 I argue against the claim of Parfit that in fission the mental life of the original is carried on in the minds of the offshoots on the ground that personal identity is necessary for psychological continuity. This undermines his argument that identity is "not what matters." So, I am assuming that the offshoots of fission are two persons distinct from the original and that each possesses the mental abilities to make it seem (at least while in ignorance of the fission) that he is identical with the original. In Hirsch 1991, Eli Hirsch denies both of these assumptions. On the assumption which he thinks (incorrectly, I believe) that he shares with Parfit, that in fission there is one person throughout but two streams of consciousness, he poses difficulties in how in each stream of thought the same person is to understand his own thoughts. From these problems he concludes that the streams of consciousness would not carry on the mental life of the original, thus attempting in his own way to refute Parfit's argument. Notice, first, that whereas Hirsch attempts only to refute Parfit's argument, I attempt to refute the conclusion itself. Second, I make the assumptions I do about fission only in order to illustrate a case in which—as Parfit intends it—there is a loss of identity even though it seems to the "copies" that there is not. Even if Hirsch is right about the way fission actually takes place in humans, surely Parfit's argument could be launched with respect to another example, such as the case in which an exact replica is produced without disturbing the original person or his body. From the point of view of the replica (at least in ignorance of his origin) it will seem that he is the original. Parfit can then argue just as before, that his relation to the replica is insignificantly different from his relation to his own self. For the details of this argument, see Chapter 3.

17. Wiggins 1980, Ch. 6, "Personal Identity."

tify myself, really is this organism. This leads him to say, among other things, that we can survive even complete and irreparable amnesia.[18] If I were permanently to lose not only my conscious memories but also all acquired dispositions of character, personality and skill, and my body were to be revitalized in Afghanistan, becoming that of an Afghan rebel, Wiggins would say that the rebel is me, despite the complete break in psychology. Yet the psychological still plays a role in Wiggins's account. The plausibility of the fact that it is the biological entity which sees, imagines, thinks, and otherwise bears the mental states is certainly a large part of why Wiggins chooses it as "the body" with which to identify the person. But just as Parfit pays only the slightest respect to the physical consideration with his "non-branching" criterion, Wiggins downplays the importance of the psychological. It is clear that the admission that we are physical beings is vague enough to permit very different accounts of our identity.

How should we decide between such accounts? I want to propose a certain method for deciding more sharply the kind of physical things we are, the adoption of which will be the most distinctive feature of this work. We have arrived at the point that our question is in effect how to apply the concept of identity to ourselves (as physical things) in the interpretation of relevant empirical data. But what justifies applying the concept of identity at all? By seeing how to apply the concept in the first place we may hope to see more clearly how to apply it in specific instances. This general strategy is analogous to one that is familiar in ethics. To resolve a disagreement over what action is right or what consequences are good one might try to show what is the general justification for applying such concepts at all. Thus an effective argument for Utilitarianism or The Categorical Imperative might well be enlisted to resolve particular ethical issues. But to make sense of this whole strategy, we must understand what would be involved in not applying the concept in question at all, so that we can see the effect of introducing it in general. In ethics one might initially take the stance of the moral skeptic and then argue that the concept of moral right or good has some general rationale. For us to adopt this same kind of strategy we must understand what it would be like not

---

18. Ibid., pp. 176–78.

to apply the concept of identity at all. We will see how this can be done in light of important work, done especially by Peter Strawson. In the next chapter I will argue that we are among the first things to which the concept of identity will be applied in the interpretation of experience, so that whatever general rationale for applying the concept at all will pertain somehow to ourselves. In the fourth chapter I will argue slightly more specifically that this first application will be to "continuants," which genuinely persist through time, thereby claiming to have established that we are continuants. We have seen already, however, that we know how to identify ourselves only by seeing ourselves as physical objects, and thus as members of a larger system of such objects. To defend the application of identity to ourselves as such objects will therefore go hand in hand with the application of the concept to other things, including things of other kinds. This means that our account of personal identity will have to be couched within a more general ontology of physical objects. Since this is a highly controversial (though not unique) way of approaching the question, let me repeat what motivates it. Our hope is to justify applying the concept of identity to ourselves by seeing how to apply it in the first place; but because we will know this with regard to ourselves only by seeing ourselves as members of a larger physical system, we will need to know how to apply the concept more generally. The fifth chapter presents an account of what justifies applying the concept of identity in the first place. The sixth chapter extracts from this general rationale a generic conception of the identities of the physical objects with which we find ourselves in interaction. By developing this generic conception in the following two chapters our account is able to offer solutions to a host of problems in current analytical metaphysics. In the final chapter we see how, in this developed form, it is sharp enough to yield an account of our identity.

Since other authors have felt the need to address more general questions of ontology in dealing with the question of personal identity, I have not said what is unique about the method we will adopt for this purpose. Transcendental arguments, as I understand them, begin with some assumption which is, in some relevant way, unavoidable, and draw out from this a desired conclusion. Although the whole argument thus takes the form of merely a conditional, the conclusion is supposedly forced on us by the unavoidability of granting the starting point. In ethics one might, for example, begin with the assumption that one has good reason to do something or other, and then derive from this one's favored general principle of morality.[19] The idea would be that anyone who wonders what to do is assuming that a good reason to do something can be found; this being so, anyone who bothers to see the strength of the transcendental argument will thereby grant the truth of its conclusion. We will make an analogous assumption. Although I said at first that we will assume that we can know the conditions of our identity, this would be to assume in effect that we are justified in applying the concept of identity. But since we will try to see how to apply the concept to ourselves by seeing more generally how to apply it in the first place, our transcendental arguments will make a more fundamental assumption than that we can know our identity. Following Ross Harrison, we will (in the fifth chapter) assume only that we can make true judgments, specifically empirical judgments, and I will argue that this requires applying the concept of identity. It is this argument which will support the generic conception of the identity conditions of the physical objects of our ontology. This conception will be, in fact, recognizably Aristotelian.[20] For the identity over time of our objects is determined by an essential tendency, distinctive of their kind, to contribute to their own future states. What they *are* is a matter of what they naturally tend to *do*. To fit an account of personal identity into this framework I will argue (in the last chapter) that our identity is determined largely by the fact that we have a tendency to make decisions, both theoretical and practical, presumed to be based on reasons. It will be in this sense that we are "essentially" rational beings. But I hold that this psychological criterion only

---

19. Alan Gewirth adopts such a strategy in Gewirth 1978.

20. Terence Irwin has thoroughly explained how Aristotle himself uses transcendental arguments to support his metaphysics (see Irwin 1988). But by his account, Aristotle begins with the assumption that "we speak of some persisting bearer of properties" (Ibid., p. 270). This means that he starts with the assumption in which the concept of identity is already being applied. Irwin clearly acknowledges this when he allows that Aristotle's conclusions can be avoided by the skeptic who adopts a property-instance language in which the subject-predicate distinction is not drawn (Ibid., p. 188). Our transcendental arguments will start from such an "identity-free" level in order to see what justifies introducing the concept of identity in the first place. For a penetrating discussion of how our approach is more Kantian and how this differs from an Aristotelian one, see Thompson 1983.

"largely" determines our identity, because, like Wiggins, I will make more of the fact that we are publicly observable physical objects than most authors do. If successful, this will show how a "Kantian" epistemological method leads to an "Aristotelian" metaphysics and account of persons (in senses of these terms which are not broad). And it will give to transcendental arguments a new application which, if successful, will provide a very deep justification for an account of our identity.

I have said, then, what will be our starting and ending points. I will begin with the austere (though anti-skeptical) assumption that we can make true judgments about the empirical world and I will end with a rather tight "Aristotelian" conception of the identities of a system of physical objects, including ourselves and those objects with which we interact. I expect both that there will be no disagreement among philosophers that if these distant connections can be made a significant amount of philosophical movement will have been achieved and that many will think it is unlikely that I will succeed. As to the latter point, I suppose it depends on what counts as success. I will be taking many steps and trying, of course, to force these as much as possible, trying to make the alternatives as unattractive as I can. I do not think that I must show that these alternatives are impossible or inconceivable, though I will do my best to push them to these limits. Transcendental arguments are not different in this respect from other arguments in philosophy. As we understand them, they begin with some relevantly unavoidable starting point (such as our assumption of justification) and try to derive "consequences" of this. Alternatives to these consequences are not necessarily ruled out as inconceivable or logically impossible, though it is best to have the connections this tight, and one should always shoot in this direction. But in general all that one can do is to make clear what one is assuming in making steps, to anticipate alternatives (which depends on what one thinks a reader will think of or be bothered by), and to try to make these as implausible as one can.

In deriving a certain generic conception of identity from our initial starting point, I will not thereby have shown that no other conception could be given such reputable credentials. Although I do not know how to rule these out in general, there is one principle against which I do argue, which has general appeal and great relevance for the problem of personal identity. This is the idea that similarity, regardless of whether it is caused, is itself a basis of identity. The converse is evidently that change itself somehow counts against identity, so that all change is like destruction. This general metaphysics has perennial appeal, being espoused, for example, by Heraclitus, Buddha and Hume. We will see, for example, that Parfit silently assumes it when he argues for his view that personal identity is determined by (non-branching) psychological continuity. Since the fourth chapter is devoted to refuting this general metaphysics, some reason beyond the mere absence of proof will be given for rejecting the idea that (causally unproduced) similarity is a ground of identity or that change in general is like destruction.

I have touted the transcendental method which we will adopt so far solely on the ground that it promises a level of justification which is very deep. I have, however, another, more specific reason, for choosing this approach. Although the theory I will present will deal with a host of problems, not only pertaining to our own identity, but to the identities of such things as artifacts and lumps of stuff, there is one problem with which we will be mostly concerned. We saw that Parfit holds that what determines our persistence is (non-branching) psychological continuity, which obtains by overlapping strands of psychological connections. Normal human life exhibits psychological continuity, since it does not involve such complete breaks in psychology as was involved, for example, in our imaginary case of the Afghan rebel with my body. So, Parfit holds, as we normally do, that identity is preserved in these cases. Nevertheless, he makes much of the fact that his position runs counter to the way we ordinarily think of ourselves, since even though he agrees that identity is preserved, he holds that the claim of identity, especially over long periods of time, is relatively *trivial*. This is because the *basis* of psychological continuity, psychological connectedness, *diminishes* over time, in particular, with each psychological disconnection. He thinks this is especially pronounced with changes in our deepest affections and ideals. In such changes the claim that we become a "different person" is not, according to him, merely a dramatic way of speaking. And yet he thinks (correctly I believe) that however important these changes are to us, we ordinarily think that our own existence is not diminished by them. We think that the claim that it is still *ourselves* who exist after them is not at all trivial. In opposition to our ordinary conception of our identity, Parfit borrows Hume's analogy of thinking of persons as being like nations. To say that an older person who has undergone a good deal of psychological change (or disconnections) is the same person as the young person with his body, though true, is as unimportant as saying that Austria today is the same nation as that of the Habsburgs.[21] In both cases it would be wrong to stress the claim of identity to make something out of it, such as the fact that the older person is responsible for the young person's actions. It is this view of our identity that I want most of all to consider and ultimately to refute. Because of its contrast with the way we ordinarily think, Parfit describes it as "revisionist," in Strawson's sense.[22] The special reason that I have for adopting the transcendental method is that it allows us to mount an effective attack against even revisionist views of our identity. As I will explain shortly, the most popular method of addressing the question of our identity is bound to beg the question against Parfit by relying on the metaphysics of ordinary thought and talk. But by descending to an assumption that even the modern revisionist will accept, the possibility of making justified empirical judgments, and by showing that our common view of ourselves rests securely on this basis, a satisfactory defense of that view will be provided.

What makes the whole question of personal identity especially interesting is the practical significance that the answer seems to have. When considering whether to administer punishment or to reward compensation for a past action, it seems crucial to know if it was the *same* person who did the wrong or who was wronged. By holding that assertions of identity are relatively trivial in such cases, Parfit places less weight on claims of desert, thus associating himself with consequentialist theories in ethics, such as Utilitarianism, which downplay the importance of "backward-looking" considerations. It is not that his unordinary view of our identity directly argues for consequentialism, but that it lends supports to it by requiring that

---

21. Parfit 1984, p. 316.

22. Ibid., Introduction, p. x: that his view of personal identity is revisionist is obvious and is implied in his chapter title, "How We Are Not What We Believe."

deontological theories such as Kant's be given an application more like that of their adversaries. Parfit's claim of triviality can also change our attitude toward the future. If our own persistence is not as full-blooded as we ordinarily think, with each psychological disconnection it is as we "die a bit."[23] I sympathize with Thomas Nagel, who finds this aspect of Parfit's theory especially depressing.[24] In the third chapter I will defend the practical significance the question of our identity seems to have. This is meant to enhance the interest in our whole project. By using the transcendental method to rebut Parfit's revisionist account, I will defend the "backward-looking" claims of responsibility we normally make and the idea that we are not constantly "dying a bit" throughout our biological lives.

I have defended our adoption of the transcendental method to deal with the problem of personal identity. The depth of justification attempted is philosophically desirable in itself and provides a vantage point by which to rebut effectively Parfit's revisionist account. Since I expect this approach to the question of our identity will be appreciated by philosophers, even those who predict its failure, I suppose that it is not actually necessary for me to criticize any other method which happens to be popular. Nevertheless, in the rest of this chapter I hope to stimulate more interest in the transcendental method by criticizing two popular alternative approaches to the question of our identity.

In the first approach (of which I will discuss two examples), it is assumed that the presence of a certain feeling or attitude reveals our identity. Peter Unger, for example, relies repeatedly on what he calls the "avoidance of future pain test."[25] I will, for example, endure some pain now to avoid greater pain after eating a bowl of tomato soup. This provides, according to Unger, "presumptive evidence" of what I "deeply believe" about my identity. Our transcendental method, by investigating the conditions of justification, aims for a good deal more philosophical penetration than any investigation of what we "deeply believe." But aside from that, I deny that this test provides even what Unger claims for it. Many philosophers discuss the "special concern"

---

23. See Parfit 1984, p. 280.
24. See Nagel 1986, p. 224.
25. Unger 1990. The test is first presented on pages 27–34.

that one has only for oneself. For example, I anticipate my *own* torture with a concern that is different from the altruistic concern that I experience when expecting the suffering of *others*. What Unger is doing is using the presence or absence of this special feeling as evidence of (what we believe about) our identity. Let us grant for the moment that I have this feeling only when I believe the future person is myself. To use the absence of this feeling as evidence of non-identity is to miss the logical point that the occurrence of this feeling may require some other condition besides the belief in one's identity. When I contemplate the future suffering of the Afghan rebel with my body I do not have that special feeling of dread. But might this not be due to the complete break in psychology? (Recall that all of my acquired mental characteristics will have been expunged.) Normally, when I anticipate my own suffering there is something I can do about it; at the very least, I can steel myself for the experience. But all such efforts will be pointless, since my intentions will be lost. Normally, I would envisage a stream of connected experiences leading up to the event. I may, for example, expect to wake up each morning with the disquieting knowledge of my fate. But this knowledge will also be gone. The general point is that normally there are psychological connections between me now and my future self which, plausibly, are necessary for me to feel that special concern, so that the absence of this feeling may evidence not the absence of identity but only of one of these connections. To use the absence of special concern as evidence of non-identity (or even of my belief in non-identity) is simply to ignore the possibility that special concern depends on these connections, and that identity can obtain without these (e.g., that I might be identical with the Afghan rebel). Moreover, as we will see in the third chapter, there are some philosophers who think that these psychological connections do not require identity (they obtain, for example, between oneself and the offshoots of one's fission). If this is true and the feeling of special concern is grounded in these connections, as they seem plausibly to be, the presence of the feeling will not even be good evidence of identity. So, using the presence or absence of special concern to tell whether identity obtains or not seems to beg the question in favor of a Lockean view.

When considering the practical significance that personal identity seems to have, we observed that claims of rights and duties often turn on the issue of whether it is the same person who performed an action in the past. Locke accordingly held that the concept of a person was a "forensic" one. Carol Rovane claims to develop Locke's point with the idea that ethical considerations are what take precedence in deciding questions of personal identity.[26] Rather than developing a general ontology first, as we will do, she would ground an account of personal identity by first settling the relevant ethical issues. Locke held, for example, that if someone had no memory at all of a past crime, punishment for it would seem to that person to fall as a calamity and not as just treatment. This illustrates (whether correct or not) the sort of consideration that could be adduced when taking Rovane's tack. A certain psychological relation is shown to be what it takes to make a certain moral judgment, and then, because personal identity is assumed to be an "ethical" matter, the correctness of the psychological account is inferred. But what justifies this starting point? My objection to Rovane's approach parallels that of Unger's. Grant that the moral relation in question (e.g., of responsibility) is grounded in a certain psychological one (e.g., of memory). Why is the presence (or absence) of the moral relation evidence of identity (or distinctness)? Perhaps, because of the lack of the relevant psychological connection, the Afghan rebel with my body is not responsible for my crimes even though he is identical with me. To assume that moral relations determine identity is no less question-begging than to assume that psychological ones do.

The methods of Unger and Rovane are strikingly different from mine insofar as they attempt to address the question of *personal* identity without having first addressed the question of how to apply the concept of *identity* more generally, to things of other kinds. They do not, that is, defend a more general ontology first to provide a framework into which to fit an account of personal identity. Instead, they attempt to make a shortcut by assuming that personal identity is revealed by the awareness of a certain feeling (such as that of special concern) or by the presence of a certain attitude (such as holding some-

26. Rovane 1993.

one responsible). This is to assume in effect that a certain empirically detectable relation is the one (or a one) which determines identity. But the whole question is to decide which of these assumptions is correct. Our transcendental method offers a basis by which to assess these assumptions critically. For if the claim that the physical world consists of objects whose identities are determined by a certain kind of relation follows from the austere assumption that we can make true judgments about this world, the adoption of that kind of relation as a criterion of identity will not be arbitrary.

The second and last alternative to our method that I wish to criticize is the very widely employed "method of cases." I wish to emphasize at the start, however, that I will not argue against this method in general; my complaint pertains to the peculiar natures of the concepts with which we are concerned, the concept of identity and the concept of a person. This method can be used, as with Unger and Rovane, to bypass more general metaphysical considerations or it can be used to deal with those latter considerations as well. Before I present my criticisms of using this method on the problem of personal identity, let me describe it in general.

In the method of cases we are invited to consider a variety of situations and are asked for an immediate unreflective judgment as to whether the word (or phrase) in question applies. We might, for example, in considering a case in which someone gets the truth, but only accidentally, find ourselves spontaneously thinking that it is not a case of knowledge. These judgments are called "intuitions" and are treated as data, on a par with scientific data, in the sense that they are collected to support an account of the general phenomenon which we seek (in this case, an account of the conditions of knowledge). These intuitions are called "linguistic" since what we are doing in effect is applying or withholding a certain expression (such as "know"). The assumption is that as speakers of the language we know when a certain word applies because this is at least part of what we learned when acquiring these words. But this knowledge may be only latent, and to bring it to consciousness we can see how we would apply the word by actually considering cases, imaginary or real. There is also the assumption that if we speakers think the word applies then this is good reason for thinking that it really does. There is, after all, something absurd in the idea that while all English speakers think that the word "wood" applies to the hard stuff in trees, it "really" applies to butter. One point of clarification. To say that these intuitions are data is to say that they offer (what is presumed to be) *direct* knowledge and not to say that they are incorrigible. Just as the data of scientific observation can be revised in light of enough other data, so can the intuitions of the method of cases be revised by other intuitions. In both kinds of inquiry they are considered knowledge in the sense that we are supposed to be justified in *asserting* them, so that we can genuinely *infer* the account they support and not merely say that it follows from them.

The way to adopt the method of cases for the issue of personal identity has been clearly described by John Perry.[27] We consider a person in one circumstance, then imagine a person in a different circumstance and ask ourselves whether it would be the same person. Recall, for example, the case of the Afghan rebel who has my (biological) body. Is he me? Many people will spontaneously judge that he is not, and this will then be offered as *evidence* that sameness of body is not sufficient for personal identity, since some kind of psychological continuity is evidently necessary. Recall, next, the case in which my body is destroyed and an exact replica is created who seems to remember my past life and who is otherwise mentally indistinguishable from me. The intuition of many is that he will be me, and this is supposed to evidence the fact that sameness of body is not necessary for sameness of person, and that psychological continuity (at least when non-branching) is sufficient. In the method of cases, our intuitions thus provide the basic data which we systematize in order to arrive at an account of our identity. Now, I certainly do not wish to suggest that as philosophers we are entitled to ignore these intuitions. But the method of cases is not the very unspecific demand that we adequately *explain* our intuitions—a demand I certainly accept. It holds rather, as the model of science is supposed to suggest, that there is a (corrigible) presumption that these data are true, so that the best account, all other things being equal, is the one that preserves the truth of most of these. This is what is implied in the notion of "systematiz-

---

27. Perry 1975, pp. 9–11.

ing." Just as we would reject a scientific theory which gratuitously chalked off observations to illusions and the like, in the method of cases an important goal of ours is to preserve as true as many intuitions as we can. This is because collectively they form our ultimate basis of support.

The application of the method of cases to the question of personal identity has been criticized by Mark Johnston.[28] He is impressed by the fact that our intuitions sometimes conflict, and he maintains that this ought to be recognized as a very serious problem for the method. A conflict of intuition is shown perhaps most strikingly by Bernard Williams.[29] It seems possible to imagine that I might undergo the most radical of psychological changes (such as involved in my example of the Afghan rebel), so that psychological continuity does not seem necessary for the preservation of identity. It also seems possible, however, to imagine just such a change taking place right after a record of my previous mentality is used to create a person psychologically indistinguishable from me. This person will be the only one who will seem to remember my present life and who will otherwise act and feel just as I would have if I had gone on as in normal life. When we look at things from this person's point of view, we are inclined to think that I have switched bodies. This inclination, however, reflects the opposite conviction, that psychological continuity really is necessary for identity. Johnston believes (with Williams, in fact) that despite the appearance of body-switching, the truth is that such radical psychological changes within the same person really are possible. He realizes that there is a temptation to say that body-switching has occurred, but he explains this as due to the "distorting" effect of the presence of the relation of psychological continuity between the two bodies, a relation which *normally* coexists with identity. (Notice that he could challenge the intuitions of Unger and Rovane on just this ground.) Johnston acknowledges, however, that he is entitled to chalk this intuition up to distortion only if he has an *argument* for the judgment of identity he favors, which is to say, in effect, that an independent standard is necessary by which to judge the intuitions themselves. Let us, then, look at his argument.

---

28. Johnston 1987, pp. 59–83.
29. Williams 1973, "The Self and the Future."

Johnston's alternative method consists of setting philosophical skepticism aside and appealing to the "humble and ubiquitous practice of re-identifying ourselves over time... [which is] a reliable and mostly unproblematic source of knowledge about particular claims of personal identity."[30] When we appeal to our ordinary practices we must surely be struck by the fact that we become convinced of our own identity with a person in the past by remembering that person's experiences.[31] But "if we now adopt a properly naturalistic view of our mental functioning, i.e., see our mental functioning as the characteristic functioning of the brain, it will be difficult, albeit not impossible, to resist the idea that one's mind would continue on if only one's brain were kept alive and functioning."[32] Although we must appreciate Johnston's attempt to go beyond the appeal to intuition to find an underlying ground, the question is whether his argument really cuts deeply enough to dislodge those who do not share his convictions. David Oderberg denies that it does.[33] He describes Johnston's argument as "quite simply, Lockean," since the importance of the brain is allegedly grounded on the fact it is responsible for memory and other mental functions, and Locke, as we have seen, held that this is what determined personal identity. Unlike Locke, however, Johnston requires not merely psychological continuity but that the natural thing responsible for this continuity (i.e., the healthy brain) be what determines identity. But why, Oderberg complains, should we regard this as more than merely one more intuition? Those who favor the view that body-switching has occurred in Williams' example point to the fact the person who is psychologically continuous with the original will share the same concerns for family and friends. Johnston dismisses this as a "distortion" on the ground that this sort of relation normally coexists with identity. But he is entitled to this only if his conviction about the physical basis of mentality is shown to be somehow more secure than our intuition about the continuity of concerns and affections and other psychological phenomena. In the absence of such a demonstration, the continuity of the brain is just as likely to seem a

30. Johnston 1987, p. 63.
31. Ibid., p. 78.
32. Ibid.
33. Oderberg 1989, pp. 137–41.

relation which "normally" coexists with identity and thereby "distorts" our judgment in favor of bodily continuity.

The appeal of our transcendental method is enhanced, I believe, in light of Oderberg's objection. Whatever conception of ourselves it defends will provide a deep justification for certain intuitions. I will eventually use our method to secure Johnston's intuition. This really will provide a basis for discounting conflicting intuitions; perhaps we should discount them as Johnston does, as being due to the distorting effect that they pertain to relations (such as psychological continuity) which normally coexist with identity. I have said that a satisfactory philosophical theory will have some way of explaining intuitions, or "explaining them away." I will shortly offer explanations for two important classes of cases when I come to my own objections to the method of cases. But first let us look at an account which attempts to reconcile the apparent conflict of intuitions which formed the basis of Johnston's dissatisfaction with the method of cases.

According to Stephen L. White, the appearance of conflict in an example like Williams's is due to the failure to realize that personal identity can be determined partly by such "extrinsic" relations as obtain between persons and societies.[34] To see what he means, suppose that there is a technologically advanced society which accepts annihilation and replication in distant places as a form of travel. The idea is that we cannot simply pronounce on questions of identity without taking into account the conventions of one's society and other contextual matters. There is, therefore, supposed to be no generally correct answer to the question of our identity. Which one is correct is determined "by the form and shape of society."[35]

To a metaphysician this must surely be received as a spectacular suggestion. Is it really believable that what constitutes what I am can be a matter of decision by other people? Wiggins is very bothered by the social consequences of this view.[36] I take it that the argument we are given by White is that it enables us to preserve the truth of more of our linguistic intuitions about our identity. As we have

---

34. White 1989.

35. Ibid., p. 323.

36. Wiggins 1980, pp. 179–182. I defend Wiggins's anti-conventionalism with regard to personal identity in Chapter Six.

seen, this sort of concern is at the heart of the method of cases. I will try to show, however, that many of these intuitions can be explained in such a way that reveals that we have no good reason to treat them as data on the model of scientific observations. This will undermine the method of cases and thereby refute White's argument for his conventionalistic account of our identity.

I have three main objections to the use of the method of cases in the issue of personal identity. The first is that it threatens to beg the question. When we are invited to consider whether in the different circumstance it is "the same person," what is the concept whose application we are spontaneously applying? Is it the concept of a person or the concept of identity? Very often philosophers seem to be working with the concept of a person, understood as Locke did, as having a certain psychological content. Locke maintained, no doubt with insight, that a person is "a thinking intelligent Being, that has reason and reflection, and can consider it self as it self, the same thinking thing in different times and places..."[37] Perry remarks that Locke's definition "makes it an essential property of persons that they have the power of reflection."[38] But all that this really means is the *"de dicto"* truth that it is essential *to be a person* that one has the power of reflection. It is not obvious that having this power is what determines the identity of those things which are persons. As we have seen, Locke attempts to connect the *de dicto* truth about the content of being a person to the *de re* claim that this psychological concept is the one which describes our identity over time. But this is just the sort of claim that is controversial and needs justification. Indeed, the lesson of Kant's example of the billiard balls is that the Lockean concept *cannot* be sufficient to decide the issue. When producing intuitions of "personal identity," what we must consider is the possibility that we are simply begging the question, by allowing our intuitions to be formed by assuming that it is the psychological concept of a person that is determining our immediate judgment. When, for example, we think that the Afghan rebel who has my body after complete amnesia is "not me," or that the person with my replicated body "is me," this might well be due to the fact that we are allowing the psychological concept

37. Locke 1975, p. 335.
38. Perry 1975, p. 13.

to determine our judgment. This is a natural mistake. Since I pick myself out as "me," and thus as a person in Locke's sense, it is tempting to allow this concept to guide my judgments about my identity. The *real* issue, however, is not how *this* concept applies or what *it* determines, but how the concept of *identity* applies. The issue is whether this thing, which I happen to pick out in these circumstances as a person, in Locke's sense, is *identical* with something in those other circumstances.

It might be objected that I am ignoring another intuition, the very intuition that it is the psychological concept that does determine our identity. In this vein, it would be said that it is not a simple "mistake," but rather something of a discovery that is made by invoking the method of cases. One problem with this response is that it does not take into account the quite different ways in which the psychological concept may "determine" our identity. What I have been objecting to is working with the psychological concept to the *exclusion* of physical considerations—considerations which we know from Kant's example *must* be worked in somehow. The psychological concept gives us, in a way, our *primary* access to ourselves, in the sense that we can think of ourselves in the first person "without a criterion." When we reflect on what this means, we realize that it is because we are "persons" in Locke's sense that we have this sort of self-knowledge. Whatever we are essentially must *provide* for this, but there are significantly different ways in which this might be done. Consider, for example, Johnston's idea that the physical basis for this mental activity is what determines our identity, and that this is a certain brain, with a certain developed structure, so that I would share this with the Afghan rebel. Then he would be me, despite the fact we would share no memories and the like. Still, it can be said that on this view the psychological concept "determines" my identity, since it is used to identify the physical basis which demarcates my persistence conditions. It will be, so to speak, merely a path to my identity, physically described. This is certainly different from the view, held by many Lockeans, in which the break in psychology would destroy personal identity despite the continuation of the functioning brain. The problem is how to decide between such subtle but significantly different views. My approach will be to work out a whole ontology of the physical world, based on stringent demands of justification which will enable us to make such precise selections.

I have said that I will eventually defend the more physicalistic conception of ourselves in which it is the physical basis of Lockean consciousness rather than the "extent" of this consciousness that is what is essential to us. And this will require that I "explain away" such intuitions as that of body-switching in Williams' example (supposedly effected by erasing one's mind and recreating these features in another body). Johnston suggested that the intuition of body-switching was due to the distorting influence of the fact that in normal life personal identity is attended by psychological continuity. There is, however, a much deeper explanation of this intuition, which is implicit in Kant's attack on transcendent metaphysics. There is an important class of intuitions, including that of body-switching in Williams' example, body-switching by resurrection of the body (effected by God or advanced scientists), and person-switching in the same body (as in the Afghan case) which can be produced by succumbing to Locke's temptation to think that the psychological concept of a person, which describes the first person point of view, is what determines personal identity. Kant thought that this mistake was one of the main examples of the tendency, natural to thinking beings, to give a "transcendent" employment to such concepts as that of essence and accident (an employment unconstrained by the requirement that their instances belong to the physical world). He thought that all such mistakes were so natural and compelling that even after we had properly diagnosed them we would still be drawn to them. In the present example, the Lockean illusion is due to the fact, discussed above, that as self-aware beings it must seem to us that we have a past reflected in memory and a certain kind of potential future reflected in our expectations and plans. This can make considerations about the empirically revealed body seem irrelevant. But as we saw, the example of the billiard balls shows that they cannot be irrelevant, for self-awareness in itself reveals only the appearance of our identity. All of this explains why we have such intuitions in which the psychological considerations entirely dominate and it explains them in such a way as to discredit them.[39] They are an "illusion," in Kant's sense, that they are produced by subjective necessities alone, and thus cannot be regarded, as they are in the method of cases, as "evidence" of personal identity. It is therefore pointless to base an account of personal identity, as White does, on the bare idea that it "systematizes" such intuitions.

It might be objected that the mere possibility that a linguistic intuition might have a subjective source shows only that it is corrigible, and this is something that ought to be admitted in adopting the method of cases. In the same way, it might be said, observational reports in science can have a subjective source in the form of hallucinations and the like. There remains, however, a striking difference. Suppose that I seem to see a dagger suddenly appearing before me and then just as suddenly disappearing. My judgment that there is a dagger there is best dismissed as hallucinatory because to think it is true would conflict with a vast amount of other knowledge that I have which is based on observations. My observational report of a dagger would still belong, however, to the class of observations which are presumed to be true, and this presumption would be defeated in the present case because (in light of general theoretical standards) there are many other observations which count against it. This is not analogous to the present case. What is being offered is an explanation of why we have linguistic intuitions which favor a Lockean account of personal identity which is supported by considerations *independent* of our other linguistic intuitions. It is not just that we might be wrong. A plausible hypothesis is being given for the production of these intuitions which, if true, would show that they have a subjective source which provides no evidence of the objective fact of the matter. To make an analogy with science, it is as though we knew that a hallucinogen were in the person's body, so that there is no reason even to presume that his perceptions are veridical. The reason for discrediting the observational reports in this case would not be that it is necessary to systematize best the totality of one's observations, but that there is reason for not admitting them to the original stock of corrigible data in the first place. This is what I am claiming about Lockean intuitions of personal

---

39. Unger gives a variety of other explanations for why people are attracted to psychological criteria of personal identity throughout Unger 1990, Chapter 3. I find Kant's especially interesting.

identity. The fact that they can be easily produced by restricting our attention to our own subjective perspective—a perspective which Kant showed cannot reveal our identity—shows that they should not be allowed as constituting even corrigible evidence of identity. But these intuitions are among those that would be counted as evidence by the method of cases. This shows, I submit, the superiority of the transcendental approach.

My first objection to using the method of cases in the question of personal identity was that the real issue was that of identity, and that there is a natural tendency to beg the question by letting the psychological concept of a person entirely determine our intuitions. It may seem, then, that to employ the method of cases correctly, all that is necessary is to make clear that our immediate judgments are to pertain specifically to the concept of identity. An important objection to this is that since the judgments are supposed to be spontaneous it is not clear how it is possible to follow this instruction. I think, however, that there is a further problem with this suggestion. Let us recall that the purpose of the method of cases is to reveal to ourselves the otherwise latent knowledge that we possess of how we would apply the word in question, a knowledge which we acquired by actually seeing how speakers do apply that word. And let us recall that another assumption, no doubt reasonable for many purposes, is that the word really does apply as we think it does. But clearly, this latter assumption will be questioned for many controversial words of philosophy, such as "true" or "right." My intuition to apply the word "awake," for example, when having certain vivid and coherent experiences, will hardly impress the skeptic who presents Descartes's dream hypothesis. Just as clearly, our intuitions about what is morally "right" will be viewed with suspicion by either the moral skeptic or the moral revisionary who condemns the common morality. In both cases, what is questioned is our right to use the criteria which we employ in ordinary life. In much the same way, there are no doubt commonly accepted criteria for applying the concept of identity. In ordinary parlance we frequently agree about what counts in deciding whether something is the same thing. Knowing when to apply the phrase "same cow" is, for example, part of what we must learn when we learn the sense of the term "cow." But just as there are philosophers who challenge the ways in which we ordinarily apply words like "awake" or "morally right," there are revisionists who challenge the ways in which we ordinarily apply the concept of identity. Since the method of cases is supposed to reveal the latent knowledge that we have about the circumstances in which we ordinarily apply terms like "same" and "one," and since the revisionist thinks we are mistaken in the ways in which we apply such terms, the method of cases is bound to beg the question against the revisionist and in favor of our common metaphysics. And this shows decisively, I submit, why the popular method of cases cannot be used effectively to rebut a revisionist theory such as Parfit's.

It might be thought that the revisionist is simply applying terms like "same" in a different sense, and that we are entitled to employ the method of cases since we are concerned with the sense that we ordinarily attach to the phrase "same person." For many terms, the fact that we are giving them a different application than the ordinary one really does show that the term in question is simply being used in a different sense. Anyone who regularly applied the word "wood" to butter really would be using the term in a different sense, because the sense of the word "wood" includes what Michael Dummett calls a "criterion of application."[40] Part of what it *means* to be wood is to *appear* a certain way, at least in normal circumstances.[41] But take a case of revisionism and ask whether terms like "one" or "same" are being used in a different sense. Hume, for example, claims that all that we really know that we observe are momentary bits of consciousness, so that when we blink our eyes while apparently looking at a fire, although we think we see the same fire, we really know only that we see two different "impressions." By applying terms like "same" differently Hume purports to refer to non-ordinary things. Now, whatever we think of such extraordinary ontologies, their problem does not seem so extreme as to be unintelligible. Hume does not appear to

---

40. Dummett 1981, p. 546.

41. I make the qualification "in normal circumstances" to take account of the point made familiar by Saul Kripke that it cannot be analytic that members of a natural kind appear a certain way (e.g., that gold appear yellow and malleable) since we can conceive of bizarre circumstances in which those members appear differently. This does not of course alter the fact that members of natural kinds must appear (to us) as they do in *normal* circumstances because it is only via these circumstances that we "fix the references" of the terms in question.

be using the term "same" in a different sense: if he were, then he would not really be *saying* that there are *two* impressions, and so, his talk of "impressions" would be only verbally different from our talk of fires and the like. He would not really be presenting, as he thinks he is, an intelligible alternative to our ordinary metaphysics. The fact that we understand his ontology of impressions and the like shows that we understand very different applications of terms like "same." Even if we learn numerical terms only in application to objects of certain kinds, appearing in certain ways, the fact that we understand quite different applications of these terms shows that the criteria of application that we first use do not belong to the senses of the numerical terms. That we are able to divorce the terms from the criteria by which we first apply them is evident also in the fact that we are able to understand mathematical statements and perform calculations with them with no consideration for how the terms are applied in experience. The futility of trying to refute revisionist alternatives in metaphysics by meaning analyses offers another illustration of how little this subject is concerned with logical necessity and possibility.

I have emphasized that the method of cases is not merely the unspecific demand, which I believe any philosopher ought to accept, that we respect linguistic intuitions to the extent that we acknowledge an obligation to explain them. It embodies instead the assumption that these are "data," and this means that there is a (corrigible) presumption that they are true; for it is from them that we are supposed to infer our account, just as in science our theories are inferred from observational reports. The method is therefore undermined when explanations for elicited linguistic intuitions are given which show that the intuitions do not constitute evidence. This is what happens, for example, when someone's intuitions about what is morally right are explained as arising from self interest or social conditioning. The fact that the person feels that "right" applies in the circumstance in question no longer provides evidence for thinking that it does. I previously tried to show how intuitions that favor Locke's view of identity can be explained in such a way that deprives them of the status of evidence. I want now to discredit that whole class of intuitions that supports the Humean metaphysics. This will not of course show that the metaphysics is mistaken. But it will show once again why the method of cases cannot be trusted in the philosophical investigation of personal identity.

Suppose that the body of a person is annihilated and a perfect replica is created by sheer accident. This would be an extreme case in which very similar but causally unconnected things exist in temporal succession. The essence of the Humean metaphysics is that it sees in similarity itself a ground for identity. In the following chapters we will see in a variety of examples that many real philosophers accept this metaphysics. I believe that there is no doubt that many persons, at least, have an intuition that identity would be preserved by the similarity of the replica with the original. This kind of intuition does not pertain only to persons. If a tree or watch were annihilated and replicated by sheer accident, many would feel that this would be enough for identity. The problem with such intuitions is that there is a clear explanation for them which shows why they should not be treated as evidence of identity. The most distinctive principle of identity is Leibniz's Law, the truism that if a and b are identical, there is no difference between them. Identity differs from all (other) forms of similarity by requiring that identicals share all properties and not merely certain ones. Things which are highly similar but still distinct may, therefore, easily appear much like identicals. Indeed, all that it takes for two distinct things to appear identical is to ignore their differences, and in the case of highly similar things this is relatively easy to do. Suppose, for example, that the only thing that makes the objects distinct in the present examples is the lack of causal connectedness. All that is necessary to produce the intuition of identity is to ignore this difference. But surely, the subjective fact that we can ignore a difference provides no evidence that in objective reality the difference is not there. Platonic realism results by ignoring the spatio-temporal differences between similar things so as to think of the similarities themselves; the fact that we can ignore such differences hardly shows that universals exist. My present point is not of course that the Humean metaphysics is wrong (as I want to show in the fourth chapter), but that the linguistic intuitions produced in its favor, like the intuitions produced in favor of Lockean personal identity, may well have a merely subjective source. To treat them as among the "data" to be "systematized" is simply to ignore this very real possibility. Again the point is not merely that they are corrigible. It is that a plausible explanation of the production of these intuitions is being provided which is not based on an overriding weight of other intuitions. This is why the intuitions in question should not be admitted in the first place to a class of those which constitute corrigible data for an account of identity. Since this is just how the method of cases treats them, I submit that we see once more the superiority of the transcendental method.

John Rawls has contrasted Hume's view of the self with the "Kantian" one in terms of (temporal) "length."[42] As Rawls explains, that our identity is "longer" on Kant's view is important to Kant, since the self is thereby thought of not as a container of experiences (a feature which does not require much persistence) but as something which can form and implement long range plans (for which one is responsible). Rawls claims, however, that we cannot make such decisions of "length" without a moral theory, since all that we can establish with the "philosophy of mind" (which I presume addresses metaphysical issues) is the unspecific idea that *some* sort of psychological continuity will be necessary for personal persistence, so that moral theorists will accordingly be free to choose the view of identity that suits their theory.[43] What we need to realize about Rawls's claim is that it is sheer speculation about the possibility of what can be achieved in metaphysics independently of ethics. This whole book can be looked at as an attempt to refute Rawls on this point. For what I want to show is that by adopting the rigorous transcendental method we will eventually be able to make just such decisions as regards our temporal "length" and the kinds of "continuities" that really constitute our identity over time—without, of course, first resorting to a moral theory.

I began this chapter by giving several examples of the question of personal identity. These are problematic since they present a conflict between two kinds of considerations: the mental and the physical. Mentalistic accounts of our identity are attractive. The problem is for self-aware beings to decide their own identity and self-awareness is a form of consciousness in which one's own identity seems evident. But as Kant realized, since this appearance can be mistaken, the conditions of our identity are knowable only if they are also describable in

---

42. Rawls 1974.

43. Norman Daniels reaffirms Rawls's position in Daniels 1979.

physical terms. This demand to know ourselves as "bodies" can, however, be met in quite different ways, since self-awareness can plausibly be attributed to "bodies" with quite different identity conditions.
After Kant's lesson, the philosophical problem of personal identity is
to justify applying the concept of identity in the interpretation of
experience to settle the question of which of such "bodies" we are.
Since any account of our identity will apply the concept of identity to
ourselves, we can support such an account by seeing how in general
to apply the concept. As we will find in the next chapter, we are among
the things to which the concept of identity applies in the first place.
But since we will apply the concept to ourselves only as physical
objects interacting with other physical things, including ones of other
kinds, our strategy of discerning the general rationale for applying
the concept of identity will require the construction and defense of a
more general ontology. Naturally, we want the deepest defense we
can find. But we also want one deep enough to rebut revisionist
accounts such as Parfit's. It is for these reasons that we will adopt the
transcendental method of deriving our ultimate account from the non-
arbitrary assumption that we can make true empirical judgments. Our
method compares favorably with popular alternatives. Those who start
with the assumption that our identity is revealed by the presence of a
certain feeling or attitude assume that certain relations (such as psychological or moral ones) determine our identity; but it is just such
assumptions which demand justification. By contrast, the assumption
of being able to make true empirical judgments is not arbitrary, since
it is just such judgments which will have to be accepted by anyone
who accepts any definite (non-skeptical) account of our identity. Since
this is our starting point, the transcendental method promises a vantage point capable of assessing the controversial assumptions in question. Our method also compares favorably with the method of cases.
This method is likely to beg the question in favor of psychological
criteria because of the Lockean temptation to derive our identity from
the mere fact of self-awareness, to be prejudiced in favor of the ordinary because of its reliance on our usual ways of applying words, and
to illegitimately favor Humean metaphysics because of our subjective
ability to ignore objective differences. We will not, however, really
begin to develop our general metaphysics until the fourth chapter.

For the claims of the practical relevance of the whole issue to such matters as hope and responsibility can be, and have been, challenged. The purpose of the third chapter is to show that our metaphysical investigation really is of practical importance. To achieve this I will appeal to the result of the next chapter, that I am a single thing.

2

I Am a Single Thing

I normally think of myself as a single thing, even if I do not go around saying it. If I were many things, I could think of myself as "us" or "these." But ordinarily, when I think of a plurality of individuals, I think of myself either as being distinct from each of them or as being one among them. I make this common assumption when, in asking, What am I?, I expect a single answer, a single account of my identity conditions which will tell me in which other circumstances I will find myself. I do not expect to be told that the answer depends upon which of the many things I mean by "I." I know that I am now seeing the computer, sitting up and striking the keys. I suppose that these states describe a single thing which appears in these circumstances and traces a single path in space and time. I do not suppose that there are, or can be, many such paths which converge at this point, like so many strands of thread pinched together, whose many travelers simultaneously designate themselves in concert by thinking "I." This strange view is, however, held by several philosophers today, and many more hold a view which entails it. The purpose of this chapter is to refute it.

This idea is expressed by a few philosophers in reference to the case of personal fission, as this is standardly interpreted. As I mentioned in the first chapter, this is supposed to be effected by carefully separating the halves of the brain. Based on clinical data which seemed to many to show that each half was sufficient to support the mental life of the original person, the case of personal fission has seemed to many philosophers to present the intriguing possibility of a person splitting like an amoeba, giving rise to two "offshoots," each of whom seem to carry on the mental life of the original person. This possibility is more vivid if the two brain halves are put in different bodies (perhaps similar to that of the original). Some philosophers have doubted that such operations are really possible or that the clinical data really support the claim that splitting the brain results in two points of view.[44] Such challenges do not bother me, since nothing that I argue in this work depends upon accepting what I call the "standard" view of fission: that fission results in distinct points of view, that is, two streams of thought in which, for example, at the same time different scenes could be perceived or contradictory judgments could be made. I am, however, entirely sympathetic to philosophers who have supposed this. Even if it turns out to be physically impossible for such splits to occur in human beings, it seems clearly conceivable for them to occur in other species of rational beings. Since in vertebrates the cranium provides rather good protection for the brain, there is relatively little need for redundancy in the realization of mental characteristics. But suppose that a soft-bodied species of rational beings has developed the survival strategy of producing a plurality of exactly similar central nervous systems throughout its body which are normally connected and work in unison. We might suppose that it is quite common for such a creature to suffer injuries which destroy one or more of these, but so long as only one is left the creature is able to think and behave normally. Since personal fission would be clearly conceivable for such creatures, we could raise with respect to them all the same philosophical questions of personal identity. These would, I believe, be just as interesting philosophically as those which arise from the "standard" interpretation of human fission. I will accordingly not quibble about whether personal fission according to the "standard" interpretation is possible for humans.

---

44. See Robinson 1988 and Hirsch 1991.

Suppose, then, that a fission actually occurs as "standardly" conceived, so that two distinct points of view associated with the two brain halves emerge after fission. Since we have defined the word "person" in terms of self-awareness, this would mean that after fission there are two persons who each have a different brain half. There is still, however, a metaphysical question of how to count persons throughout the transformation, and philosophers have been quite imaginative in exploring the possibilities. Many would say that the original person, like the original amoeba, would cease to exist with fission and be replaced by the two very similar "offshoots." It is possible to maintain, however, that there have been two persons all along. Even this view is compatible with the idea I wish to defend, that I-thoughts belong to just one person, if it is allowed that when the two people "cohabitate" before fission, they have numerically distinct but qualitatively indistinguishable streams of thought. Just this view is taken by Eugene Mills.[45] It is easy to see, however, that I cannot take this view of fission since before fission it would be impossible for each person to know which person he is: the one who will end up with the left brain half or the one who will get the right. And obviously, this question will not be settled after fission since before fission each person will know, for example, that the person with the left half will realize that *he* is the one with the left half. But if I am one of the "cohabitating" persons before fission, how do I know that this realization pertains to *me*? This objection to Mills's view shows that it is thus ruled out by our original assumption that we can know what we are.

Mills maintains that there are two persons throughout fission, "cohabitating" before fission, each of whom possesses his own stream of consciousness. If there is only one stream of consciousness and two persons sharing this stream, then the I-thoughts of this stream would denote two persons. Supposing that I am this person, I could say before fission that I am two things, which is just the sort of claim I want to refute. Just this interpretation has been proclaimed by David Lewis and is shared by Harold Noonan (and should perhaps be

---

45. Mills 1993.

attributed to Perry).[46] Since they describe persons as temporally extended series of momentary "person stages," they would say that right now my I-thoughts relate to one person stage here and now, and if I undergo fission, this stage will be part of two different series of person stages. (In the fourth chapter I argue that persons are not series of person stages at all.) But since one person is one such series of stages it follows that my current I-thoughts would denote more than one person, which is just the sort of claim that I deny.

I said that although few philosophers would wish to allow that I am many things, many hold a view that entails this extraordinary position. Many philosophers talk as if all that it takes to refer to something real is to make up a word with associated identity conditions for which there are empirical data.[47] This is to say in effect that in the interpretation of empirical data we are free to use the concept of identity as we please (provided that we avoid contradiction). To take an extreme example, consider Nagel's concept of day persons, who are just like normal persons for just one day, sharing their same bodies and mental lives from midnight to midnight, but not existing at other times. Just as these persons are (temporally) "shorter" than normal ones, he also imagines "longer" persons, called "series persons." Suppose that a normal person ceases to exist with the death of his (biological) body and that he is perfectly replicated in the future. The original person and his replica would be numerically distinct normal persons but the same series person would coexist with each. Now, it seems plain that the concepts of day persons and of series persons are

---

46. See Lewis 1969 and Noonan 1989.

Another interpretation of fission which may seem to uphold the view I want to refute is provided by Perry (in Perry 1972). Wanting to conform to ordinary intuitions, Perry suggests that before fission there is one person and after fission it is true that before fission there were two people. This is not to be confused with the familiar interpretation that there is one person before fission and two after fission. It is rather that the number of persons involved at a time (such as before fission) depends on the time the judgment is made. My main objection to this account is that I do not understand it. I understand terms like "one" and "two" but I do not understand terms like "one relative to the time of judgment-1" or "two relative to the time of judgment-2." Perry does have a way of avoiding these relativizations, and that is to say how many persons are involved "at any time." Since he holds that when we judge "at any time" how many persons there are before fission the correct answer is "three" (the sum of the correct answers relativized to a time) I can understand his view only to the extent to which I associate it with that of Lewis and Noonan.

47. Peter Van Inwagen deplores this same attitude to questions of ontology in Van Inwagen 1990, pp. 6–12.

logically coherent; and there are empirical data which answer to them. Is this enough to establish that there really are such things? Although Nagel himself does not adopt this liberal attitude toward ontology, Parfit does. Nagel denies that he is a series (or a day) person, saying instead that he exists just so long as his brain retains its mental capacities. But Parfit says that even if Nagel is right, there still exists the series person who "can start to speak through the mouth that both share."[48] This is clearly unacceptable. As Parfit says, Nagel would not be turning himself into something else.[49] If the series person really does exist, then he has been speaking through Nagel's mouth all along, and it is arbitrary to say that Nagel "really is" identified by the original brain, since "Nagel" and his own uses of "I" designate *both* the "brain" person and the series person. Unless we are prepared to accept this extraordinary result about I-thoughts, we cannot suppose that we are this free to interpret empirical data with the concept of identity.

It will appear to some that there is still a way left to avoid the conclusion that each I-thought really denotes a plurality of persons. If we can relativize identity to a kind, then Nagel can be series-person-identical with and brain-person-distinct from the same person. Although I will criticize this strategy more in the seventh chapter, I will mention now one objection that I think in itself is decisive. All attempts to relativize identity need to be supported by a modification of Leibniz's Law, the proposition that if *a* and *b* are identical there is no difference between them. For in this original form there will be some difference, for example, between Nagel-as-series-person and Nagel-as-day-person; after all, they do not share the same total history. Somehow, then, this particular difference must not be allowed to count against their identity, which is to say that Leibniz's Law must be restricted to guarantee that identicals share only *some* properties (such as those physical and mental ones which describe our Nagel-persons at a time they both exist). But identity differs from all forms of similarity precisely by requiring *no* differences. For any form of similarity we could contrive a "restricted" form of "Leibniz's Law" and declare "relative identity." Objects and their surfaces can thus be

---

48. Parfit 1984, p. 292.
49. Ibid.

"identified" relative to the surface features which they share. Since "relative identity" thus appears as nothing more than a misnomer for various forms of similarity, it does not offer a way of avoiding the conclusion that I-thoughts denote a plurality of persons while still enjoying the freedom to apply the concept of identity in experience as we please. It is, then, perhaps not surprising that Andrew Brennan, in his book which self-consciously develops Parfit's view, eventually allows that there are many, mutually incompatible conditions of identity for persons.[50] Since he does not relativize identity, this is to say, in plain language, that I am many things.

My argument against this extraordinary view will be a transcendental one. Such arguments, as we understand them, begin with some uncontroversial premiss which is "unavoidable" in some relevant manner. The fundamental premiss of the argument of this chapter is the assumption that we can individuate things. (We will seek grounds even for this assumption in the fifth chapter.) Since transcendental arguments are dialectical, our argument is really addressed to individual persons, so that each person thinking about it should look for consequences about what "I" think. Individuation, as we will understand the term here and in subsequent chapters, is a matter of what is thought. In this respect it differs from reference, which is something done by a speaker in using a singular term, such as a name or pronoun. When someone uses a singular term to refer to something, and I understand which thing he means, I "individuate" the thing designated. By requiring that one know of which thing one is thinking, I want individuation to conform, by definition, to what Gareth Evans calls "Russell's Principle," that one have "discriminating knowledge [of the thing] ... a capacity to distinguish the object of his judgment from all other things."[51] Although this example shows that one can individuate by having a thought symbolizable as "Fa," I want the term to be understood broadly enough to cover both what Russell meant

---

50. Brennan 1988.

51. Evans 1982, p. 89. Some question whether reference must comply with Russell's Principle: see especially the examples in Kripke meant to refute the "description theory" of proper names. If reference does not necessarily comply with this principle, the notion of reference would seem to lose a good deal of importance for epistemology. This is one reason for shifting to a technical term such as "individuation."

by knowledge by acquaintance and knowledge by description.[52] As Russell drew the distinction, knowledge by description is epistemically posterior to knowledge by acquaintance. I am acquainted with a certain thing just when "I have a direct cognitive relation to that object, that is when I am directly aware of the object itself;"[53] since knowledge by description is indirect, I individuate something by description only by uniquely relating it to some one or more things I know by acquaintance. Suppose, for example, that I am acquainted with my dog, Argus, because I see him. Then I can individuate his father, as "his father," even though I have not made his acquaintance. Russell would have denied that I am acquainted with Argus on the ground that I could be mistaken about his presence; this substantive view of acquaintance is not required by the notion of directness, and we will not adopt it.[54]

It is controversial where to draw the line between the two forms of individuation, and Russell himself changed his mind on the subject. He allowed at first that he was acquainted with himself (in having what we have called "I-thoughts") and with universals; but he eventually settled on only sense-data. His earlier idea that self-awareness involves acquaintance with oneself is Kantian, inasmuch as Kant held that self-awareness is a condition for all knowledge. Russell's later view, that we know of ourselves only by descriptions related to sense-data, such as "the subject of these experiences," is by contrast Humean; for Hume held that he could think of something such as "this blue image" without having to know which thing he is. His analogy of persons with nations nicely illustrates this epistemic relation. We know of nations by knowing first of the individual people who compose them and then individuate the nation in question by reference to these people. The United States, for example, just is the nation which was formed by certain people making certain agreements. In the same way, we are supposed to be able to know of our individual states of consciousness and then individuate ourselves in relation to them. Self-awareness on such a view is not necessary for knowledge, since one can chose to think only of the objects of one's acquaintance and

---

52. Russell 1972.

53. Ibid., p. 16.

54. The phenomenalists used incorrigibility as a criterion of directness.

perhaps some things other than the self known by description. Kant, on the other hand, would deny this view of self-awareness: Hume can think of his experiences, but he knows them only as his own. I will argue that I am a single thing by siding with Kant (and the earlier Russell) on the fundamental role of self-awareness in individuation.

Our fundamental premiss in this chapter is uncontroversial and unavoidable for anyone who, like ourselves, is inquiring into the nature of the self. By allowing that individuation covers knowledge both by acquaintance and by description, the conditions of individuation should be accepted by anyone who admits there is a self about which to inquire; and in particular, it accommodates both the Kantian and the Humean views about how the self is known. Since we want to consider in this chapter the bizarre view that the self is really a plurality of things, let us relax the notion of individuation so that "the object" picked out may, in fact, be a plurality of things. I may accordingly "individuate" my two sons, as such, or a plurality of selves with personal pronouns such as "I" or "me."

My last clarification of the notion of individuation consists of differentiating individuative thought from a more primitive kind of cognition. Consider Argus, who can certainly see the food bowl in front of him, and thus has some knowledge "about" this bowl. Although he made be said, in Russell's language, to have a "direct cognitive relation" to the food bowl, we will not say that he "individuates" the bowl unless he knows *which* thing it is. It may be tempting to describe his knowledge by using terms which are familiarly applied to humans, by saying, for example, that he knows that there is a food bowl in front of him. But suppose that all that happens is that he recognizes a characteristic visual pattern and this causes him to respond in distinctive ways. This is an example of what Henry Price once called the "recognition of universals," since, as my own description suggests ("a characteristic visual pattern"), the content of Argus's cognition would be purely general, possibly pertaining equally well to more than one thing.[55] It is the nature of "patterns" that they are universal, something which may be shared by, and exhibited in, several things. If Argus's state of awareness is adequately described as the recogni-

---

55. See Price 1953, pp. 40–41.

tion of something like a pattern, a universal, then he does not thereby know which thing is the food bowl since the content of his knowledge fails to discriminate this bowl from any other which would appear the same. When, on the other hand, we are acquainted with the bowl or know of it by uniquely relating it to objects with which we are acquainted, then we know which thing it is and thereby individuate it.

Russell chose the term "acquaintance" over Frege's term "presentation" in part to imply clearly that acquaintance is a relation to a thinking subject, the one who is directly aware of the object in question. This suggests a stronger thesis than that the self is an object of acquaintance. If acquaintance is a relation to the subject of awareness, perhaps one is acquainted with anything only if one knows how that thing is related to oneself. This stronger thesis has been held, for example, by Peter Strawson, Roderick Chisholm and Sydney Shoemaker.[56] It does not require that to be acquainted with something one must actually be thinking of oneself at that time. If I am acquainted with my dog, Argus, by seeing him, I do not have to think that I am seeing him. What the thesis would hold instead is that in order to know which thing Argus is, I must be able to think of how he is uniquely related to me. And since I can avoid thinking of any object knowable only by description while I am acquainted with things, to think of how an object of acquaintance is related to me, I must be *able* to think of myself as an object of acquaintance. What Strawson held, plausibly, is that I must be able to relate the thing to *me now*, e.g., I can think that Argus is the dog I see now. If this is correct, knowledge by acquaintance always involves the capacity to be acquainted with both oneself and the present moment. It is this claim about the fundamental role of self-awareness with which we are concerned in this chapter. Since knowledge by description is parasitic upon knowledge by acquaintance, the thesis accords to self-awareness an indispensable role in individuation in general: to individuate something one must know which thing it is; to think of how I know which thing it is, I must be able to relate it uniquely to myself, and so to think of myself directly, as an object of acquaintance. For convenience of expression, I

---

56. Chisholm 1981, Strawson 1959, p. 2–49; Shoemaker 1984, pp. 6–18.

will call this thesis "Strawson's," since it was he who developed it most fully. The argument of this chapter has two stages: first, I will begin by assuming this thesis and trying to show that a consequence of it is that I am not a plurality of things; then, I will defend the thesis itself by arguing that self-awareness is necessary for the sort of grasp of demonstratives required for individuation in general.

In abstract, my argument for the first stage is as follows. Suppose that Strawson's thesis is true, and that I have individuated something and think to myself how I know which thing it is. To do so, I must think of how the thing is uniquely related to me. If the thing is anything other than myself, I will have to think of at least two things. If I can think of only one thing, it must be myself. Suppose, then, that I am thinking of just two things. This means that I do not confuse them, but know which one is which. I have discriminating knowledge of each of them. Then one and only one is myself. Since I have discriminating knowledge of each of them, I am able to pick either one and think of which one it is. If it is not myself it must be related by a unique description to myself, in which case I am the other one of the pair and not both of them. If it is myself then I am able to think of it alone, without the other one, in which case again I am not both of them. This means that (on the thesis in question) I cannot think of myself as a plurality of two things. I do not mean that they could not be parts of me—this must be possible. It is rather that I cannot think of myself as *being* these two things (as my two sons are two things, though they form a single pair or set). This argument clearly extends to pluralities of more than two things. For to think of anything as a plurality I must be able to understand a reference to each of the several members, individually. But on the view in question, I can think of which thing anything is only by relating it ultimately to myself, which means that I must *already* know which thing I am. This is the crucial point. According to Strawson's thesis, my knowledge of which thing I am cannot be *inferred* from knowledge which I already possess about which thing something else is, since I understand which thing anything else is only by relating it to myself. But to grasp the fact that something is a plurality is to understand it as really being many things, which involves understanding how to think of the things separately. This means that once we think of something *as* a plurality, the plurality itself becomes epistemically posterior, in the sense that it is thought of only by reference to things already individuated. And since I am supposed not to be knowable to myself in this way, I must be *among* the things already individuated and therefore not identical with the plurality itself. This argument supports the common way of thinking that I mentioned at the outset of this chapter: that whenever I think of "us" I think of myself as one among the several people.

It is no objection to this argument to claim that even if I must think of myself as a single thing, it is still "possible" that I am many things. For the argument is a transcendental one, and claims only to reveal how we must coherently think from our own, finite perspectives. A more serious objection would be that although I might *initially* think of myself as a single thing I might *discover* that I am really a plurality. This would be analogous to my discovery that a dark object in the sky is really several birds (say, flying close together at a distance). Since it is possible to discover that something we once thought was a single thing is really many things, why could this not happen in the case of ourselves? Suppose that I come to think of the black object as several birds by seeing them separate. Then, according to Strawson's thesis, I am able to relate each of them to myself. I may, for example, see where, in relation to me as an observer, each one is; I may think that there is above me a single object, the black one, of which each bird is a part; or, I may even think of the place which had something black in it (which I now see has several birds). It is possible, however, to discover that something is a plurality without being able to individuate the members themselves. I could be told, say, by someone with binoculars, that the black object is really several birds without being able to discern a single one. But then I would individuate the plurality of birds by reference to something else, such as the black object of which they are parts or the place with something black in it, and I would know which object this is only by relating it to myself. In the same way, I can discover that the particular quantity of matter of which I am composed is really many atoms, even though I can individuate no single atom. But then I am individuating the plurality of atoms only by already knowing which thing I am. The general point is that I can discover that something previously thought to be a single thing is really a plurality of things only if I can come to individuate the members individually or relate them as a plurality (of a certain kind) to something already individuated. But I could not discover in either way that I am a plurality of things (on the thesis in question). If I could, then I could individuate either each member of the plurality or something else (such as a certain place or something composed of them) to which they are all related in order to explain to myself which thing I am. But then I would have to understand which things these are without knowing which thing I am, which contradicts the thesis in question. The "necessity" of thinking of myself as a single thing is not merely that it is temporally first, but that it is epistemically first, so that it really is impossible (given Strawson's thesis) to discover that I am many things.

I have said that we must not confuse the claim that I am a plurality with the claim that I am composed of parts. The idea that I am not composed of parts at all, that I am "simple," is an extraordinary view, held only by such non-materialists as Descartes and Leibniz. The idea that I am composed of parts is of course compatible with the idea that I am a single thing, since I can distinguish parts of myself from me just as easily as I can distinguish from myself things that are spatially distanced from me. A plurality is not merely *composed* of several parts: it is *identical* with these several parts. It is because of precisely this difference that pluralities as such must be epistemically posterior. To understand the claim that something is composed of parts does not require that one be able to think of these parts individually before understanding which thing is the whole thing, since the parts can be differentiated from the whole. But to understand the claim that something is a certain plurality of things is to think of it as identical with these several things, which requires either a prior understanding of which things these are or an ability to relate them all to something else. This is why, to think of myself as a plurality, I would have to be able to individuate things other than myself without already knowing which thing I am.

Let us see how this rather abstract argument would be applied in a concrete case. We saw before that Lewis and Noonan describe the case of fission as one in which two people share a body and a stream of consciousness before fission and then part company. Suppose that I am these two people about to undergo fission. How could I (we) individuate either one? One will be the one which ends up with the left half of the brain and the other the one which gets the right. Now, if I could individuate brain halves without already knowing which thing I am, there would be no problem. This is the sort of thing I will discuss in the second stage of my overall argument. If, for example, I could refer to "this" brain half or the one right "here" without already knowing which thing I am, then I could go on to explain to myself that I am identical with these two things. But this would contradict the thesis we are assuming. Lewis uses phrases like "your present person stage" to explain which thing he means; Noonan uses phrases like "my present use of 'I.'"[57] There is no problem with these if we can individuate person stages and tokens of words without already being able to individuate ourselves, for then the reference to oneself can be made by a description related to these things. But this is just what is denied by the thesis in question. And according to this thesis, I can think of which thing I am by thinking of myself alone. If, then, I am the two persons Lewis and Noonan have in mind, I can think of which things "we" are without individuating anything else. As a plurality, I can know who "we" are only by being able to individuate each one. Since "we" are the person who will get the left half and the person who will get the right, I can, for example, individuate the person who will get the left half. But then, by the thesis, either I can know who this person is by thinking of him alone, in which case I am identical with this person and not the plurality, or I must relate this person to the one who will get the right half, in which case I am this other person, and once again not identical with the plurality.

I have argued that Strawson's thesis supports the common view that I am a single thing. At the heart of this thesis is the idea that individuation *terminates* in a certain way. I individuate all things other than myself only by being able to relate them to myself and I know myself directly, as an object of acquaintance. But what if the chain of references can be otherwise terminated, not with a direct reference to myself? A very plausible idea is that this can be accomplished with demonstratives such as "here" and "there" or "now" and "before." It was such a view to which Russell was led when he abandoned his

---

57. Lewis 1969, p. 22 and Noonan 1989, p. 138–39.

original idea that the self is known by acquaintance. Since he came to think that he knew only his own sense-data by acquaintance, he thought he could demonstrate them to himself, as Hume thought of "this blue image," and thereby think of which things they were without also thinking of himself—without thinking of them as *his*. With respect to ordinary objects, we might wonder why I have to think of Argus as being in front of *me* now? Why can I not think of him simply as "that dog" or "the dog over there"? In the example of Lewis and Noonan, the suggestion would be that I direct my attention to one brain half and think of "the person with *this* brain half." Strawson argued clearly for the need to add *something* to a purely general description (such as "dog") to ensure that it applied to just one thing. But do not such demonstratives by themselves supply just such an extra element? It seems just as clear that there cannot be more than one dog "over there" as it does that there cannot be more than one dog in front of "me" now.

Now, it is obviously possible to refer to Argus in the sense of speaking about him without explicitly mentioning oneself. I can simply refer to him as "that dog" with the appropriate ostension. But individuation is a matter of knowledge, not of speech. The crucial question is whether in *understanding* these words one must be able to think of oneself. And it is certainly not obvious that a listener can interpret my use of "that dog" without being able to think of himself and how he is related to a certain dog.

I called Strawson's thesis "Kantian" because Kant held that the capacity for self-awareness was a condition of knowledge (and hence of individuation specifically). One has knowledge, for Kant, only by having a representation which one can put in its place within the totality of what one knows, and this capacity so to organize one's knowledge is signaled by the recognition that one's representations are one's own. The capacity for self-awareness is, on this view, necessary for being conscious of the representations themselves, and thus to have what Kant would call knowledge.[58] Whereas the brute can certainly *have* representations such as a visual experience of its master, it is not thereby conscious of its own

---

58. Kant 1968, A 122: "it is only because I ascribe all perceptions to one consciousness (original apperception) that I can say of all perceptions that I am conscious of them"; Kant 1968, A 123: "The abiding and unchanging 'I' (pure apperception) forms the correlate of all our representations insofar as it is to be at all possible that we should become conscious of them."

visual experience, and is consequently not able to "put in place" this representation within a system of knowledge. It cannot, for example, take the fact that it sees its master as confirming what it thought a moment before when it heard the door opening. It thereby lacks what Locke called the power of "reflection," the capacity to be aware of one's own mental states. And Locke, too, as we have seen, thought that this involved awareness of oneself as such. Creatures like us not only see things but simultaneously know that they do, thus exercising both their visual and reflective capacities. Kant holds that self-awareness is necessary to be aware of the mental states, since we gain awareness of our mental states only by being able to relate them to others, and we do so only when we think of them as our own.

The problem with all of this for the present purpose is that it is not yet clear enough to show that this kind of self-awareness is actually necessary. As I understand Kant, he relies on the supposedly evident fact that the function of "I" is precisely to combine the various mental states or representations. And even if we grant him the point that this is *sufficient* for reflection and thus for "thinking," it is not obvious why it is actually *necessary*. For it is not obvious why we could not restrict our thought to the grasp of such demonstratives as "here" and "there" and "now" and "before" and still "combine" or "unify" our various mental states into something which we can *then*, as something of an afterthought, describe as *"our* conscious life." To say that "I" serves this function of combination makes it sound as if it is analytic that I cannot be directly aware of a variety of mental states without thinking of them as mine. And this is hardly obvious. As we have seen, it will rejected by anyone who follows Hume in thinking that the self is known only by a description, such as "the subject of these experiences." Parfit even embraces what he calls the "impersonal" view that all the facts of the world can be expressed without mentioning persons as such.[59] He would hold, for example, that the fact that I feel a tingle is nothing more that the fact that this tingle is occurring. And in support of this view he cites with approval Russell's argument for the definability of "I" in terms of other demonstratives.[60]

---

59. Parfit 1884, pp. 225ff.
60. Ibid., p. 252. The reference is to Russell 1956.

Russell's view about the definability of "I" was based on a famous remark of Hume's: that when he looks about his "perceptions" (his immediately evident mental states) nowhere does he find himself. Russell concurs and concludes that he is thus forced to treat "I" as a kind of "description" for oneself: "Hume's inability to perceive himself was not peculiar, and I think most unprejudiced observers would agree with him. Even if by great exertion some rare person were to catch a glimpse of himself, this would not suffice; for "I" is a term which we all know how to use, and which must therefore have some easily accessible meaning. It follows that the word "I," as commonly employed, must stand for a description ..."[61] It is remarkable that the basis of Russell's view, upon which Parfit leans, is at best a tendentious view of introspection. According to the Kantian view which I will defend, in introspection one is directly aware of oneself by perceiving how one appears to *oneself*. To be aware of anything one must be aware of it in some way. By regarding states of consciousness as mere states of the subject, it is the subject which is the object of awareness, and the states are merely the ways in which this object appears. Just as one perceives a dog by knowing how it appears, one can perceive oneself by realizing how one feels or how it looks. On this view, to feel a tingle is to feel oneself in a certain way. This does not prevent one from attending to the way one feels and giving a term such as "tingle" to describe it. We can then generalize about this kind of shift in reference from the original objects of awareness to the ways in which they are perceived, and we can give a term such as "state" to refer to the ways themselves. When, on the other hand, Hume and Russell observe only the states of consciousness and not the self, the states become the objects of awareness—"sense-data"—and are no longer really *states* of the self. Russell's argument for the definability of "I," to which Parfit appeals to support his "impersonalist" claim that the facts of the world can be stated without mentioning persons as such, thus relies on the sense-data conception of perception. That this is not a view to which any unprejudiced observer would consent is evident by considering the alternative description of introspection, and perception generally, which I associated with Kant. We are not, therefore,

---

61. Russell 1956, p. 164.

compelled by the fact of introspection to deny that the self is an object of acquaintance.

I have attributed to Strawson the thesis that individuation in general requires self-awareness because one knows of which thing one is thinking only if one can relate that thing uniquely to oneself. In holding this thesis Strawson was concerned primarily to explain how we are able to individuate things which are not presently perceived, and he argued that this was possible because "we ourselves ... and our own immediate environment, provide a point of reference..."[62] Since he did not, however, consider the possibility that the things perceptibly present be individuated with demonstratives such as "there" and "now" without needing to think of oneself, we need an argument for his thesis, since it was just this thesis which we used to support the main claim of this chapter, that I am a single thing. Let us begin by considering why Strawson would want to explain how to individuate things which are not perceived by relating them to things which are. Why, that is, should we suppose that individuation in general somehow rests upon the individuation of things which we are currently perceiving, so that we can individuate at all only if we can do so by understanding demonstratives such as "there" and "now"? I think it must be admitted that this is, in a broad sense, an "empiricist" assumption. For what it amounts to is the claim that we are acquainted with things only by knowing them from our individual perspectives. Demonstratives in general are singular terms which depend on the context of utterance to achieve their reference.[63] One does not know which time is meant by "now" or which place is meant by "there" simply by understanding the term; one must take into account the time or place of the actual utterance of the term. To do so is to consider how things appear to a particular person understanding the demonstrative in question.[64] To require that we are acquainted with things only if we can designate them with demonstratives is, therefore, to deny that we can individuate

---

62. Strawson 1959, p. 18.

63. I am using the term "demonstrative" instead of Peirce's "indexical" since it is more familiar, although David Kaplan points out that the former term, unlike the latter, suggests the need to understand a demonstration such as a pointing gesture.

64. Colin McGuinn points out that when we focus on demonstrative *speech* we are impressed by the shift from occasion to occasion, but when we focus on demonstrative *thought* it is the perspectival character of our understanding that is conspicuous. This is important to us, since we are concerned with individuation, which is a matter of what is thought rather than of what is said. See McGinn 1983, p. 17.

things just by thinking of how the world must be independently of how it appears in sense-perception. Such a requirement would be denied, for example, by theists who think they can know of God's existence and uniqueness on purely a priori grounds. I believe that Strawson's empiricist assumption is justified by Kant's refutation of the Ontological Argument, since to individuate something is in effect to know that a certain concept is instantiated, and we can know if a concept (such as the concept of God) is instantiated without needing any sensory confirmation at all only if the fact that the thing exists can be somehow be deduced from the concept itself. Since I do not wish to argue the point further than Kant, however, let us simply confine our attention to those things, including ourselves, which we know through sensory perception.

Our problem thus becomes that of seeing why self-awareness is needed for the understanding of demonstrative references. For we have seen that knowledge by description is dependent upon knowledge by acquaintance, and we have adopted the "empiricist" assumption that we are acquainted with things only by the sort of thoughts we have when we understand demonstratives. The main feature of demonstratives upon which I will focus is emphasized by Strawson.[65] This is the fact that they allow us to "separate" qualitatively indistinguishable things. The point is that even if we are presented with two things of the same kind which appear the same, a demonstrative like "this" or "here" enables us nevertheless to distinguish them. Two coins may look the same, but we can still individuate one of them by thinking of it as "this" one. So also, two mental states may appear the same in introspection. A recurring tingle may feel the same and yet I am able to think of different occurrences of it: "this tingle is just like the one that occurred before." This characterization of demonstratives clearly depends upon a contrast with the way things appear, so that the element which is added by the demonstrative itself does not contribute to the content of the appearance. This seems correct, at least in many cases. In thinking of "this" tingle or the tingle which is occurring "now," the demonstratives do not describe how the tingle appears, how it is felt. Nevertheless, there is a kind of demonstrative

---

65. Strawson 1959, pp. 9–10.

use which does describe such qualities, and we need to understand this phenomenon in order to understand my main argument.

Evans explains how a demonstrative element can be involved in the way something appears.[66] Suppose that I throw a ball to my dog, Argus, and it enters his visual field from above. He does not simply recognize the shape of the ball, since his reaction shows awareness of its direction. He reacts differently when the ball is above than when it is to the left, and since this is something he has learned, we must credit him with some kind of awareness of spatial direction. When we describe the content of his awareness, we must use some demonstrative, such as "this" or "above." But there is an important difference in the content of this kind of awareness and the kind of awareness that we have when we grasp the meaning of such words. For all we know from Argus's behavior he may be doing only what Strawson calls "feature-placing,"[67] which, as Strawson explains, is a form of Price's universal recognition. Feature-placing is a form of cognition the content of which is described by combining a general term with a demonstrative, as in "There is water over there." I will, however, describe feature-placing with hyphens to bring out the aspect of it which I wish to emphasize. Let us suppose that Argus is only feature-placing. Then I will describe his cognition with a phrase like "Ball-here." Because this describes the result of universal recognition, Argus thus has a cognition which is just like one he would have on another occasion of throwing the ball from the same direction, or perhaps it is just like that of another dog who is also seeing a similar ball coming from the same kind of direction. "Ball-here," despite the presence of the demonstrative, describes a universal and in particular a way something appears. "Ball-there," let us suppose, describes a different way things look to him. Now, the crucial thing about hyphenating these expressions is that even though we understand that there is something in common between these two kinds of appearance, we cannot suppose that Argus

---

66. Evans 1982, p. 154ff. In Doepke 1989 I ignored this primitive grasp of demonstratives, thus supposing that Strawson's feature-placing would involve a pure grasp of demonstratives and thus individuation. I am indebted to John Perry for bringing this mistake to my attention. I still agree with the main point I wished to make, that a pure grasp of demonstratives goes hand in hand with the abilities to individuate and to draw the distinction between appearance and reality.

67. Strawson 1959, pp. 208–16.

does. It may well be that these are simply two different universals, two kinds of patterns that he recognizes. The fact that he distinguishes these two is shown by the difference in the way he responds. So also, he responds differently to different kinds of smells and shapes and patterns of behavior. It does not follow that he knows anything about the *similarity* which we notice on two occasions of ball-here and ball-there. He may have nothing like our thought that it is a *ball* which is coming in from here and also the same kind of thing which is coming in from there.

I will describe the kind of grasp of demonstratives which is involved in feature-placing as one that is not "pure." Argus does not (let us suppose) grasp the demonstratives "here" and "there" purely, since he grasps them only in certain complex patterns such as ball-here and ball-there. We, on the other hand, grasp these demonstratives when things *appear the same* and we nevertheless distinguish the different things appearing by adding the demonstrative elements. Suppose, for example, that I am confronted with two balls and that I attend to these in succession, so that each of the two balls looks the same at each of the two moments. Argus could do the same thing, and so we could credit him on both occasions with cognitions with a certain content, expressed, say, by "ball-in-front." Since Argus's cognitions have the same content at both moments he does not "separate" the two balls. But when we think of the first ball as "this" one and the second one as "that" one, we do just that.

The difference between "here" and "there" is, in an obvious sense, subjective. There is no contradiction in something's being both here and there (at the same time) if it is here and there to different subjects. When we understand the description of Argus's cognition as "Ball-there" we accordingly think of it from his point of view. Of course, Argus does not have to think of himself in order to think ball-here precisely because he does not have a pure grasp of the demonstrative "here." He is aware of the ball and is sensitive to its direction. He does not have to know that *he* is confronted with a ball which is related to him in a certain way. But we are capable of grasping the demonstrative purely. Now, the demonstrative specifies the direction in relation to a certain subject. When we grasp the import of the demonstrative *as such* we must therefore *know which* subject is in question. When, therefore, I have a pure grasp of the demonstratives "here" and "there," as I do when the two balls look the same at different moments but I nevertheless think of them as here and there, I must individuate *myself*, since I am the subject in relation to whom these demonstratives describe different directions. To *understand* the "pure" difference between being here and being there in the case in which I use this difference to distinguish the two apparently identical balls I must be self-aware.

What I have said so far applies only to the case of spatial demonstratives. It is not obvious why this applies to others. This is important, for unless this can be shown, for all we know individuation might be able to terminate with these other demonstratives. I think, however, that we can generalize our latest reflections so as to show that the point holds for all demonstratives. When we individuate things by grasping a spatial demonstrative purely, our thought about that thing is based on our perception of it. As such, the subject is "immediately aware" of the object of perception in the sense that the object is individuated in the non-inferential thought the subject has on the basis of that perception. Suppose, for example, that I know directly (non-inferentially) that I see just one dog in front of me now. Then I am "immediately aware" of that dog. Suppose further that I think of Bubba by thinking that the father of the dog before me now was large. Then I am aware of Bubba only "mediately" in the sense that I individuate him only by a description in which he is uniquely related to something of which I am immediately aware. The notion of immediate awareness is similar to Russell's notion of acquaintance, except that Russell wanted acquaintance to be a form of knowledge that did not require being actually aware of the object.[68] Russell sometimes uses "this" in a special sense that is appropriate just when the entity designated is an object of attention. I want to borrow this idea and use "this" in a special sense to apply to anything of which I am immediately aware. If I see Argus, I can refer to "this" dog. On the thesis of Strawson, I can also refer to myself as "this" person without any suggestion that my knowledge of myself is known by inference from current experience, as Russell (and Hume) would have it. I want now to

68. See Russell 1988, p. 17.

generalize the point I made about spatial demonstratives to apply to "this" in our special sense.

The point I wished to make about spatial demonstratives is that they enable a subject to transcend the level of universal recognition and achieve genuine individuation. We supposed that Argus could recognize (the universal) ball-in-front but could not grasp the import of thinking of *this* ball, since this would require a grasp of the subjective relation to himself. Now a similar point can be made about "this" in general, in our special sense. As explained above, what this term indicates is a certain epistemic relation, specifically that the entity designated is the object of attention. But this relation, like that of spatial directedness, pertains to a subjective relation. Just as something can be above one person and not above another, something can be an immediate object of awareness of one person and only a mediate object of awareness of another. Whenever we apply the term "this" to indicate an object of immediate awareness, to grasp the special contribution of this term we must accordingly realize that it is known in this way. Since, however, it is not just known absolutely this way, but only by a certain person, we must know *who* it is that is immediately aware of the entity. And there is no doubt that it is oneself, since there is nothing more fundamental in our knowledge of ourselves than that each of us is the person who is immediately aware of the object in question.[69] I discover, for example, that a tingle is *mine* just by feeling it. Now, the point about transcending the level of universal recognition can be made more generally. In any case of immediate awareness I can use the term "this" to express my individuating success. For example, I can refer to this tingle. But to really understand this, to be individuating and not merely recognizing the kind of sensation in question, I must be able to do more than recognize the universal, *tingle*. I must understand the special import of "this," which, we have seen, is to indicate an essentially subjective relation. *This* tingle is the one I am feeling. Without self-awareness, I am arguing, one will not be able to distinguish "this tingle" from "tingle" and will be confined to the level of universal recognition.

I have argued that self-awareness is necessary for individuation

---

69. In the first chapter we saw that this thought was the basis for Locke's theory of personal identity.

on the ground that it enables one to mark the distinction between immediate and mediate awareness.

It is clear that this is connected with our "empiricist" assumption that we are acquainted with only such things as we can demonstratively designate from our individual finite perspectives. For the ability to grasp a demonstrative distinction "purely" is just what is needed to distinguish between something of which one is immediately aware and something else qualitatively indistinguishable from this. And marking this sort of distinction is itself just what is needed to count things on the basis of perception. I assume that we can count things that are not perceived, such as things which existed long ago and those that are too small to see, only when we know of them by inference from things we do perceive. When we do perceive several objects of a certain kind, what enables us to count them, and thus to individuate any one, is that we make a distinction between the one immediately perceived at each step of the count and those already counted and thus only mediately individuated. It is true that we can recognize several things of one kind in a moment without counting them. A pair of coins has a certain look with which one might be quite familiar. But a pair of coins does not look like a single coin, and to see the pair as two coins one attends to each in turn, which requires distinguishing between "this" coin and the one just observed. Since self-awareness is required to draw this distinction, we must be able to think of ourselves to think of anything at all.

It may seem that my position is subject to the same objection I leveled against the Humean view. I said in effect that to understand which tingle is this tingle one needs to relate it to oneself. It may seem that underlying this objection is a view of individuating that is viciously regressive. This would be the idea that to know which thing is meant one must be able to relate it uniquely to something else. Since this would never allow individuation to terminate, nothing could be individuated in the first place. But then the objection could be raised that since we must stop at some point, it is not obvious why it should be with oneself (in self-awareness) and not, say, with this tingle. Put another way, the objection is that to terminate a chain of individuation some demonstrative must be grasped, but, for all we know, it might as well be "this" and not "I." This objection is mistaken, however, since it fails to take account of the unique way in which one individuates oneself in self-awareness. It is true that demonstratives in general can switch reference from one context to another, but personal pronouns switch reference only by switching persons. This means that whenever I understand my own use of first person pronouns, such as "I" and "mine," I think of the same thing, regardless of the change in context. When I think of something by understanding a demonstrative singular term such as "this tingle" or "now," I am thinking of something such as a feeling or a time which belongs to kind of which there are (or can be) many others like it, many others which could be before my mind but which are not. This is why I need to know something more than the general way in which such things appear to pick one of them out. Since all that I know about the one in question which differentiates it from the others is my epistemic relation to it, I need to be able so to relate that thing to myself to think of which one it is. But since the only person who appears to me in the general way in which persons appear to themselves is myself, I do not need to be able to relate the person who so appears to me to something else to know which thing it is.

My main point about the dependency of "this" (in our special sense) upon "I" was that being able to grasp the sense of "this" requires self-awareness and is necessary to rise above the level of universal recognition and reach the level of genuine individuation. To be vivid, I gave kinds of sensations as examples of universals recognized: feelings and perceptual experiences. But these are not the only things that philosophers have attempted to individuate with demonstratives independently of self-awareness. In presenting a "neo-Lockean analysis" of personal identity, Rovane rebuts what I have called the (Kantian) thesis of Strawson by reducing self-references to descriptions such as "the thinker of this thought."[70] In order for the thought in question to identify the thinker it must not of course be general, a certain proposition, but must be rather a particular episode of thinking. Although such a particular will not have the phenomenal quality of a sensation like a tingle, I think it is clear that the objection I raised will apply just as surely against such analyses. Suppose I think that Locke was English

---

70. Rovane 1993, pp. 86–88.

and I am aware of this (particular) thought. Other people may also have particular thoughts with this content, but I can know that they do only inferentially, e.g., by inferring the presence of a thought from what I hear them say. By contrast, I am aware of "this" thought directly, by being immediately aware of it (assuming that we can individuate such things at all). And just as the individuation of this tingle must be more than the recognition of the kind of sensation, the individuation of this particular episode of thinking must be more than thinking that Locke was English. In both cases that "something more" is effected by realizing that the thing in question is an object of immediate awareness, known directly by oneself.

Since this completes the second stage of the two-stage argument of this chapter, I would like to clarify the assumptions and the basic steps. Overall, the subject has been the conditions of individuation, of that knowledge in which we know of which thing we are thinking. In the first stage we assumed the Kantian thesis of Strawson that I know of which thing I am thinking only by being able to think of how that thing is uniquely related to myself. Since knowledge by description is parasitic upon knowledge by acquaintance, this means that I must be acquainted with myself, not knowing which thing I am only by a description such as "subject of these experiences." Assuming that we really are as we can only know ourselves to be, I argued that this view entails the main conclusion, that I am a single thing and not a plurality of two or more things. According to this thesis, I cannot identify myself only by relating myself to things already identified, since I use my self-knowledge to know which things these are. But since a plurality can be known as such only by knowing already of things which form the plurality, or by relating them all to something else, I cannot, according to this view, know myself as a plurality. In keeping with a broadly empiricist view of the possibility of individuation, we accepted Strawson's idea that demonstratives are needed for individuation. With this idea, the claim that I am a plurality can be sustained only by embracing the Humean view of demonstratives, that they can be understood without needing to be able to individuate oneself. The second stage of the argument meant to refute this view. Although demonstratives can be used to express feature-placing, in the "pure" use that they have in individuation they can be understood only by being able to individuate oneself. I cannot dispense with demonstratives such as "I" and "mine" in favor of ones such as "this" and "there" since these can switch references for me. To know which thing is meant I must know that it is the one of a certain kind to which I am attending. Without this ability to relate the thing to myself I know only its general appearance, in which case I am merely feature-placing and not individuating. This is the proof of the thesis of Strawson that was shown in the first stage of the argument to yield the desired conclusion.

In any justified view of myself I will be able to individuate myself. In such a view I will appear as a single thing. In the next chapter I will attempt to show how this common assumption supports another one: that knowledge of our identity is practically important.

3

The Importance of the Metaphysics of Personal Identity

There is, I believe, little room for doubt that the question of our identity is *theoretically* important. Aristotle realized that there was a kind of explanation, which he called "formal" explanation, in which a property of a thing was derived from its essence. To point out that something *could* not be other than F, that being F is (at least part of) what x is, is a way of explaining its being F. A child who asks why a triangle has three sides might be told simply, "That's just what it is to be a triangle." So also, anything derivable from its essence would be similarly explained. Whatever our identity turns out to be, the discovery of this will therefore have theoretical importance, importance in explaining things about ourselves. If, for example, we are essentially disposed to try to make our beliefs coherent (as I think we are), then the fact that someone who discovered that he had contradictory beliefs began an investigation of them would not be some mysterious fact that called for explanation. That we are concerned with such incoherencies would be part of "what we are." This would not mean that we could not fail to be bothered by contradiction, but that such failures, and not such concerns, would be what call for explanation in the form of intervening factors. In the same way, all organisms might turn out to be essentially alive, so that when they are actually engaged in their form of life, the fact that they are calls for no explanation. We can, of course, ask why there *exist* such things, but this is a different fact to be explained. If life is essential to living things, it will be the fact that they are *not* engaged in their characteristic form of activity that will need explaining. Sleep and comas will be explained largely at least by the interference of the external world. In this sense, the activity in question will be "natural" even though it is not always present when the thing exists. What will be *necessary* is only the *tendency* to perform the activity. This sort of phenomenon will then illustrate Aristotle's idea that sometimes the "formal cause" coincides with the "final": what a thing *is* will be a matter of what it has a tendency to *do*. The purpose of the next two chapters is to lay the groundwork, through transcendental argument, for just such an ontology, in which *all* the things which appear to us in experience, including ourselves, owe their identify to a form of activity that is distinctive of their kind.

In the present chapter, however, our concern is with the practical importance of the question of our identity. It is clear and uncontroversial that this question seems to have such importance. Perhaps the most obvious example pertains to what I will call "self-involved desires." My desire to see how my children will turn out is "self-involved" in the sense that its satisfaction requires my involvement: I cannot get what I want without *my* seeing my children in later years. By contrast, I want altruistically that they prosper in these years, but this desire could be satisfied even if I am no longer around. The question of whether some future person is *me* seems obviously to have a great deal of importance beyond the merely theoretical, since (it seems) it is only then that many of my desires (the self-involved ones) can be satisfied.

In the first chapter I mentioned Parfit's troubling idea that in the course of normal human life it is as if we are gradually dying a bit as we undergo psychological changes. In a variety of examples, he suggests that with losses of deep affections and concerns it is especially trivial to think that personal identity is preserved.[71] It is easy to see why this is troubling. My continued life (it seems) is very important

---

71. See, especially, Parfit 1984, p. 305 and p. 327.

to me largely because it is necessary for obtaining many of the things I want very much. I suspect that what troubles most people about "short" views of our identity is this point, that they deny us the satisfaction of self-involved desires. This is what bothers us so much about the prospect of our death. Some people think there are holy ones who finally purify themselves of such desires and by doing so overcome their concern with personal survival. I will argue later in this chapter that this goal is at best an unreachable ideal. But even if it were possible, it would not follow that such desires are actually irrational or immoral. This being so, for persons like me who have many of them, our persistence, while perhaps not of cosmic importance, certainly seems very important to us.

I also mentioned in the first chapter Parfit's claim that his "true" view of our identity should alter the way in which we assign responsibility for past deeds. If identity over time is a rather trivial matter, so—it seems—are claims of responsibility for "our" past actions.

Since Parfit's view is the main target of this book, and since Parfit himself seems to offer a variety of arguments for it, I want to be clear about what exactly is our target. As I mentioned in the first chapter, he holds that personal identity is determined over time by non-branching psychological continuity, a relation which obtains by overlapping psychological connections. Such connections obtain whenever, for example, a belief is retained, a desire is fulfilled or an intention is carried out. But with changes in belief, loss of desires and abandoned intentions, there are psychological disconnections. Now, so long as there are still other connections which bridge these changes, there is still psychological continuity and hence (if there is no branching) there is supposed to be persistence of the same person. But since the *basis* of the ground of personal identity is *diminished*, claims of personal identity are held to be proportionately *trivial*. I believe that the inference that Parfit is making is correct. *If* the basis of claims of personal identity is eroded, as Parfit says it is, then this really should change our attitudes about such matters as responsibility for past actions. The main purpose of this chapter is really to defend this sort of claim. But as a preliminary, let us concede (what will soon be doubted) that personal identity is necessary for the satisfaction of self-involved desires and the retention of responsibility. And let us concede (what I want ultimately to refute) that personal identity is diminished in the circumstances Parfit says it is. Then, claims of personal identity are thereby used correctly to *ground* the practical attitudes in question, and these in turn are *grounded* in a basis which diminishes with psychological disconnections. I take it as obvious that the relation of grounding is transitive, so that whatever grounds the claim of personal identity would in turn ground the practical attitudes. But then as the former diminishes, so does the latter.

Parfit often contrasts his view with one which he associates with Descartes. This is the idea that there is a "separate self," the identity of which is a "separate fact" over and above what can be empirically discerned through observation and introspection. And he sometimes suggests that our common convictions about the practical importance of our identity are based upon embracing this view. This has lead some, such as Unger and Johnston, to suppose that they can rebut Parfit by showing that these convictions are not dependent on this "metaphysics" (in the pejorative sense of being a form of transcendent metaphysics).[72] This is fine as far as it goes, but I am urging that there is an interesting challenge that Parfit throws down which does not depend on this claim. To suppose, as Parfit often seems to, that the choice is between his "short" view and the Cartesian view just described is to present a false alternative. For one can maintain a "longer" view which coincides with common sense and is just as wedded to the empirical as is Parfit's. All it takes to support a "longer" view is to deny that the breaking of psychological connections in general erode the basis of identity. Perhaps with the loss of even deeply held values, claims of personal identity are not at all trivial. This is just what I will eventually maintain. But I can still hold that there is another empirically ascertainable relation which obtains through many psychological disconnections and determines full-blooded personal identity. In the last chapter, I will argue that so long as the tendency to make rational decisions is physically realized in the same kind of body, claims of personal identity are not at all trivial, even if many psychological disconnections have occurred. My present point, however, is that the really interesting argument that Parfit makes is the one

---

72. See Unger 1990, pp. 326–32, and Johnston 1992.

defended in the last paragraph. To refute this argument, it is not enough to show that our common convictions about the practical importance of personal identity do not have a Cartesian source. One needs to refute the "short" view (which, I have argued, requires establishing a general ontology) or the claim that our identity is really connected with the practical attitudes in question. The following chapters are largely devoted to the first of these tasks. Since this concern with the "length" of personal identity is motivated by the conviction that our identity does have such practical significance, we do well to consider first whether this conviction is warranted.

In spite of Parfit's claim that personal identity really is important in assigning responsibility, it is Parfit himself who is famous for challenging, in another context, the "importance" of our identity. As we will see, all the practical importance can be called into question by generalizing his original point. Parfit realizes that most of us are very concerned with our own *continued* existence. But in an ingenious argument he concludes that this is irrational. The argument is based on the fission case, mentioned before, in which the two halves of a person's brain are carefully separated so that each, it seems, would carry on the mental life of the original person. In the last chapter we saw that the self is a single thing, as most of us unreflectively suppose, and so this cannot be a case, such as Lewis and Noonan thought, of two persons parting company. Not unless we resort to an unknowable view of the self. And so we are forced to conclude, as most would anyway, that the original person is distinct from each of the two "copies." What Parfit seizes upon is the apparent fact that the original is related to each of his two offshoots in the same way that he would be related to himself if instead of fission he had continued to exist (say, by having just one brain half destroyed). But then it seems that even though identity is lost, all that is important to the original person in his continued existence is not only preserved but doubled![73] If so, then even in normal life it is not really the fact that we continue to exist that is important, but rather that we continue to be related to ourselves in the way in which we would be importantly related

---

73. Ibid., pp. 261–62.

to the offshoots of our fission. And this relation, Parfit suggests, is psychological continuity.

It might seem that the result of our previous chapter, that I am a single thing, easily shows what is wrong with Parfit's conclusion about the unimportance of my continued existence. As I said before, many of my desires are self-involved, for example, that I see how my children turn out. If I am a single thing, then even if my offshoots see how my children turn out, it will not be I who sees this, and hence my desire will not be satisfied. I will eventually argue that there is something importantly correct about this. But the very example may well seem to show just what is wrong with the argument. What Parfit can hold is that "self-involved" desires, in an important and perhaps obvious sense, *can* be fulfilled by someone else. What is shown by the fission example, he can say, is that such desires do not really require the same self for their satisfaction. Perhaps we should not, then, *call* them "self" involved, but this may seem to be a trivial linguistic point. Parfit makes a similar reply at some length about the propriety of saying that the offshoots have "memories" of the original person's life. Even if it is analytic that I "remember" only my own past, it is easy to coin a term, like "quasi-memory," which has a sense just like "memory" with the sole exception that it does not require personal identity.[74] In the same way, it may be suggested, we can speak of "quasi-self-involved" desires. These do not require for their satisfaction that numerically the same self be involved in their satisfaction, and they are paradigmatically satisfied by my offshoots seeing how my children turn out. Anyone who is persuaded by Parfit's claim that my offshoots are related to me in the same way that I would be related to myself if I had continued to exist will surely have difficulty in seeing why the satisfaction of self-involved desires is superior to the satisfaction of their quasi correlates.

As I said, Parfit himself does not say that the question of personal identity has no practical importance, since he uses his view of our identity to support consequentialist theories in ethics, such as Utilitarianism, and this accounts for a great deal of the interest that his whole project has generated. Nevertheless, this connection has been

---

74. This was first suggested by Shoemaker in Shoemaker 1984, "Persons and their pasts."

questioned. Wiggins, for example, once claimed that "a malefactor could scarcely evade responsibility by contriving his own fission."[75] Since Wiggins believes that fission would result in the destruction of the original person, what this means is that he thinks that personal identity is *not*, as Parfit and most of us ordinarily think, required for assignments of responsibility as in compensation and punishment. What he is saying, perhaps very plausibly, is that the offshoots, even though non-identical with the original person, would still be punishable for his crimes. If so, there must be some *other* relation which obtains and which accounts for the preservation of responsibility. It would be a short step to conclude that identity is never what really matters in cases of responsibility. Perhaps it is a relation like psychological continuity which (supposedly) is independent of identity. If so, then metaphysical investigations which disclose our identity would have no bearing on ethical matters pertaining to desert.

Just this position has been elaborated by Christine Korsgaard.[76] She calls the "other" relation which really accounts for responsibility the "authorial" relation. This relation is explained by her construal of Kant's conception of the distinction between the noumenal and the phenomenal. Korsgaard thinks (correctly, I believe) that this is best explained not as a distinction between two "worlds" but between two perspectives or viewpoints on the common world. The phenomenal standpoint is the theoretical: adopted when concerned with explanation and prediction. We consider ourselves this way when we want to explain what we have done or predict what we will do. We take the noumenal or "authorial" standpoint when we make decisions, about what to think or do. Whenever I have conflicting beliefs or desires I find myself in the position of a judge. In any court, there must be one judge: even if there are several people they must act as one in order to settle the issue. Just so, we must regard ourselves as a unity when adopting the authorial perspective, and it is just this sort of unity, she thinks, that is expressed by personal pronouns such as "I." But—and this is important to her—this unity is only "practical"; it is not "metaphysical," in the sense that it need not be matched in reality by the numerical identity of the person in question. This possibility is

75. Wiggins 1976, p. 146.
76. Korsgaard 1989.

evident, she thinks, over time. In Wiggins's case in which a malefactor contrives his own fission Korsgaard would say that even though identity is lost the authorial relation would still obtain and hence responsibility would be preserved. With Parfit, she thinks that the malefactor could "quasi-intend" to do things that the offshoots would carry out. The original person's responsibilities would transfer to the offshoots because he would be the "author" of their actions, even though these offshoots are numerically distinct from him. This is her "answer" to Parfit: personal identity is not what matters in assigning moral responsibility; the authorial relation is. A crucial part of her answer is an assumption she shares with Parfit: that quasi-intending really is possible so that the authorial relation is independent of identity. It is only this that enables her to question the relevance of discovering identity in assignments of responsibility. In this same general way, Parfit must also believe in quasi-intending and the like in order to think that psychological continuity is independent of identity and so to conclude that identity is not what matters in personal survival.

It is not difficult to make a case for Korsgaard's view that it is the authorial relation which primarily bears the relation of responsibility. In accepting that I ought to do something, I implicitly accept responsibility and the appropriate measure of censure for failing to do it. I cannot now consistently accept the obligation while denying that my future self is blameworthy in the event that he fails to do what I ought now to initiate. But then what makes him responsible, it seems, is not really the fact that he is identical with me, but rather the fact that he is the one whom I get to do things just by deciding to do them. I "directly" control him, or, as Korsgaard would say, I "author" his actions. If this relation really is independent of identity then I can "author" the actions of my offshoots and, by the present argument, they would inherit my duties, and presumably, my rights as well.

Wiggins, like Parfit, does not think that the question of our identity has no practical importance. He maintains that our identity through time is determined, not by the fact that we are persons, but more specifically by the fact that we are members of a certain biological species.[77] This is practically important, he argues, since it makes our

---

77. Wiggins 1980, pp. 179–82.

identity more determinate, and this helps to restrict the ambitions of social planners who like to regard our nature as more plastic.[78] What Wiggins wants especially to oppose is the view that our identity is not entirely natural but is determined conventionally to some (appreciable) degree. This is pernicious, he thinks, because there is a tendency of social planners to underestimate the potential for variation and change in human desires, to suppose that future people will want pretty much what they now want. The biological view that Wiggins favors would encourage them to realize that present desires are merely a manifestation of an obscure underlying nature that happens to find itself in certain contingent social circumstances. With this conviction in a real human *nature* that has to be discovered and cannot be declared on the basis of its present appearance, social planners would be more open to possibilities of constructive social change.

The problem with this argument for our purpose is that it seems to pertain more to the continued identity of the human species than to the identity of individual humans. The important fact that Wiggins wants to establish seems to be that human nature itself should not be judged by how it appears in present social circumstances: that humans in currently unimagined forms of society might have unimagined desires. What seems important is the fact that the creatures in such societies would still be human and not that any of them would be numerically identical with any humans today. The social planners that Wiggins want to restrain deliberate more about future human societies than societies in the future which are populated by the people actually living today. It might be countered that if human nature itself permitted such variations then surely this would imply that any individual human could undergo such changes. But this is not certain. Human nature might permit such variations only across generations, so that the variations would actually require that they appear in numerically distinct individuals. And even if it could be shown that each of us has an underlying nature that permits us to reappear in different forms of society with quite different desires than those we now have, we will know why this will be important only if we know why our numerical identity with that person is important.

---

78. Ibid., pp. 173–89.

Perhaps my relation to myself in such a different circumstance will be like my relation to the Afghan rebel who ends up with my body. Even if he is identical with me, does that matter? Perhaps the fact that he has become adapted to such a different society makes him different in such a way that there is no practical significance to the fact that he is identical with me. We do not know until we know why personal identity itself is practically important.

Although neither Parfit nor Wiggins themselves deny the practical importance of the question of our identity altogether, it is not difficult to imagine one who would. (Perhaps Korsgaard?) There is clearly something suggested in Parfit's position about our continued existence which can be generalized. All that has to be said is that there are one or more other relations, independent of identity, relations perhaps like psychological continuity or the authorial one, which normally coexist with identity but which bear the practical importance. It would be such a relation which we would look for in praising and blaming and which we would hope will link us with a future person when considering those desires we normally think of as "self" involving. The whole appearance of the importance of the metaphysics of persons might be due only to the fact that such relations normally coexist with identity. But once we realize which relation or relations are the really important ones, metaphysical discussions of our identity which aim for practical relevance will seem a sham; the issue of our identity will seem a red herring, distracting us from the (perhaps easy) question of whether this or these other relations obtain.

I hope it is clear from our discussion that such a position will need to rely heavily, as Parfit and Korsgaard do, on the notion of "quasi" states. I have mainly discussed only two kinds of practical importance that questions of personal identity have seemed to have, pertaining to self-involved desires and moral responsibility. I do not know if there are other considerations that are not instances of these. But these are certainly issues of great human concern. The satisfaction of self-involved desires, as we have seen, will certainly require a quasi correlate if identity is not important. I have also argued, on behalf of Korsgaard, that the authorial relation is what bears the relation of responsibility, so that if this can link numerically distinct persons, Parfit's quasi-intending must be possible.

Before I argue against this position, I would like to spell out how my own is different. Perry once argued that all of the practical importance of personal identity is due to the fact that our concerns are relatively stable, so that, for example, my continued existence is important to me because my future self is likely to share many of my present concerns and is therefore likely to work for the things I now want.[79] Parfit realized that this is to say that my future self is valuable to me now only as a *means* for getting what I now want; and he pointed out that this supports his own view, since copies of one would presumably inherit these same concerns.[80] In arguing for the practical importance of personal identity, it is of course not necessary to deny that copies of oneself would be of some, indeed even very great, value to oneself. The question is whether the loss of identity would also be a serious matter.

In order to convince us that the offshoots of our fission would be psychologically continuous with us, Parfit claims that if he knew he were about to undergo fission he could form intentions, or rather quasi-intentions, for each of them: he could quasi-intend that one roam the world and that the other stay at home.[81] This claim is of the utmost importance to him, since it is only on the basis of the fact that he will be psychologically continuous with the offshoots that he can claim that he is related to each of his offshoots in the same way that he would be related to himself if he continued to exist. And as we saw, it is only this that enables him to conclude that all that is important in continued existence is preserved in fission (indeed doubled) despite the absence of continued existence. If the mere loss of identity would break the psychological continuity, he could not say that identity is unimportant. For he realizes that the possibility of quasi-intending is particularly important. If our offshoots could, for example, quasi-remember our experiences but we could not quasi-intend things for them to do, then a great strand of psychological continuity would be lost. We are not merely remembering beings, but intellectually active beings, capable of acting with conscious purpose. So Parfit must hold that he would be linked with his offshoots by this aspect of our mental life in

---

79. Perry 1976.
80. Parfit 1984.
81. Parfit 1984, p. 261.

order to make his case that identity itself is not what matters. I deny that he can form such intentions for his offshoots. I claim that if he knows that he is about to undergo fission and he thinks, as Parfit does, that this will be the end of his life, he cannot make plans to do things after the fission. He can at most plan how he will be at the end, knowing that he will be "copied." He can, for example, decide to stock his head with arguments that he knows will be immediately available to his offshoots, in the hope that these will influence the decisions that they will make. But in this respect they are no different from his children: each will make his own decisions. And by the argument that I gave on behalf of Korsgaard, this will mean that he will not "author" their actions and will not be responsible for them. I also claim that I have self-involved desires for which there can be no quasi-correlates, so that the boundaries of my existence determine not only what I can plan to do but what I can hope for in the fulfillment of these desires.

Before I begin my argument I want to deal with the objection that my conclusion is counterintuitive. I expect the main resistance to come from the conviction, first expressed by Wiggins, that a copy of mine, even though distinct from me, would still bear my responsibilities. Suppose, for example, that there is a machine which annihilates and quickly replicates a (distinct) person. Is it really acceptable to allow, Wiggins would ask, that a criminal could "evade responsibility" by jumping into it, knowing that his replica would spring out laughing? There are several observations to make about this case. First, knowing what kind of character the replica will have, we have good reason to protect ourselves. Second, what matters is what is the truth and not what he thinks about what is happening. If a criminal were to commit suicide with a laugh because he was sure that he would be reincarnated, this would obviously not be enough to hold responsible the person whom he thought he was to become. If our criminal jumps in, thinking that this is not really going to destroy him, then he is simply wrong. If, on the other hand, we suppose that he really does understand what is about to happen, then we must consider what a serious matter this might be. According to the argument I will present, since he will understand that he literally cannot plan to do anything at all after he steps into that machine, he can plan at most to make himself a certain way at the end, knowing that he will be copied. But he must regard his replica as a distinct person, with his own will, just as his replica will divorce himself from memories of the crimes which he knows were not really "his." By my account, if a criminal were to jump eagerly into the machine, his behavior would show that he did not really understand what was about to happen.

Parfit's claim that he can form quasi-intentions for his offshoots may well seem plausible only from the third person point of view. We think of Parfit's decision-making as something going on in his brain, leaving a microstructure which is then duplicated. But what about from his own point of view? Can he think, for example, "When *I* have the left brain half *I* will roam the world and when *I* have the right half *I* will stay at home"? This seems absurd, and the argument of the last chapter explains exactly why it is: since I am a single thing I cannot plan what "I" will do when the person I have in mind is someone distinct from me. Rovane is sensitive to this sort of objection and suggests it can be overcome by thinking not what "I" will do but what "I*" will do.[82] Although genuine I-thoughts, she can allow, are directed only to a single thing, I*-thoughts are what correspond to quasi states and differ precisely in not being restricted to just myself. Again, the charge against my position would be one of triviality. Although it may be allowed that *I* cannot decide what I will do after fission, I can decide what *I** will do. And the claim is that there is no important difference, so that even though genuine I-thoughts are circumscribed by my identity, this is also unimportant, because I*-thoughts are not.

Rovane's suggestion does not really lend further support to Parfit's view that quasi-intending is possible. It shows only that we cannot defeat his view by the cheap linguistic maneuver of just saying that intentions are expressed by "I." But any plausibility in the idea that I can animate my offshoots by deciding what I* will do is due entirely to Parfit's idea that I can quasi-intend what they will do. The asterisk is designed only to give verbal expression to this idea.

We must also realize that the question is not of what one can *say* but of what one can *think*. It is obvious that I can coin the *word* "I*" so that when I say what "I*" will do I am not committing myself to the fact that I and not a copy of mine will do it. The question is what I

---

82. Rovane 1990.

must *think* when I decide what to do. I may linguistically express my decision to roam the world without a personal pronoun like "I," by saying, for example, "Let's roam the world." But the question is whether in *understanding* my own utterance, or in being aware of my decision without the use of any words, I must think of myself as such.

In the last chapter I defended the Kantian thesis of Strawson that individuation terminates with I-thoughts, and I argued that the self-awareness of such thoughts is the awareness of just one thing. A consequence of this is that in understanding my own use of Rovane's word, "I*," I must distinguish between the case in which it is a distinct person, such as a distinct replica of mine, and the case in which it is merely myself. Without making this distinction I would simply fail to individuate anything. In the first case I will understand "I*" by means of a description such as "my only replica"; the second will involve just the I-thought. The use of "I*" to express our intentions, or quasi-intentions, is accordingly always dispensable. To suppose that I can quasi-intend in the case in which I realize that it is the distinct replica whose future I am planning, is thus to suppose that I can quasi-intend by deciding what "my only replica" will do. But there is surely something strange about this, and it is certainly not clear that this involves doing anything but deciding how to make myself (now and until I end), knowing that I will be copied.

To begin to see what is strange about it, consider the fact that this situation is not significantly different from that in which I continue to exist (and know it) and also know that I will be perfectly copied at a certain time in the near future. Suppose I realize that in five seconds I will still live but also that a perfect copy of me at that moment will be created. I know that my current decisions will *affect* how he will be, but in this respect he is no different from a shadow of mine. Suppose that I watch my shadow against a wall and make it go upstairs with me. I might even watch the shadow "walk" up the stairs and say to myself such words as "Now I take these steps." This, I contend, is like thinking of a copy of myself and verbally expressing my intentions with the contrived expression, "I.*" This word game with my shadow does not of course show what I am actually thinking. And it seems plain that what I would really think is how to make *myself* now (lifting my leg slowly to the next step), knowing that this will affect how my shadow will look. The case in which I think of a copy of mine is not significantly different. As Parfit says, I know that he will "inherit" my intentions in the sense that his brain will have the same micro-structure which presumably realizes my intentions. But in this respect the fact that I am annihilated is irrelevant. Whatever relation I have to a copy of mine created after I exist is the same that I have to a copy of mine when I continue to exist. But the way in which I animate such copies is no different from the way in which I animate my shadow. There is simply no reason to accept the idea, that is so important to Parfit, that I can get my copies to do things directly, just by deciding to do something.

I have tried to cast suspicion on the notion of quasi-intending when the person is making decisions for someone he realizes is distinct from him. We have observed that the most obvious objection to quasi-intending is that intentions are expressed with I-thoughts which, we have seen, belong to one person; our challenge now is to avoid the charge that this is a trivial fact. Let us consider, then, why intentions are expressed with such thoughts. According to the thesis of Strawson, which I supported in the last chapter, I am able to individuate things other than myself only if I can think of how they are uniquely related to myself. Since self-awareness thus serves to anchor my individuation of things in general, it offers a way of thinking of myself which does not in turn require my being able to relate myself to something else. This means that I am different from all other persons in that to know who anyone else is I must be able to differentiate him from myself with a description which relates him uniquely to me. There is a consequence of this to which Evans pays a good deal of attention.[83] When I know that a predicate "x is F" applies to a person without needing such a description to think of who it is, I automatically know that the predicate applies to myself. When I know that someone feels a tingle just by feeling it, I know that I am the one feeling the tingle. The main point I want to make now is that predicates which express knowledge of practical decisions are normally like this. It is possible to know that a predicate like "x will roam the world" applies to myself without knowing that I satisfy some individuating description like "the

---

83. Evans 1982, p. 209ff.

person who is speaking now." This is certainly true of such predicates as we normally use them. Ordinarily, when I decide to roam the world I am aware of this decision with the same kind of directness as when I am aware of my tingle. By contrast, when I come to know that the lights are on in my car by being told that the person with the blue sedan has his lights on, I have knowledge of myself which is in this sense indirect. It strikes me that *my* lights are on only because I realize that I am the one with the blue sedan. This is not the normal way in which I come to know of my decisions to do things. The question now is whether there is some rationale for why our knowledge of our own decisions comes to us directly in this way.

In the last example I came to know something about myself which did not contribute to my knowledge of which thing I am. I learned that the owner of the blue sedan has a car with its lights on, but until I realized that this was me I could not add this fact to the stock of knowledge which together marks me out as a single individual. It is through I-thoughts, through self-awareness, that I realize both what I have been and what I can be. Let us ask what sorts of I-thoughts I must have in order to individuate myself. What sorts of properties must I ascribe to myself in self-awareness in order to know which thing I am? We have addressed this question to some extent before. The lesson of Kant's example of consciousness being passed through subjects like motion through billiard balls was that we need to know more than what is available by thinking of ourselves only from the current subjective perspective. We need to presume that from this perspective we view ourselves and other things as members of the physical world. Now, if we can see why this requires that we ascribe to ourselves properties of a certain kind, then we will have an expla-nation for why such properties are ascribed directly, in the sense that when one knows that such a property applies without needing an individuating description for the bearer, one knows that it applies to oneself. The ascription of such a property will result in a genuine I-thought, for it is only these that express our knowledge of which things we are. It is clear that among such properties will be ones by which we discover our own intentions, since it is only through acting on these that we manifest our presence in the physical world as a rational being. This is why I can know that a predicate such as "x will roam" the world applies to me directly, expressing my self-awareness. If I could apply such predicates as I applied the predicate "x has a car with its lights on," only by knowing first that the predicate applies to someone and then realizing that it applies to me because I fit some description, then I would be able to know which I thing I am without knowing any of my intentions. For I would need to have individuated myself already in order to understand the descriptions of me by which I come to know of my intentions. But this is impossible, since I would not know myself as a physical being. This explains why intentions are known to us through genuine I-thoughts. And by the argument of the last chapter, the "I" in question will denote just one thing, so that it will not pertain to someone, such as a distinct replica, known to be other than oneself.

Let us consider how my knowledge of my intentions is used by me to know which thing I am to see what was wrong with the idea that I can form quasi-intentions for someone I realize is distinct from me. A consequence of our assumption that our identity is knowable objectively is that we must be able to affect objects distinct from us. To see ourselves objectively is to see ourselves as we see other persons, which involves those persons having an effect on us. We must see ourselves as "bodies," as physical objects acting upon and being acted upon by other objects, being, in other words, one among a number of physical objects in interaction with one another. Now, to use this sort of fact to know which thing I am, I make a distinction between what I do *immediately* and what I do only as a *result* of what I do immediately. For example, I move my pencil mediately since I move it by moving my arm, but I move my arm immediately since I do not move it by moving something else. Many things which I "do" to things around me are not done intentionally. I affect the cushion I am sitting on by depressing it, and it in turn does something to me. It resists my force, and I am thus aware of it as an object distinct from me. My awareness of this interaction helps me to know which thing I am. Since, as I have argued, I will also have to use my intentions to individuate myself, I will also have to see myself as being in interactions in which I affect other objects intentionally, as when I move my pencil in order to write. The distinctive manner in which the pencil resists compression and movement offers me knowledge of an object distinct from me and thus helps me to see which physical object I am. Some philosophers are attracted to the idea that all of nature is God's body; if His omnipotence renders unnecessary resorting to indirect influence, every movement in nature would seem to be an expression of His immediate intentions. God would not see Himself in interaction with anything and it would thus be a mystery how He could see Himself distinct from anything else. We would be in this predicament if we could not make a distinction between what we do immediately and what we do mediately. Since these doings include those that are intentional, to avoid this predicament we must distinguish between what we *will* and what we do merely as a *result* of what we will. Now, the point I wish to emphasize is that we are not *in general* free to ignore this distinction. Yet the defenders of quasi-intending hold that in the case in which someone is a copy of mine, even though I think of him as a distinct object, I can ignore the difference between him and me and just go ahead and form intentions, or quasi-intentions. Even though I realize that my current decisions will animate him (as I animate my shadow) only because they affect how he will be copied, I can ignore this fact, focus on his future, and decide what to do. It might be protested that if this is the only case in which I ignore the distinction between myself and another object in thinking of what I will do, there will surely be enough other facts to individuate myself. I will still know, for example, that my body stops at the cushion and at the pencil. But why are we entitled to ignore the distinction in one case and not all others? Defenders of quasi-intentions, such as Parfit, claim that it is arbitrary to draw a line between me and my distinct copy. But what is really arbitrary is to suppose that I can ignore the line in this case when it is just such lines in general which are necessary for the individuation of myself and hence of all other things.

It might be objected that all that this shows is that there must be some intentions of mine which are expressed with genuine I-thoughts and not some quasi correlates. It shows that when deciding what to do I am not *always* free to shift from thinking what *I* will do to thinking what *I** will do. We have seen that the latter really boils down to thinking either what I will do or what a distinct copy of mine will do. So the defender of quasi-intending is left with the idea that there is a special kind of intention, other than that by which we individuate ourselves, which we can form while directing our thoughts to someone known to be distinct from us. But at this point there is nothing to recommend the idea. What we have instead is an explanation of why intentions belong to that class of phenomena which are known by persons to apply to themselves directly, and in which they think of themselves as single things. In light of this explanation, the claim that there are nevertheless other "intentions" which are not like this appears to us as mere words. If our arguments for this explanation are correct, they show something of the nature of intentions that rule out the possibility of quasi-intending for persons known to be distinct from us.

This reveals to some extent the practical importance of metaphysical investigations concerning our identity over time. A convincing investigation of this sort will result in a belief about the extent of our persistence. If we do not believe that we will live beyond a certain time we must contemplate that time with utter passivity. Of course we can try to make an *effect* on what happens then. But this is palpably different from planning what to *do* then. Parfit presents the cheery possibility of planning what to do when contemplating the life of a distinct copy of oneself. The present argument rejects this possibility. Just because I think of my copy as distinct from me I must restrict my plans to my own life, knowing only that I will be copied at my end. As we ordinarily think, the end of my existence is a kind of wall beyond which I cannot extend my will. And if Korsgaard is right in thinking that the "authorial" relation is what determines responsibility, the end of my existence circumscribes my sense of responsibility. For Korsgaard held that the authorial relation bridges the gap between two persons when one quasi-intends what the other does. Since I cannot quasi-intend that my replica do anything, neither he nor I will see ourselves as linked by the authorial relation. By the argument I gave on behalf of Korsgaard, there will be no evident reason to think that he is responsible for what I decide to do. For I attribute obligations to my future self only because this is required for taking responsibility for my current decisions. Since I can only make decisions for someone I believe is myself, there is no basis for attributing a transfer of obligation to my replica.

I have argued that I cannot quasi-intend that someone do

something when I believe that person to be distinct from me. Marya Schechtman has objected that this does not show that personal identity as such has practical importance: all that I have discussed is what we think about personal identity and not what is really the case.[84] I have a couple of remarks to make about this objection. First, it is not clear why it is really an objection. Metaphysics, like any intellectual discipline, though it aims for truth, achieves this only by creating beliefs. The metaphysics of personal identity can therefore have a practical effect just by changing our beliefs. It does seem correct that what I believe about my identity would have quite an effect even if I were wrong. If I thought I were to be hanged at sunset I would not make plans for tomorrow even if in fact I would later escape. But let us consider a case in which I am not aware of my annihilation and replication and I am making plans that pertain to the time of my replica. In what sense would he "carry them out"? Suppose that he also is unaware of the switch and says to himself, "Since I decided with good reason to do this, I will now do it." How should we interpret this remark? Evans imagines a similar case in which a person thinks he is both seeing and feeling a cup, but there are really two cups, and he attempts to refer with "that cup."[85] He argues that we are not entitled to assign a referent to "that cup" since the person is merely in a muddle. So also he would say that my replica would be in muddle in saying "I will do it" since he mistakenly supposes that it was just one person who both decided what to do and then acted on this decision. But if we cannot assign to him the I-thought in question, how can we say that he is "psychologically continuous" with me? We will not, in particular, be able to say that he is doing what I decided to do, since my decision is expressed with an I-thought that we cannot attribute to him. In defending Korsgaard's position about the importance of the authorial relation in assigning responsibility, we took the first person point of view to see why a person attributes obligations to his or her future self. Even if the original person and the replica do not realize that they are distinct, if it is really true that they are, then in the true description of what is intended or what is done there will be no evi-

---

84. Marya Schechtman made this point at the conference on personal identity at Santa Clara University in April, 1990.

85. Evans 1982, pp. 249–250.

dent reason to transfer obligation to the replica. For the true description will take the point of view of the two persons *as if* they are aware of the switch; and we have seen that from this point of view there is no reason to hold the replica responsible for the deeds of the original person.[86]

Having argued against quasi-intending, what can be said against the quasi-correlates of our self-involved desires, such as my desire that I see how my children turn out? Although I suggested before that "short" views of our identity are most bothersome because they threaten to limit our hopes in satisfying our self-involved desires, if these have quasi-correlates they would be satisfiable by distinct persons sufficiently similar to ourselves. To see whether our metaphysical inquiry into our identity has practical importance with respect to our ability to satisfy these desires we might ask whether our rejection of quasi-intending carries over to them. It may seem that these are quite distinct issues. My desire to see how my children fare is, for example, not a desire to do something but merely to enjoy a certain experience. I believe, however, that our self-involved desires are related to the will closely enough so that our previous argument against quasi-intending can be enlisted to show that only we can satisfy them. The first thing I wish to point out is that at least many of our self-involved desires spring up in the context of forming intentions. Whenever we intend to do anything at least part of what we envisage and want to bring about pertains to how we alone will be. There is, in fact, in every intentional action a concern for oneself that it is only rational to have. Since it is necessary to perform the act that one be able to do so, a desire to be personally equipped to succeed is a desire to have the necessary means to one's end. Even in deciding to stroll through the woods I will need a sufficient amount of physical ability. In light of the previous argument about quasi-intending, we see that the desire for this ability is one which no one but myself can satisfy, since no one else can carry out my decision. In many of our intentions what we envisage for ourselves is not merely that we be able to act on them but that the end result will improve our own situation. In trying to extricate my finger from a mouse-trap I am not merely trying to equip

---

86. I am indebted to Grant Gillett and John Perry for urging me to make the second point of this paragraph.

myself for future action. And there is, of course, nothing irrational about such actions, since there are some things concerning ourselves, such as eliminating pain, which we cannot help but care about. The point to emphasize now is that whenever our intentions pertain to how we will be, the desire to be that way must be a self-involved one for which there are no quasi-correlates because of the fact that only we can fulfill our own intentions.

What this shows is that those desires which pertain to how we will be in acting on our intentions are genuinely self-involved, having no quasi-correlates. Although it must be admitted that many of our self-involved desires are of this kind, it is not obvious that all of them are. I admit that there can be exceptions, but I believe that these are quite unusual. Let us recall the Afghan rebel who has my body after I suffer extreme amnesia, so that he has none of my acquired mental characteristics. Although I believe with Wiggins that he would be identical with me, I do not look forward to his seeing how my children will be with the same concern that I do now, even if we suppose that he has come to care for them deeply.[87] What this shows is that my actual desire to see my children is not *merely* that it is I who sees them. I want further that my future self be psychologically connected with me, in particular by being the one who carries out my current intentions. I might also wish myself all the best as an Afghan rebel, but if I do, this would be an example of what I mean by a quite unusual "self-involved" desire. My only point now is that when I survey my own self-involved desires I am struck by the fact that what I want is not merely that I am involved, but that this involvement results from the unfolding of my current plans. It is worth observing, perhaps, that I can make the same point by adopting a more Lockean criterion of personal identity, such as Parfit's. Suppose that my biological life is extended and that my future self, though psychologically continuous with me, is so different psychologically that he does not even remember what I am like now. Even though most Lockeans would admit that he is identical with me, I must say that I feel just as strongly that

---

87. Van Inwagen denies that any psychological connection is needed with his future self in order to have selfish concerns for him (Van Inwagen 1990, p. 184). This would make personal identity itself even more practically important than on my account, since I require personal identity plus a psychological connection to satisfy my self-involved desires.

his seeing my children does not really satisfy my present desire. What I am suggesting, then, is that we normally get self-involved desires as a result of forming intentions that depict (in part) how we will be in acting on those intentions. I want, for example, to *conduct* my life so that I get to see the lives of my children. Since the argument about quasi-intending shows that no one but myself can fulfill such desires, the metaphysical question of my identity bears on the practical question of whether I can get what I want. A "short" view of my identity, such as Parfit's, would limit not only the extent of my responsibility but also the range of things I can hope for.

It may be possible to discern an even deeper point about the practical importance of personal identity if we reflect a bit on how self-involved desires arise when we form intentions. I take it that genuine intentions are formed only by creatures like us who have the foresight to imagine future consequences of our actions. The object of our intention appears, at least at the time we act, as good, as worthy of pursuit. Without this foresight there would be no basis by which to distinguish the values in the things we seek intentionally from the objects of our desires . What we foresee is the possibility of realizing what we value by performing an action that takes time. If quasi-intending were possible, the preservation of personal identity would not be necessary to perform such actions, and thus we could discover such values even if our continued existence was not assumed. But since intending is possible only for oneself, our future existence must be assumed whenever we rationally reflect in order to discovery what is worthy of our intentional pursuits. If I thought that my existence were confined to the present moment, there would be no practical point in rational scrutiny of my desires; if this were the fate of every person at every time, values could not be recognized in distinction from present urges. Perhaps the most important philosophical reason for acknowledging the practical importance of personal identity is that our continued existence is necessary to act intentionally, and thus to see our actions as worthy of performance. It is only by assuming our continued existence that we are able to perform the sort of actions that enable us to see our lives as well spent.

Since this completes the argument of this chapter, I will summarize it and show how it combines with the result of the last chapter.

The metaphysical question of personal identity has seemed to have more than theoretical importance. There are desires of mine which seem to require my future presence for their satisfaction and there are past actions for which I now seem to be responsible only if it was I who performed them. "Short" views of personal identity seem to deny me some of these satisfactions and absolve me of some of this responsibility by denying that, at least in the normal full-blooded sense, it is *I* who will satisfy the desire or who did the deed. What called into question the apparent importance of the temporal extent of my existence was the alleged possibility of quasi mental states. Quasi-intending was especially important, in part for the reason suggested by Wiggins and Korsgaard, that responsibility is transmitted by the "authorial" relation, or the exercise of will. If I can animate someone distinct from me, such as a copy of mine, just as I animate myself, just by deciding to do it, then it would seem that he would inherit my responsibility despite the absence of identity. Quasi self-involved desiring was also important. If my copy can satisfy desires that I normally, but only trivially, think of myself as being able to satisfy, then my hope that these will be satisfied does not depend upon my continued existence, so that once again the issue of personal identity will be irrelevant. I argued that at least many of our self-involved desires are connected with intentions. Whenever I intend to do something, I always envisage and want myself to be some way, even if this is only to have the ability to perform the action. I suggested that the self-involved desires we normally have are connected with intentions in this way, and I explained how our intentional actions carry value in our eyes only because they promise to satisfy self-involved desires (to perform the action in question) which arise in rational reflection. If quasi-intending for a distinct person is impossible, these self-involved desires will also have no quasi correlates. Now, intentions are normally expressed with I-thoughts, and in the last chapter we saw that the "I" of such thoughts denotes just one person. Such thoughts cannot, therefore, be directed to someone else, such as a copy of oneself. Defenders of quasi-intentions claim that this is a trivial fact, due only to the meaning of the word "intention." The notion of quasi-intention was introduced to cover the case in which one animates a copy of oneself just as one animates oneself, just by deciding to do something. I argued that this is impossible. There is an underlying rationale for the fact that intentions are expressed with I-thoughts. Such thoughts are necessary for the individuation of oneself, and we individuate ourselves in part by seeing how we intentionally interact with other things. To see this requires distinguishing what we will from what we effect as a result of our will. I animate a distinct copy of myself only as I animate my shadow or the pencil in my hand, only by deciding what I will do, knowing that this will affect the external object in question. To suppose that we can ignore the difference between ourselves and our copies when forming intentions is to suppose that we can ignore a distinction of the sort that is necessary for individuation. It is not trivial to insist that only I can do what I decide to do since the distinction between what I do immediately and what I do as a result of this is among the distinctions that together enable me to know which thing I am. Death is necessarily bad inasmuch as it is a wall beyond which our wills cannot reach. If I am to be replicated by a distinct person I can only plan to make myself a certain way at the end knowing I will be copied. It is true and important that our non-self-involved desires can inspire action up to our death. But our own activity in such projects ceases with our death. This may have seemed obvious, but its defense has required the refutation of the doctrine of quasi-intending.

Our conception of our identity really does have practical importance. Since to justify such a conception is to find reasons for applying the concept of identity to ourselves, we want to know more generally what justifies applying the concept at all. The pursuit of this question will require the development and defense of a more general ontology within which we will be able to locate our own identity.

4

The Priority of Continuants

We saw in the first chapter that Hume's view of the self reflected his general metaphysics, which questioned the reality of persistence or permanence. We commonly think that the manifest properties of experience, the shapes, colors, smells and the like, are born by "bodies" which continue to exist even while unperceived and which undergo changes in such properties, so that the very same thing exists at different times with different properties. Just because there is a difference does not mean there is a different thing; a person can be different without being a different person. But Hume thought that, for all he knew, the manifest properties were borne instead by momentarily existing "impressions." In the world he knew there were not things that "underwent" change: one impression ceased to exist and was replaced by another. It is therefore of the essence of this metaphysical outlook that all change is construed on the model of destruction. The thing before you does not really "survive" a change in properties: it goes out of existence and is replaced by a similar but numerically distinct thing. It is therefore not surprising that when he came to consider himself, his own identity over time seemed similarly a kind of fiction. He was not something which accidentally possessed his impressions and other "ideas," changing with respect to them over time, but was instead the mere collection of these. He accordingly held that disputes of personal identity were merely verbal. Since one can arbitrarily mark the extent of "the collection" to which the present states belong, the temporal extent of our existence would seem to be a matter for legislation rather than for discovery.

Hume's metaphysical outlook has been attractive to many philosophers (though certainly not all). It reminds us of Heraclitus's picture of all in flux and of Buddha's denial of permanence. In the present day it finds expression in the idea that instead of "continuants," which exist continuously through time, there are series of momentary "stages."[88] Stages are different from Hume's impressions in being objective. They are not creatures of the mind but things with material composition. Although the stage ontology reflects the rejection of the subjectivism of Hume's day, it still embodies the denial of real permanence underlying manifest change.

The purpose of this chapter is to refute this metaphysical outlook, thus defending the reality of persistence and permanence.[89] This will not in itself prove a "longer" view of personal identity, but it will support it indirectly by removing what would have been a powerful support for a "shorter" view. Although Parfit himself does not deny the reality of permanence in general it is, I submit, not unfair to see him, as well as many others, under the influence of this metaphysical outlook. Parfit's example of the "Combined Spectrum" consists of a

88. Endorsements of the stage ontology can be found in the following: Russell 1954, p. 286; Russell 1958, p. 329; Quine 1960, p. 160; Quine 1973, p. 131–37; Quine 1981, pp. 10–13; Smart 1972; Hirsch 1982; Lewis 1986, pp. 202–04; Brennan 1988; Noonan 1989.

Against the idea that the stage ontology is useful for solving problems about continuants, Roderick Chisholm claims that this ontology "presupposes" that of continuants, since to say how the stages associated with one continuant are unified we will refer to a continuant or assume that we can (Chisholm 1976, pp. 143–44). The stages of one river are, for example, associated with that river, or that river bed, or with a person observing it. My complaint with the stage ontology is similar, but weaker. For if Chisholm is right, even God (who is not restricted to a finite empirical perspective) could not see how the river stages were unified without relating them to continuants of some sort. Brennan can be seen as answering Chisholm, by describing a generic relation of "survival" in terms of causality and continuity of form that would link the stages (see Brennan 1988).

Perhaps the most serious attack against continuants is that they violate modern physics. This is why Mellor's rebuttal is important (see Mellor, pp. 128–32); further comments on these lines are in Simons 1987, pp. 126–27.

Some philosophers have doubted whether an ontology of continuants can avoid

range of persons beginning with himself and ending with a replica of Greta Garbo; intermediate cases result in succession by replacing Parfit's cells a few at a time with those of the replica.[90] Parfit claims, plausibly enough, that each person in the series would be very similar to his or her successor, both physically and psychologically, and he concludes from this fact that it would be trivial to draw a sharp line where he ceases to exist. Evidently, the sheer fact of apparent similarity is supposed to provide grounds for re-identifying the same person from one case to the next. But this is merely the other side of the coin that finds difference in appearance a ground for numerical distinctness. David Lewis is under this same Humean influence when he thinks that the great change in personality in a person like Methuselah would evidence a change in persons.[91] When we see what is wrong with the Humean metaphysics we should no longer be tempted to these sorts of inferences. The appearance of similarity will be no evidence of identity and the appearance of difference will be no evidence of distinctness.

Before I begin my somewhat complicated argument I want to make clear exactly what it is that I am arguing. First, I do not deny that the Humean metaphysics is logically possible. I do not think that it can be shown wrong in the strong sense that it is logically incoherent. This has become a familiar theme for us. Like Kant, I have admitted that many things are possible in this sense and turned instead to the

---

the apparent contradiction of attributing contradictory properties to an object which has changed. For a subtle and appealing defense of continuant ontologies against this charge, as well as citations on this literature, see Merricks.

Haslanger argues (in Haslanger 1989) against stages on the ground that their causal influence over time is mysterious, whereas continuants are able to survive so as to exist with the things they affect. It seems to me that the same problem would exist with regard to the causal effect of spatially separate things. She complains that temporally separated stages would need an occult power to exert influence. Why not say that an occult power is necessary to bridge spatially separated influences?

Wiggins complains (in Wiggins 1980, pp. 25–27) that the linguistic transformations required by a stage ontology have been greatly underestimated. Although I do not disagree, the present chapter lodges a more serious complaint.

89. An earlier version of this argument was presented in "The Indispensability of Continuants" at the Pacific Division meeting of the American Philosophical Association in Berkeley in the spring of 1989. I am especially indebted to my commentator, Mark Hinchliff, and to Peter Simons for many helpful criticisms of that version, and also to Barry Smith for his comments on a later version.

90. Parfit 1984, pp. 236–243.

91. Lewis, p. 30ff

question of what we can know or justify. This stance was warranted by the admittedly substantive assumption that we can justify a view of our own identity, so that we are investigating conditions not merely of the logically possible but of the justifiable. I want to show that any justified view of what there is will contain concepts of continuants. Although I will not actually deny the existence of momentary stages, if I am right, concepts of continuants cannot be *replaced* by concepts of stages and their sums. In technical terminology, we cannot "reduce" continuants to sums or series of momentary stages. Although I personally see no reason to admit the additional existence of stages, what must be realized, if my argument is right, is that if there are sums of stages their existence is really *additional*. If I am a continuant, it will not do to say that "in reality" I am a temporally extended series of momentary stages. No continuant can be identical with a sum of stages. This is because a continuant does not have temporal parts. It persists through time instead of being extended through time.[92] Just as water is ordinarily thought of as spatially continuous, existing here and there, rather than having parts here and there, "continuants" are meant to be temporal continuants, existing now and then, and not merely because they have temporal parts existing now and then. This is why continuants are said to be "wholly present." A sum of stages is "present" now only by having a stage here now, just as I am in the cookie jar only by having my hand in it. Since no continuant is identical with a sum of stages, if there are sums of stages they must coexist with continuants. Although I technically allow this, once the necessity of continuants is seen, the attraction of stages may well disappear. But as I said, I want only to argue for the irreducibility of continuants.[93]

---

92. I do not require, as does Brennan (Brennan 1988, p. 84), that continuants cannot have temporal gaps in their existence. By my definition, which I think is more fundamental, they may have such gaps, just as water has spatial gaps by existing continuously through space but in spatially separated portions. There is a good reason in the case of (temporal) continuants for not allowing such gaps, which is clearly implicit in the argument of Guyer's, which I explain in Chapter 7, for why the disappearance of a thing would never provide evidence of its passing into nothing. It is better to argue against temporal gaps than simply to define continuants as not having them.

93. I hope it is clear that among the positions against which I will be arguing is the conventional attitude toward ontology that is espoused in Carnap 1958, p. 30ff.

I will be arguing specifically for the "priority" of continuants in the sense that they will be at least among the only things that we can individuate without individuating things of other kinds. I say "at least among" since, for all my argument is meant to show, knowledge of continuants will be possible only with knowledge of entities of another kind. To see what I have in mind, let me just say that it might be that we can justify thinking of continuants only by justifying thinking of changes they undergo or times in which they have their properties. It is not important for my overall argument that such entities also be admitted as indispensable for knowledge or justification, and I would welcome a way of avoiding this conclusion. But since I am not convinced this can be done I want to argue not that continuants are the only things that we can know without knowing things of other kinds but that they belong to this class. Within this class, however, they form a special group, since (as I will try to show) they are the things to which we must ascribe the manifest properties of experience—the shapes, colors and so forth. Just as Hume wanted to ascribe these instead to his momentary impressions, the modern stage ontologist wants to ascribe these to momentary stages and sums of them. I will not actually deny that their entities also bear these properties, but will argue that we must think of continuants, at least, as bearing them, so that we cannot ascribe them to stages *instead* of to continuants.

It is crucial to realize that I am speaking of epistemic rather than temporal priority. W. V. Quine is willing to allow that continuants are temporally first in the sense that they are literally the first things about which we purport to speak and think.[94] This is an important point for him since he uses it to explain (away) the intuition that continuants are somehow necessary for thought. He supposes, though, that continuants can be replaced by stages as the parts of a ship are replaced in a journey. On this view, continuants are not really necessary. Since he thinks that the stage ontology can be empirically supported, this leads him to his grand view that ontology is the province not of transcendental philosophy but of science. Against this, I will argue that the continuant ontology really is necessary. Although we may be able

---

94. See especially Quine 1969, 292–93.

to add planks to the ship, there are certain ones without which it just won't float.

More specifically, I will argue that we cannot *individuate* anything without at least implicit reliance on the individuation of continuants. I will not actually deny, for example, that we can individuate stages or their sums; I will claim instead that they can be known only in *relation* to continuants which are, therefore, already individuated. I will allow, for example, that I can individuate the frog stage before me now, but only by thinking of it as the present stage of the continuant frog before me now. Aristotle held in his "Categories" that continuants like this man and that horse were somehow "primary": other things, such as their shapes and places and colors, were somehow "differentiated" from them. I will be defending in effect an epistemological interpretation of this doctrine.

It might seem that I am the the only thing that is primary to myself, since I can individuate myself alone. This is a consequence of Strawson's thesis, discussed in the second chapter, that I individuate things other than myself only because I can think of how they are uniquely related to myself. Although it is true that I can think of myself alone by thinking of myself only from my subjective perspective, we have seen that to know my identity I must still have knowledge of the physical world, since it is only by knowing myself as one physical object among others that the appearance of my identity in introspection can be objectively confirmed. This means that I am not really the only thing that is epistemically prior to all others: to individuate myself I must know which thing I am, and I can have such knowledge only if I can see myself as merely one among a system of physical objects which all together comprise the epistemically primary things.

Since my method will be "transcendental," and since Kant himself argued for the reality of permanence (in his "First Analogy"), should I not simply look to what he or his sympathizers have said? The reason why I think that this is not enough is that their arguments have not been addressed against the specific alternative of the stage ontology, so that it is at least not clear why the stage ontologist cannot simply accept the point of these arguments. Since I do think it is worth substantiating this, let me illustrate how it applies to the excellent reconstruction of Kant's argument by Paul Guyer.[95] A crucial part of Kant's game-plan, according to Guyer, is to establish the need to distinguish objective from subjective change. Ultimately this is because we are supposed to be committed to thinking of objective change even within our subjective states in order to have any empirical knowledge at all.[96] The Analogies in general lay out conditions for knowing when a change is really objective. As regards the First Analogy, suppose that we perceive something objectively changing, say, going from hot to cold. It may seem that all that is necessary to realize that a change has really occurred in the objective world is that incompatible properties are instantiated. But as Guyer points out, the incompatibility is due to the fact that they cannot be instantiated at the *same* time in the same object. What if the hot and cold things are two ends of a metal rod? We seem to need to think of a continuant which undergoes the change in order to be forced to the conclusion that the properties were instantiated at different times and thus that a change really took place. Now, the problem with this is that while it may be natural to say that it is the same object undergoing the change, it is not obvious that a series of momentary stages would not do as well. Surely, the stage ontologist will simply say that just as a continuant may not bear these properties at the same time there can be a series of stages which can bear these properties only by having different stages bear them in succession. Guyer realizes clearly that we will have to think of the continuant in question as being of a certain kind. For we can conceive of some kind of thing that could simultaneously appear in these circumstances to be both hot and cold. To judge from the appearance that this is not so we will have to think of the continuant as having a nature which rules this out. Since we must do this for continuants, it seems open to the stage ontologist to say that we are confronted with a series of stages which by its nature does not allow that the same stage appear both hot and cold. By claiming that his stages are of a kind which does not allow them to appear in these circumstances to be both hot and cold, the subjective appearance of hot and cold will provide evidence of objective change. So, it is not clear why the stage ontology is not

---

95. Guyer 1987, pp. 215–35.

96. As I explain in the next chapter, I believe Ross Harrison finds an even deeper assumption in Kant.

adequate to ground the distinction between objective and subjective change. This being so, the Kantian argument, as explicated by Guyer, does not really show why we must accept the reality of genuine persistence through change.

What this discussion is supposed to show is that if transcendental arguments are to be really effective against the modern denial of permanence or persistence, the reduction of continuants to sums of stages, they must do more than argue for the "same thing" existing at different times and must address specifically the difference between continuants and sums of stages. After all, there is a sense in which the sum of stages corresponding to a continuant exists "at different times": it has different temporal parts at these times. What must be shown is the need for something which exists at both of these times but *not* merely by having different temporal parts or stages at those times. It is only this that will show the need for a (temporal) *continuant*, something which is at least relatively permanent by genuinely *persisting* through time.

I said in the first chapter that transcendental arguments, as I understand them, draw out implications from some relevantly unavoidable starting point. The starting point of this chapter (as it was for the second chapter) is that of individuation itself. I will be assuming that we can individuate something and then argue that among the things we must be able to individuate are continuants. If correct, the alternative is to avoid individuation altogether. It is not obvious how extreme an alternative this is. Would this, for example, involve giving up all possibility of justified thought itself? This will be the central topic of the next chapter. I will argue then that the exercise of rationality itself requires individuation. This may seem obvious, but we will find that it is in need of much argument. If this argument is successful, it will strengthen the result of this chapter, since it will show that recognizing continuants is needed not just for individuation but for justification itself. But even the weaker starting point of individuation will not appear arbitrary to stage ontologists, for they certainly think that they can individuate stages and sums of them without acknowledging continuants. Can they?

Once again it is crucial to realize that the question is not of what we can say but of what we can think. It is obvious that one can *refer* to a stage (supposing, as we will, that they too exist) without explicitly mentioning a continuant. I can say, "That frog stage is green," without uttering words which refer to the frog. But I can also refer to its shape. I can say, "That's a strange shape," while pointing in the direction of the frog. This hardly shows that in *understanding* my remark you or I can think of the shape without thinking of the frog which has it.

How can we show what one must think? I will now explain and defend the method we will adopt. Let us imagine that we are challenging the stage ontologist to show that he can think of stages and their sums without reliance on thought about continuants. If he cannot actually show this, the idea that he still "can" do this is of no interest to us, for it is only an abstract, merely logical possibility. I will assume that if he can individuate such things he will do so on the basis of attributing empirically manifest properties to them, such as shapes, colors, textures and so forth. The reason for this is essentially the Kantian (or empiricist) one that the only way in which we can find justification for actually applying concepts is through experience. There are of course things such as the particles of physics about which we have empirical knowledge and which do not have such manifest properties, but we know of them only by inference from knowledge that we have about manifest objects. The stage ontologist, to make his case, ought to be able to individuate stages with the shapes, colors and so forth that are empirically manifest. I expect no resistance on this point, since these are the sorts of objects that are usually discussed anyway. I will also assume that if he is able to show that he can individuate stages and their sums (without continuants), he can do so by speech. I am not assuming that individuation can be shown only linguistically. (Indeed, the discussion of the next chapter is meant to shed light on how the power of individuation is non-linguistically exhibited.) The speech situation is supposed to provide only a convenient way of reflecting what he thinks. As I will explain shortly, there is a certain distinction that one must notice in order to be individuating anything. All that I am asking is that the stage ontologist show that he can mark this distinction without reference to continuants. To see what he notices it is convenient to imagine him expressing his distinctions in words. So, the game will be to imagine him trying to refer to a stage or a sum of them without referring to a continuant. As we will see, he will lose the game by being unable to mark the distinction in question.

Before I explain what is required for individuation in general I want to show that our stage ontologist, to make his case, will have to individuate not a sum of stages of such a temporal extent that it has parts lying beyond the present moment but an individual stage which is only momentarily present. Suppose that he is in the presence of a frog and imagine properties it might appear to have at that time. A continuant frog would possess these properties at this time and the very same thing, after undergoing changes in these properties, would possess different properties at different times. Suppose that this has happened. The sum of frog stages corresponding to this continuant frog "has" the present manifest properties only in the sense that it has a temporal part with them. If the frog croaks, the only sense in which the sum of stages croaks is that a (temporal) part of it does. As I said before, this is like saying that I am in the cookie jar when my hand is. Now, the important point is that I can thus attribute the croaking to the whole sum of stages only by inference. I must first know that the momentary stage croaks and then infer that the whole sum does (in the sense of having a part that does). In an analogous way, in order to know that I am in the cookie jar, one must infer this from the fact that my hand is in the jar and that it is part of me. Since to know in what sense the sum itself "has" the present manifest properties one must first know the sense in which the present momentary stage has them, one must be able to individuate this stage (and other stages at other times in the same way) before one can individuate the sum itself. To know of such a "longer" sum we must first know of the various momentary stages which comprise it. Continuants are strikingly different. Since the frog is "wholly present" in the sense that it is it and not a temporal part of it which is present, there are not two senses in which we attribute the present manifest properties, one epistemically prior to the other. The continuant frog "has" the manifest properties in the same epistemically primary way in which the present momentary frog stage does, but the sum of frog stages "has" these only in an epistemically posterior sense. Since the stage ontologist must individuate momentary stages before temporally extended sums of them, the issue comes down to whether he can individuate something like this present frog stage without reference to a continuant like the ordinary frog.

My argument against the stage ontologist relies heavily on a discussion by Evans on the nature of predication.[97] Evans points out that a subject shows that he is truly predicating a property only when his thoughts can be distinguished from feature-placing, and this occurs only when he distinguishes between internal and external negation. To explain this, let us recall (from our discussion of the second chapter) that feature-placing is a form of what Price called the recognition of universals. Strawson used the term "placing" to indicate that the universals in question might incorporate spatial directedness, as when my dog, Argus, distinguished between ball-here and ball-there. But with or without such an element the basic idea is that a creature who is restricted to this form of cognition would only distinguish between the presence or absence of a certain kind of situation. The content of its cognition might be rich and subtle, say, by representing a distinct and finely structured surface appearance. A feature-placing (or universal recognition) sentence could be framed for any such cognition. But since the creature who only feature-placed would discriminate between only the presence or absence of such a "feature," we could report its cognition with either the feature-placing sentence in question or its negation. The crucial point is that in the case of negation, it would be the whole sentence that is negated, thus representing a case of "external" negation. But it is the very nature of predicates that they themselves can be negated. We who predicate can say, for example, not merely, "It is false that the frog here is pink"; we can say, "The frog here is not pink." Russell, in his theory of descriptions, realized the difference: only the second "internal" negation entails the existence of the frog here. What Evans is getting at is really clear and obvious on reflection. To *individuate* something is to know *which* thing is being thought about. To do this, we must think of it in some *way*, which means that we must think of it *as* having some property. But the whole idea of feature-placing or universal recognition shows that there is a difference between merely *recognizing* manifest properties and *ascribing* them to a certain thing. The point about the need to mark the

97. Evans 1985, "Identity and Predication."

distinction between external and internal negation is simply that one can think of something *having* a certain property only if one can also think of it as *lacking* a property. That something lacks a property is just what internal negation expresses. In negating the feature-placing sentence, "It is raining now," there is no difference between saying, "It is false that it is raining now," and saying, "It is not raining now," just because the "It" is not really a term by which we are individuating something.

My claim is that our stage ontologist will not be able to mark the distinction between internal and external negation and will thus not be able to show that he is truly individuating and not merely feature-placing. It is easy to see how he could mark the distinction with the "crutch" of referring to the associated continuant. If he can refer to this frog stage as the present stage of this continuant frog, then of course he can go on to say any number of things about which properties this stage lacks. This frog stage will not, for example, be of a different shape or in a different place. The same ease of internal negation is possible for any "secondary" entity. By reference to the continuant frog I can think of its shape, and think that this shape is not a color and not identical with a triangle. These will be genuine internal negations because, if true, the shape in question exists. This is just what nominalists will not allow; but they will agree to the external negations. They will say it is false that the shape of the frog is not a triangle because it is false that there are such things as shapes. The point is that for secondary things in general the availability of primary things as reference points makes genuine individuation easy and unproblematic (aside from the question of whether the secondaries really exist). But this way of introducing references to stages is obviously illegitimate if one is to take seriously the claim of the stage ontologist that continuants can be replaced by or reduced to sums of stages. It is telling, I suggest, that this is the only way that *examples* of stages are mentioned. Our attention is called to a certain momentary stage, such as the present stage of this frog, as if the reference to the continuant is innocuous, merely a convenience. But if it is merely a convenience, as it *must* be if we are to take seriously the dispensing of continuants, then this should be proven. I claim that it is not a mere convenience since the reference to continuants is indispensable.

My next point is that one cannot show to what kind of thing one is referring while restricted to a single circumstance, with respect to only the present manifest properties. The stage ontologist wishes to make reference to something which possesses these properties but which, in being momentarily existing, does not exist at other times. The continuant ontologist wishes to ascribe these same properties to something else, something which exists not only at these times but at other times as well. The objects in question differ in the kinds of things to which they belong, in our sense of "kind," which means that they satisfy different (incompatible) identity conditions. Since all that our stage ontologist has to go on to show to which object he is referring is that it possesses these current manifest properties, and since there is a continuant which possesses the same properties, the mere ascription of these properties in the present circumstances will not make clear that he is succeeding in individuating the stage without reliance on the continuant. If all that he says is, "That frog stage is oblong," we have no reason to think that "that frog stage" is referring to a momentary stage or to a continuant.

In fact, the problem is even worse when he is restricted to only the present moment, since his attempt to individuate the stage will not appear different from merely feature-placing. This has nothing to do with the stage ontology in particular, since the same problem would arise for the continuant ontologist. To see the problem clearly, let us suppose that "Ben" is the name of the present frog stage and our stage ontologist tries to show that he is thinking that Ben is oblong. Now, in classical logic there is no difference between internal and external negation when a name is used since all names are automatically assigned objects. There is accordingly no difference between saying that it is false that Russell was dimwitted and that Russell was not dimwitted. But in free logic, since names without objects are allowed, the difference re-emerges. We of course want to see names in the latter way since we want to be open to the possibility that the stage ontologist is failing to refer with the name, "Ben." (We could even think of "Ben" as merely an abbreviation of a demonstrative description such as "that frog stage.") Let us suppose, then, that our stage ontologist, in attempting to ascribe the manifest properties to Ben, which is all that he has in the present moment to show that he is individuating

Ben, utters the sentence, "Ben is oblong." For all we know from this slender bit of information "Ben" is equivalent to the "it" of "It is raining." He could try to deny that Ben has certain properties, by saying, for example, "Ben is not triangular," but this would not—in these very circumstances—be distinguishable from the feature-placing sentence, "It is not triangular." On reflection the point is really clear. When restricted to the present moment he cannot show that he is individuating anything since all that he can do is attempt to ascribe the manifest properties. But this cannot be distinguished from feature-placing since to attempt internal negation, the idea that something lacks a property, he can only attempt to deny that properties incompatible with the present ones are possessed. This attempt, however, cannot be distinguished from feature-placing since all that is evident is that these other properties are not present. He or any ontologist will not be able to show that he is doing more that merely recognizing the presence or absence of the manifest properties. Any creature who exhibits awareness of only what is here and now provides no grounds for thinking of him as individuating instead of merely feature-placing. (This result will be of great importance in the next chapter when we consider what justifies individuation.)

It might be worth observing that the argument applies just as surely to the case in which one gives evidence of individuating oneself through self-awareness. Suppose a creature is trained to go about uttering such things as, "I seem to see a tree" whenever a tree is before it, and "I do not seem to see a tree" whenever there is not one there. On the basis of this evidence, we would have no reason not to see its cognitions as merely feature-placing. We might as well report them with more modest sentences such as "Tree-here" and "Not-tree-here." If the claim that I am really individuating myself when I utter first person pronouns is defensible, I ought to be able to demonstrate it by doing more than our feature-placing creature. According to the present argument, to defend the idea that I am genuinely aware of myself, that I really do know which thing I am, and that I am not merely feature-placing, I must show that I can think *now* about how things are which are *not* here now.

Since individuation cannot be exhibited in a single moment, our stage ontologist must turn to other circumstances and other manifest properties. As we have seen, he cannot just forget the first circumstance, since the same problem will arise whenever he concentrates on only the present moment. What he must do somehow is to connect the different circumstances: in Kantian jargon, he must "synthesize the manifold of sense." The problem with the stage ontology comes down entirely to the fact that when he turns to other circumstances the original stage is not there. Because of this, there is no evident difference between saying that this stage lacks certain properties and that it is false that it has them. Of course there is a difference between the two facts. The point is that to show that he is aware of this difference without surreptitiously and illegitimately thinking of the continuant he must show that he is marking the distinction in response to his manifest circumstances. And the problem is that because stages exist only momentarily, we never see that he has *grounds* for thinking of a stage as *lacking* any manifest properties. To put the point in slightly different language, the problem is that the manifest properties of a stage are all *essential* to it, so that when it loses any one it ceases to exist. This is the whole idea of stages. They do not really "undergo" changes; whenever a change occurs one ceases to exist and is replaced by another. But just because of this, it is never directly evident that we are confronting a stage which lacks manifest properties. Whenever it lacks its manifest properties it no longer exists. And as we saw before, what differentiates internal from external negation is precisely the fact that internal negation still requires the existence of the thing in question. Continuants, by contrast, have at least some of their manifest properties only accidentally. It is only because of this that they can be found directly in experience as lacking properties, the original manifest ones that they shed in undergoing a change. Suppose that the continuant frog has changed in shape, being no longer oblong. The stage ontologist when turning to other circumstances can say, "Ben is not oblong here." But he will have no evident reason for this which is not also a reason for saying, "It is false that Ben is oblong here." If, on the other hand, "Ben" had been the name of the continuant frog, the genuine reference to Ben could have been discerned. For "Ben is not oblong here" would be true when Ben is still here in a different shape but would be false when we turn to still other circumstances where Ben does not exist.

To see why it is continuants alone which can be shown, without reference to other things, to bear the manifest properties, it is necessary to reflect on the fact that no one is ubiquitous. Continuants undergo change and thus end up in other circumstances, but no one of them ends up in *all* other circumstances. It is rather that they form a system of separate individuals. Suppose that we attempted, as we did with a stage, to individuate independently a single, omnipresent thing. Now when we turn to circumstances other than the original ones to show which thing we mean, we attempt to refer to The One in every other circumstance. Since every manifest property is purportedly ascribed to The One, however, no evident difference is marked between ascribing these properties and merely feature-placing. "The One" would add nothing more of semantic import to such sentences than does the "It" of "It is raining." As we have seen, however, when we try to show what we mean by a term for a continuant, such as "that frog," we can both apply it and withhold it in a variety of circumstances. But "The One" would never be withheld. Since "it" would always be present, there would be no occasion in which "It is false that it is F" would be true and "It is not F" would be false. Since The One would always have the manifest properties, we can never find it absent; but all negations cannot be internal since there would be no contrast with external negation; it would be as if in each feature-placing sentence, such as "It is raining now" or "It is snowing over there," we mysteriously interpreted the "It" as denoting The One. Monistic visions, such as occur in mystical experiences, cannot be taken as providing full descriptions of reality. (It is significant that Spinoza's monism was supported entirely *a priori*, attempting to individuate without dependence on experience, which we have despaired of doing.) We are able to individuate The One only by reference to the totality of continuants, some of which must be already known. We cannot avoid thinking of these without collapsing into feature-placing. And if we try to report the monistic vision in feature-placing alone, there will be no evident unity among the features. The world can be unified only by taking its diversity seriously.

I hope my discussion has made clear that the problem with stages is the same problem, at the opposite extreme, as that of monism. Individuation is possible, in the first instances, only by steering between the Scylla of momentary things and the Charybdis of monism. Since stages never appear without their original manifest properties they can never be directly observed as lacking these properties. Since The One always has the manifest properties there can never appear its absence. Since continuants undergo change they can be found lacking the properties which they lost; and since no one is everywhere at all times the absence of each can be discovered. Since only such things permit the palpable differentiation of internal from external negation, individuation is impossible without them.

My target in this chapter has been the modern version of that ancient and perennially attractive view that persistence or permanence through change is not real. Although the view is logically possible and may perhaps be allowed as a mere picture of some heuristic value, it cannot be taken as a true view of what kinds of things there are. For to take it as such would involve individuation, presumably backed by reasons. But such reasons, we have agreed, would have to come not purely from the intellect but from experience. The modern rejection of persistence attempts to substitute for each continuant a mere series of momentary objects. Such series or sums would "have" the manifest properties of experience only in the secondary sense that their temporal parts have them, and could thus be individuated only by reference to these parts. But these individuals cannot be picked out directly from their environment. In a single moment, the attempt to ascribe manifest properties cannot be distinguished from merely placing them. But since stages cease to exist as these manifest properties themselves disappear, they never appear without them, and thus their lack of these properties appears no different from their merely being absent. Since genuine individuation involves the complex thought that a certain thing has a property, it requires being able to think as well that the thing lacks a property. Grounds for this are found in experience for a continuant since it can be found after a change as lacking the lost property; and this is different from its merely being false that it has it, since this is true even when the continuant is not there. Since continuants alone meet this necessary condition of individuation, stages and the like can be justifiably admitted, if at all, only as genuine additions to an ontology which includes continuants and thus respects the reality of persistence or (relative) permanence.

It follows that we are continuants. Since, as we saw in the second chapter, Strawson was right in his Kantian thesis that individuation terminates with and thus depends on self-awareness, we must be among the things that are primary. I could not, for example, individuate the members of a system of continuants and then individuate myself only in reference to these as a sum of stages. Although there might be other primary things, such as changes or times, it is clear that I am not one of these. Like the frog, I, too, am a bearer of manifest properties—at least only this view makes my identity knowable. Since only continuants are both primary and characterized by the manifest properties, we are continuants. If there are person stages, then I am only *correlated* with a numerically distinct sum of them. Since this sum will not *be* me, we will pay no more attention to it in the following.

We have seen that if we are justified in individuating anything, we are justified in applying the concept of identity over time to re-identify continuants, including ourselves. The question of the next chapter is, What justifies applying the concept of identity at all? This is relevant to our general project. Since we ultimately want to know how to apply the concept of identity to ourselves, we do well to consider what justifies applying it in the first place.

5

The Justification of Individuation

Our eventual goal is to know what we are, insofar as this is a question of what determines our identity over time. The strategy announced in the first chapter is to see more generally what justifies applying the concept in the first place. I call this the "general rationale" for the concept. If our own identity were evident merely by taking the current subjective perspective, as Descartes and Locke thought, it could be argued that what justifies applying the concept of identity in the first place is just to take this perspective: I would be justified in applying the concept implicitly insofar as as I ascribe various properties to the same subject in having the variety of I-thoughts which describe how it is for me now. Kant's objection, which I discussed at length in the first chapter, requires a very different answer. Since this perspective provides only the appearance of my identity, to know my identity requires supplementation by an objective conception as well. Following Kant, we supposed that this will be provided by a conception of ourselves as one physical object among others. In the second chapter we saw that all individuation terminates in self-awareness, so that we will be justified in individuating anything only if we are also justified in individuating ourselves in self-awareness. But Kant's crucial point adds another requirement. Self-awareness is possible only if we can also individuate ourselves as physical objects. The clue to our identity is not merely that we are self-aware, as Descartes and Locke thought. It is that we are also physical objects, specifically among the epistemically primary ones that we encounter in experience, as objects of perception. Whatever justifies, most fundamentally, applying the concept of identity at all must therefore apply to ourselves, as physical objects. The last chapter added a certain detail to the picture of the kind of physical objects we are: we are not merely strings of momentarily existing objects but we are, as we commonly think, things which genuinely undergo changes, "persisting" through time. This conclusion, though highly general, is still of some importance to the topic of personal identity, since it refutes a view that would have lent support to a "short" account of our identity. If all change were like destruction, all identity over time, including our own, would be less full-blooded than we ordinarily think. That we are continuants does not really decide, however, between "short" and "long" views of our identity, since both can be interpreted in terms of criteria for continuants. To decide between such views, which is our main goal, we need to see with a good deal more clarity how to justify applying the concept of identity over time. The present chapter adds more detail to the picture of our epistemically primary physical objects by discovering a general rationale for concepts of them. It is by seeing what, most fundamentally, gives us the right to think there are such things that we hope to see eventually what *kinds* of things they are. That is, we hope to use our general rationale to form a generic conception of the identity conditions over time of our primary continuants, and thus of ourselves. The next chapter will begin to articulate this conception.

To see more clearly what we want to establish in this chapter it helps to see how little we are helped by Kant's requirement that to know our identity we must admit our status as physical objects. I take it that the bare notion of such an object requires only that, by existing in space, it can exist independently of our perception of it. Even when we add the very general requirement that it genuinely persist through time it is clear that quite different conceptions of what determines its identity through time are possible. Our whole strategy is recognizably Kantian: it is to turn from analytical questions about what is contained in the bare notion of such an object to questions of what gives us the right to think of them at all. It is by imposing on these objects the requirement that they satisfy the perhaps rather stringent conditions which make them knowable to us that we hope to gain a far richer conception of these objects than we can ever obtain by merely deducing what is involved in the notion of being a physical object or a physical continuant. We want, in other words, a general conception of how these objects appear to us, when we are justified, most fundamentally, in thinking of them. Again, if it were legitimate to individuate only oneself in self-awareness, by taking the current subjective perspective, with no knowledge of the physical world, then physical objects would be known to us only by inferences from knowledge about ourselves as subjects of subjective states.[98] This might greatly affect our conception of how such objects legitimately appear to us. But we know that we can individuate ourselves in self-awareness only if we are able to individuate physical objects. Moreover, because self-awareness is necessary for any individuation, we will see what justifies individuating physical things only when we see what gives us the right to apply the concept of identity in the first place.[99] It is this justification, the "general rationale," that we hope to establish first in this chapter; then we will use it to develop a notion of the kind of physical object that appears to us when we are justified in individuating anything at all. By being demanded by the general rationale, a very deep justification for thinking of these kinds of physical objects will have been provided. I will close the chapter by contrasting our account of what justifies thinking of such things with a complementary account of what advantage this gives us in anticipating the future. In the next chapter we draw lessons from the first account about what, in general, determines the identity over time of these physical objects.

Metaphysicians often operate from a certain limited ontology and wonder whether there is reason to admit other things as well. Are there universals as well as particulars? Are there generable and perishable objects in addition to the basic things of which they are

---

98. This strategy of proving the existence of the "external world" has, of course, been popular since Descartes.

99. I equate the conditions of individuating with that of applying the concept of identity because even though one individuates a thing by applying one predicate to it, one must be at least prepared to apply others and thus implicitly to apply the concept of identity to re-identify the same subject of predication.

composed? When, however, we are considering how to apply the concept of identity in the first place, we have no other things to think about, no things which we can fall back upon. How, then, can we even make sense of the question? What would it be like not to have the concept of identity at all? Reflection on the predicate calculus with identity suggests that the removal of identity would sweep away quite a bit else with it, what Quine calls the whole "individuative apparatus": names, predicates, quantifiers and the like. It may even seem obvious that one could not think at all. After all, it might be said, in any thought there will be a subject and a predicate in the traditional sense that it will be about something and say something about this, and to grasp this distinction will involve understanding what it would be for the same subject to have a different predicate.

For our purpose, Strawson's discussion of feature-placing is invaluable.[100] For it shows why it is not obvious that thinking requires using the concept of identity. Even if, for example, every thought has a subject, it is not obvious that the thinker himself must individuate it. This possibility appeared clearly in our discussion of my dog, Argus. When, as a result of learning, he makes a distinctive response to a high-flying ball, we are entitled to credit him with the feature-placing thought or cognition, Ball-above. The subject of this thought, we may say, is the ball in question. But as Strawson clearly saw, one can recognize the shape of a ball, or the visual pattern of a ball coming from a certain direction, without actually individuating the ball. The latter *involves* the recognitional ability, but it also involves the ability to think of a ball in another circumstance as being the *same* ball. If the thought of a creature were restricted to feature-placing, it would have knowledge with contents which none of the "individuative apparatus" would describe. By understanding what it is for one's thoughts to be restricted to feature-placing or to the recognition of universals, we can make sense of what it is to be deprived of the concept of identity and will thus be able to address our question of how to justify applying the concept in the first place.

I have spoken, as did Strawson, of the "thoughts" expressed by feature-placing sentences. This might seem objectionable. Many phi-

---

100. Strawson 1959, pp. 208–16.

losophers reserve the expression solely for something rather sophisticated. It is often said that thoughts are of such a nature as to have a logical structure which reflects the entailment relations in which they stand to one another. Now, feature-placings have no such structure. This is why I used hyphens, as in "Ball-above," to report their content. For as we saw in the second chapter, the creature, such as perhaps Argus, who is restricted to feature-placing does not have a grasp of the demonstrative distinctions themselves. Hyphenating "Ball-above" helps to remind us that the feature-placer is not really aware of such distinctions as being above or below. Such hyphens are generally appropriate for feature-placing sentences; since the feature-placer is merely responding distinctively to the presence or absence of some general feature, it is not aware of differences within this feature by which it could consciously connect this feature with some other. Accordingly, it lacks "thoughts" in the sophisticated sense. But why can it not have unsophisticated thoughts? The point is more than merely terminological. Strawson's feature-placing sentences, such as "There is water here" and "There is gold there," are certainly capable of expressing truths, so that there is a clear sense in which the feature-placer is having propositional attitudes, even if the contents are not logically interrelated.

Since the feature-placer has representations, assessable as true or false, it can accordingly act with reasons, so that there is thus a sense in which it is a "rational being." When Argus leaps for the ball because he knows Ball-above, this cognition is one of the reasons upon which he acts. Let us call this sense of rationality "primitive" and contrast it with "conscious" rationality. A creature is "primitively" rational if it merely *has* reasons. "Conscious" rationality requires awareness of reasons as such. The consciously rational creature is one like us who can be aware of something as a reason for something. Only such creatures are capable of making *inferences*. In his *Groundwork* Kant observed that while all things in nature act in accordance with laws, only a rational being can act in accordance with a conception of laws.[100] Kant's "rational" being is what I have in mind as a consciously

---

101. Kant 1959, second section. Although Kant is concerned here to describe practical reason, I want us to understand the capacity to be aware of reasons as such to extend to theoretical reason as well.

rational being. If a computer were constructed to operate in accordance with a rule of inference, that in itself would not mean that it made inferences, for this requires *following* the rule and thus being aware of the rule itself. At least this is how we will understand the term. To appreciate the difference between these two forms of rationality, consider a certain marine snail which is expertly discussed by Fred Dretske.[102] This snail has actually been conditioned to alter its behavior to light, coming to avoid it by being punished with turbulence. Since this behavior is not instinctual, but learned, it evidences genuine consciousness of its environment. Dretske argues about conditioning that it always involves "procedural knowledge": a rat conditioned to get food by pressing a bar does not merely know *how* to press a bar but *when* to press it. So, even the humble snail knows when to alter its motion. Since procedural knowledge takes the form of a rule, such as "When there's light, change direction," even the snail has knowledge, gained from experience, of a rule. Thus even the snail counts as primitively rational: by being aware of light it has a reason for turning. We know that the snail is conscious of light and turbulence and that it *knows* a rule. But as Dretske explains, this knowledge is only *tacit*, in the sense that it is exhibited in only this one form of behavior. The snail's knowledge would be *explicit* if it were in the service of projects other than that of avoiding turbulence when there is light.[103] To see how this difference in knowledge is manifested in behavior, we can adapt an example of Evans's discussed by Dretske in this same context. Suppose that the snail, after learning to expect turbulence when there is light, exploits this knowledge by attempting to orchestrate the behavior of other snails by shining light on them.

---

102. Dretske 1988, p. 206.

103. The notion of tacit knowledge was used by Noam Chomsky to describe the kind of knowledge of grammar that a speaker of a language has. The sort of "tacit" knowledge which I am attributing to "primitively" rational creatures such as snails seems tantamount to what Stephen Stich calls "subdoxastic states" which are not available to consciousness and are inferentially isolated. See Stich 1978. Thomas Kuhn attributes the notion to Michael Polanyi and uses it to describe how a paradigm of science might be known (see Kuhn 1962, p. 44).

In this case of the imaginary snail conscious rationality is manifested non-linguistically. I do not mean to imply, however, that this possibility shows that a creature without linguistic ability could be consciously rational; for all I have argued, it may still be that one shows that one has an explicit grasp of rules only if one also shows in other contexts that one can speak.

Or suppose that it attempts to stop the turbulence by extinguishing the light. Assuming of course that it had not also been conditioned to these activities, such novel behavior would show an awareness of the rule in question that ordinary snails clearly do not have. What I am claiming is that only such behavior would reveal, not merely primitive, but conscious rationality. Only by such behavior could we tell that the snail knows that the presence of light *is a reason* for expecting turbulence or for changing direction. Without such behavior we have no evidence that the snail is *aware* of the rule itself, which is the kind of rule by which an inference is made and which thus expresses the concept of a reason.

We want to understand the difference between primitive and conscious rationality. The present discussion shows clearly, I believe, that having explicit knowledge of rules is necessary for conscious rationality. After all, conscious rationality is the capacity to make inferences, and this involves being aware of a connection between a reason and what it supports. It may not be clear enough, however, that such explicit knowledge is really sufficient for being consciously rational. If it is not, then we underestimate the difference between primitive and conscious rationality by explaining it in terms of the difference between a merely tacit and an explicit grasp of the rules in question. I think, however, that if we reflect on what having explicit knowledge of rules requires we will be assured that only consciously rational creatures have such knowledge. The important point, I suggest, is that a creature does not display explicit knowledge of one rule in isolation; we have evidence that it is aware of one such bit of knowledge only when it combines it with other knowledge of this kind. Consider Dretske's snail. Suppose that it has observed snails changing direction when light is shined on them, so that it has come to expect this. As we have seen, the creation of this expectation shows only a tacit grasp of the rule in question. But suppose also that it has observed that when snails move in a certain direction a coveted food stash is gobbled up, and that it comes to expect a loss of food when seeing them on this path. And suppose finally that it has discovered that when it runs over a certain button the light comes on. So long as we see evidence of only these several expectations, we have no reason to credit the snail with explicit knowledge of the rules. But now suppose that, without being conditioned to do so, it runs over the button to alter the path of snails away from the food. Now it shows awareness of the rules since it combines them to produce new knowledge. Each rule takes the form of a conditional, such as "When light hits the snails, they change course." To have a grasp of such a rule which is explicit, to see that the antecedent is a reason for thinking the consequent, is to see that the conditional has these two parts. But the creature does not show the awareness of the two parts of the rule unless it shows an awareness of the parts in *other* complexes. And it does this only by combining different bits of knowledge to make an *inference*. This is what it does when it shows that it uses the (new) rule, "When I run over the button, the snails change course." Knowledge becomes explicit only when the light of reason comes on.

Having seen the difference between primitive and conscious rationality, the question arises as to what is the importance, for our purpose, of being conscious of reasons as such, of making genuine inferences. The answer is not difficult to find. The conditions for making inferences or seeing that something is a reason are of clear epistemological importance, for any view which violated these would be untenable. Now, we are ultimately seeking justification, or reasons, in support of a certain view of our identity. What if making inferences itself required use of the concept of identity? This would provide a very strong form of justification for the concept, since it would show that no view of the world is "justified" in the sense of supported by reasons (which are consciously offered) which does not apply, at least implicitly, the concept of identity. It is on precisely these grounds that I wish to justify the concept.

There are powerful reasons for thinking that Kant made just the link we want, showing that individuation is necessary for conscious rationality. Many commentators expound the transcendental arguments of Kant's first critique by beginning with Descartes's *Cogito*, the assumption of self-awareness. This would be unfortunate for us, if correct, for as we have seen, the possibility of thought without self-awareness is clearly presented in the form of feature-placing. In several places, however, Kant grounds self-awareness in consciousness of a representation.[104] I take his point to be that self-awareness is what makes consciousness of a representation possible.[105] Argus *has* a representation of the ball when he has a visual experience of it. This does not, however, itself require Locke's "power of reflection," the power of being aware of the visual experience itself. Now, if we become aware of the experience by ascribing it to ourselves, then this requires that we be able to "unify" it with other representations, thinking of ourselves as having other such properties as well. If I become conscious of my visual experience by thinking of it as mine, then for this addition of self-ascription not to be idle or otiose, I must be able to think of myself as the bearer of other properties. Again, I take Kant's point to be that these properties at least include those by which I think that I have other representations, such as thoughts or other sensations, so that this "manifold" is "unified" by self-awareness. If this is correct, it is clear how using the concept of identity is necessary for conscious rationality. The consciously rational being will be conscious of representations since it is only then that he can assess them as true or false and thus see them as supported or refuted by reasons; if this in turn requires ascribing the representations to oneself, such a being must also grasp the concept of identity, for in ascribing different representations to himself it is implicit that he is the same subject being differently described.

Although I will eventually defend Kant's view, as I have presented it, what we need to see now is that it stands in need of defense. The problem is that it is not obvious why consciousness of a representation actually requires self-awareness. In an extraordinarily careful and subtle presentation of a system of transcendental arguments, Harrison

---

104. Kant 1968, A 122: "it is only because I ascribe all perceptions to one consciousness (original apperception) that I can say of all perceptions that I am conscious of them"; Kant 1968, A 123: "The abiding and unchanging 'I' (pure apperception) forms the correlate of all our representations insofar as it is to be at all possible that we should become conscious of them."

105. In Schwyzer 1990, Hubert Schwyzer interprets the "I think" that is necessary for thinking not as genuine self-awareness in our stipulated sense (involving genuine individuation of and predication to oneself), but as expressing only the "for me" kind of consciousness that we persons have. This seems to me remarkably close to Harrison's starting point, discussed ahead. And although Schwyzer is not concerned, as we are, to see how the need to use the concept of identity is rationally required, it is noteworthy that his final account of how the "for me" factor is achieved depends primarily on the fact that we have explicit knowledge of rules.

has explicitly denied that it is obvious.[106] Transcendental arguments, as we understand them, begin from a point which is in some relevant way unavoidable. Harrison begins from the austere assumption that a subject is capable of making judgments. Not all cognitions automatically qualify as judgments in his sense. In judgment a subject *consciously* selects a proposition as true. A creature who simply acquired knowledge passively, without actively making a selection between a proposition and its negation, would not be "judging." The fact that Argus has representations which are in fact true does not mean that he regards them as true. Harrison's starting point is thus strikingly similar to the one I have attributed to Kant, that the subject be aware of his own representations.[107] But Harrison realizes (what I mentioned before) that even if his thoughts must have subjects, it is not obvious that he must individuate those subjects. To be careful in avoiding unnecessary assumptions about what judgment involves, Harrison suggests, as he puts it, that we suppress the referential element of thought in favor of the descriptive. Since this is to imagine a form of thought which entirely lacks the concept of identity, Harrison is in effect scouting the possibility that the judger is merely a feature-placer. This is reflected in the fact that the contents of the judgments of his imagi-

---

106. Harrison 1974, p. 84 and p. 87.

107. Harrison himself considers an interesting set of candidates for what was Kant's actual starting point of the Transcendental Deduction (Ibid., pp. 81–88). I am using Harrison's not primarily because I think it was actually Kant's, but because I think it is the best, for exactly the reasons Harrison gives.

108. Considering the feature-placing alternative is essential for defending the Kantian argument against skepticism concerning the external world. To his credit, Jonathan Bennett is careful to acknowledge that other animals have forms of cognition, but he claims that this constitutes a "genuine gap" in Kant's argument (Bennett 1966, p. 116). To defend Kant, he observes that this form of awareness is less than we can expect the skeptic to admit. For the skeptic will admit to having a "story to tell," about what things are like (empirically) *for him*. I admit that the skeptic in question should be prepared to "tell a story," but what Harrison sees and Bennett misses is the fact that it may be possible to tell this story in feature-placing terms, with no self-ascription at all. If the skeptic shifts to the terminology of feature-placing, he will still be able to make empirical judgments, and it will not be obvious that he must accept all the conditions of self-awareness (since he individuates nothing, not even himself).

In Strawson 1966, Strawson identifies the ultimate premiss of Kant's argument as the "standard-setting" definition (p. 25) that experience involves the duality of concept and intuition, the recognition of a particular instance as falling under a general kind of thing. (See also p. 20 and pp. 100–01.) It is not clear to me that this is supposed to encompass the feature-placing alternative. It is not clear that it does, since the whole idea of recognizing something as being of a general kind surely sounds like that of

nary judger are reported with simple propositional constants like "p" and "q" (and with their negations) and not with any devices of the predicate calculus.

This is a radical idea of Harrison's. Although a thinker, in the sense of a judger, will be conscious of thoughts, it is not obvious to Harrison that he will ascribe these thoughts to himself. It is not obvious, at least, that a thinker in this sense will have Locke's "power of reflection," awareness of his own mental states *as* his own. It is not obvious that, as Kant thought, this thinker will be aware of his mental states *by* unifying them through self-ascription.[108] Although it is not obvious that it is impossible to make judgments by feature-placing alone, it is by seeing that and how this really is impossible that we hope to see what justifies using the concept of identity in the first place.

I have been emphasizing the importance for our purpose of addressing the alternative of feature-placing. I dare say that without reflecting on the subject of feature-placing it is impossible to have an adequate account of how to justify the concept of identity and thereby have an adequate account of personal identity. The reason why feature-placing is so important is that it seems clearly, as Strawson said, to constitute that level of thought or cognition "just below" the

---

individuating and predicating, which is not involved in feature-placing. And if we attempt to extend it to feature-placing Strawson's next steps seem not compelling.

Strawson argues that the recognitional component incorporates the "thought of experience itself," which seems to mean that the subject must be able to think of how things "seem." But why is this obvious? Why can he not simply make feature-placing judgments such as that there is blue there or that it is hot here? Strawson argues from the supposed need to think of how things seem to the need to think of oneself, in self-awareness. But since it is not immediately obvious why judgment itself requires thinking of how things seem, I follow Harrison's more cautious construal of judgment.

Paul Guyer's attempt to defend Kant also misses the possibility of empirical judgment in feature-placing form. Guyer clarifies Kant's starting point (at Guyer 1987, pp. 292–95) as the realization that the mere succession of representations is not sufficient for the recognition of this succession, so that knowledge of the objective world is necessary to defend knowledge claims to the effect that the subject in question is having experiences in a certain temporal order. Guyer claims (at Guyer 1987, p. 301) that "it is difficult to imagine any serious skeptic—surely any known to Kant—who could put [such knowledge of an actual temporal succession] in doubt." But even if Kant did not think of a skeptic who would resort to feature-placing, his argument is successful only if this attempt to escape the conclusions regarding the objective world can be blocked. I hope the present chapter will be seen to complement these attempts to derive anti-skeptical conclusions from the fact of self-awareness, since I want to show that empirical judgment cannot be restricted to feature-placing alone, and really does require self-awareness.

individuative level, so that it shows us exactly what is involved in not having the concept of identity and therefore must be considered to assess the effect of having it. The intuitive idea is that feature-placing is what is left if we strip from our thought only the concept of identity and all that it carries with it: the "individuative apparatus," of names, quantifiers, predicates and so forth. That feature-placing is genuinely "below" the individuative level is due to the fact, explained by Evans and discussed at length in the last chapter, that in feature-placing there is only external negation, only the presence or absence of a general feature is noticed. This seems "just" below the individuative level since it is still a form of "thought" or cognition, and fundamentally differs from individuative thought only in lacking internal negation, the idea of something *lacking* a property. But once this distinction is "added," individuation is achieved, for the idea of a negated predicate carries with it the idea of something which can be *identified* with or without the predicate. Now, it may seem that Strawson himself, in a chapter called "Language Without Particulars," discusses what is involved in the "step" from feature-placing to individuation.[109] But unfortunately for our purpose, this is not really so, since his "language," as he makes clear, includes terms for identifying places and times instead of "ordinary" particulars. He is accordingly discussing a choice between two ontologies rather than the adoption of an ontology in the first place.

In a fascinating discussion of why we think of "bodies," Hume also seems to be thinking of a choice between two ontologies.[110] He believes that since we are not justified in thinking of bodies existing independently of our impressions, the fact that we do calls for psychological explanation.[111] Hume imagines, for example, that he hears a creaking sound while his back is to his door. Since he knows from past experience that this sort of sound has come from this door, by supposing that even in the present case this particular sound is coming from this same door, even though he does not now perceive this door, he bestows "on the objects a greater regularity."[112] Hume is care-

---

109. Strawson 1959, pp. 220–32.

110. Hume 1968, Bk. 1, Part 4, Section 2.

111. For an excellent discussion of how Hume typically presents his skepticism as a necessary prelude to his psychological explanation, see Stroud 1977.

112. Hume 1968, p. 197.

ful to distinguish the question of what is contained in our notion of a body from his psychological question of why we think of them. What is fundamental to the notion is just that they exist independently of our subjective states, so that they continue to exist even while unperceived. It is this fundamental feature which he uses in his psychological account. If he regards the creaking sound as merely an impression then he has no explanation of why it is occurring now. But by thinking of the door as continuing to exist when his back is turned he is able to regard the creaking sound as the *effect* of something. His psychological account is supposed to work, we may say, by adding to the bare notion of a body that a body is a *source of power*, something that is potentially *active*, and in particular, capable of exercising this power by *affecting us*, by being responsible, to some extent, for how things *appear* to us. And although it retains this power even when unperceived, the *sort* of thing it can do has actually been witnessed by us *repeatedly* on other occasions. (We think the creak is coming from the door even while not looking at the door since we have experienced the creak with the vision of the door on many earlier occasions.) Although Hume appeals to these quite new features to provide a purely psychological account of why we think there are bodies, perhaps we can extract from his psychological account one that is truly justificatory.

Although Hume seems to think of the shift from thinking of impressions to thinking of bodies as a shift from one ontology to another, my argument of the last chapter shows that it is thought of better as the shift from feature-placing to individuation. Since Hume's impressions are momentarily existing and do not really undergo change in manifest properties, they cannot be epistemically primary. To be restricted to impressions is therefore really to be restricted to feature-placing. Hume's thought of "this creaking noise" while turned from the door is better regarded as the feature-placing thought, Creaknow. And since Hume's "bodies" are the continuants which we found are really the epistemically primary bearers of the manifest properties, the shift to bodies really is the shift to individuation itself. I do not mean, of course, that we should actually interpret Hume's words this way. I am saying that by re-interpreting his examples we may hope to benefit from his great insight. Unlike Strawson's discussion of a language "without particulars," Hume's discussion really does offer a vision of the "step" to individuation itself, the adoption of an ontology in the first place from the level "just below."

We are interested in Harrison's account of judgment because in taking care not to assume that judgment involves individuation, he provides a model that may enable us to see what justifies applying the concept of identity in the first place. Although Harrison does not proceed with our question in mind, I think his account is rich in sharp insights that will eventually allow us to transform Hume's psychological account of why we think of bodies into a "general rationale" of why we are *entitled* to think of them.

From his starting point of a subject who is capable of judgment, Harrison's next step is to argue that the judger must be able to make other judgments which support his previous ones. His point is that since the judger's selection of a proposition over its negation is conscious, he cannot think of this selection as arbitrary, for then it will appear to him that the selection of the negation would be just as good and he would not really be thinking of the original selection as true. But this commits him, according to Harrison, to thinking that there are reasons for his judgment, themselves expressible as further judgments, which support this original judgment. The point is not that all judgments are inferred, for this would be infinitely regressive. It is rather that even his direct, or non-inferred, judgments will involve a conscious selection regarded as non-arbitrary, so that there will have to be reasons which *confirm* the direct judgments. These reasons do not have to be actually possessed by the subject but must be *available*. The judger must think at least that there are other facts "out there" which if discovered would show his direct judgment not to be arbitrary.

In saying that our direct judgments must be regarded as confirmable by other judgments, it may seem that Harrison is denying that there is incorrigible knowledge. And if so, it may be doubted whether his account of judgment is correct. Those, such as the phenomenalists, who think that knowledge rests on a base of incorrigible thoughts would say, for example, that if I know that I feel pain now, I could not be wrong. So, why would such a judgment have to be "connected" with other, confirming judgments? Although Harrison does not address this issue, I would like to defend his account. I want to suggest that Harrison can allow the phenomenon of incorrigibility while still preserving the idea that our direct judgments must be confirmable by other judgments. Consider a good candidate for incorrigible knowledge, such as my feeling pain now. What should be noticed is that when I am sure that I am in pain I never make only one judgment to that effect. In knowing that I am in pain I will normally be aware of the pain over a stretch of time, so that at each successive moment the judgment that I am in pain at that moment confirms the similar judgments that I made before. And typically I will be aware of more than the feeling; in particular, I will realize that I am disposed to try to free myself from the pain. Now consider what it would be like to make just one relevant judgment. All that it could amount to would be a sudden momentary conviction that I am in pain. But without any other relevant thought, without continuing to feel pain or without perceiving any desire to rid myself of the pain, why would I think of this as anything more than a strange passing thought? What Harrison would emphasize is that the only way I could be aware of the pain is by making the judgment that I am; I cannot stand outside of myself and see the pain causing me to think that it exists. It is clearly possible that I could have a sudden, momentary conviction that I am in pain that is due not to a pain but to some physical or psychological malady. This being so, if I had such a conviction that was utterly unsupported by other bits of knowledge, I would have no reason for thinking that it is true. In the absence of any supporting context I would lose the conviction, regarding it as some sort of mental aberration. What I am suggesting, then, is that any one of our direct empirical judgments is corrigible. This is compatible with the idea that a small cluster of them could cohere in such a way as to provide incorrigible knowledge. I am not committing myself to such knowledge; I only want to show how the admission of it does not refute Harrison's point.

If I am wrong and there are individual judgments which are incorrigible it can still be argued that not all of a judging subject's judgments can be. Suppose that a subject made only incorrigible judgments. As judgments they would be regarded by the subject as nonarbitrary and so supportable by reasons. As incorrigible each would not be supportable by a different judgment. So each would constitute its own sufficient reason. For each such proposition p to see what reason there is for thinking p is true the subject would think p is true because p is true. But this is no different for him from just thinking p is true. There is accordingly no reason for us to say that he ever makes genuine inferences, and so no reason to grant this as a genuine possibility. So, even if a subject can make some incorrigible judgments not all of his judgments will be this way. By investigating the conditions of being able to make corrigible judgments Harrison really is investigating the conditions for being able to make any judgments.

Let us consider a typical case in which a direct empirical judgment is confirmed. For example, my judgment that I see a coin on the ground would be confirmed by such further judgments as that I feel it when I reach to pick it up. Now, Harrison makes two points about these confirming judgments that will prove important to us in the chapters to come. The first is that the confirming judgment must be logically independent of the original. If I am in doubt about the original it will not help to confirm this by merely deducing some consequence of it. If I doubt that what I see is a coin it will not help to deduce that if it is, it is a form of currency. I must make the confirming judgment through independent contact with the world: judging, for example, that I feel a coin.

Harrison's first requirement for empirical judgment would appear to establish that the subject capable of judging must be able to make judgments about states of affairs that are *causally* connected. He has argued that the judgments which link such states of affairs must be connected, but that this connection must be weaker than a logical one. That the connection is a causal one is evident from the fact that the direct judgment in question needs to be connected with another one which *confirms* it. If the first judgment is that p and this is confirmed by the judgment that q this can only be on the strength of the conditional that, in some sense of "if," if q then p. I call this "causal" since, having ruled out the stronger sense of logical implication, it seems clear enough that what we want is the weaker form which is involved in counterfactual conditionals. The truth of my judgment that I really see the coin "depends" on the fact that I will feel it when I reach down to pick up it in the familiar sense that if I come to feel it follows that I saw it—provided that I do not feel it due to some incidental reason, such as its being put there by coincidence just before I reach down.

We have not yet seen why we need to transcend the level of feature-placing to that of individuating things. We cannot yet suppose, therefore, that we have found justification for thinking of Hume's "bodies," which are sources of power, causally active in such a way as to affect our senses. But by establishing that our direct judgments be about states of affairs that are causally connected, Harrison has laid a groundwork for imposing this conception on the continuants that we will be primarily justified in individuating. It is in the development of the next requirement that we see why empirical judgment must involve applying the concept of identity.

Harrison's second main requirement is that the two judgments must be connected by a rule which has general applicability. Suppose that the rule by which I support my original judgment with the second confirming judgment has no generality, so that it applies to only this one occasion. Then the rule itself, which is also something which is judged to be true, will have no ground of support and its choice will be arbitrary. Suppose that our first judgment is that p and its support is that q. If we are restricted to just this occasion, then all that we have to make this inference is the rule that if q then p. By why not apply the rule, "If q then not-p," to judge that the original was false? Both rules are available in this situation and there is no reason to choose between them. The only way that "If q then p" could be favored is by knowing that p was true. But the truth of p was in doubt and the judgment that q was supposed to confirm it. We cannot therefore use the truth of p to choose the rule, "If q then p," since it is this rule which is supposed to support the judgment that p. In light of Harrison's ingenious argument, it seems clear that a rule which allows us to confirm direct judgments must be general, since it is only other applications of it which will provide grounds for favoring it over the alternative. If p is regularly followed by q, if we have many experiences of this connection, and none or few of not-p followed by q, we have reason to think that on this occasion the fact that q supports p rather than not-p.

Since it is still not clear why the judging subject cannot remain at the level of feature-placing, we still have not found what justifies thinking of Hume's "bodies." But we are a step closer. For these things are not merely sources of a power to affect our senses: we discover *how* they affect our senses by experiencing their effect on repeated occasions. Hume came to realize that his door was responsible for his hearing the creaking sound because he had experienced this connection on many occasions. Different things may be responsible for different ways of affecting our senses: a dish of butter will not emit such a sound. We will see that it is owing to this fact that our epistemically primary continuants divide into different *kinds* of things.

From his second requirement it is easy for Harrison to favor rules of greater generality. This thesis also will prove to be of the highest importance for us. If the rules in question find their support in other instances, rules of greater generality have more potential for greater confirmation. The point is not the crude one that merely adding numbers of confirmation is the only way of increasing support. After taking the boiling point of water at sea level many times, there is little reason to repeat the experiment. As is well recognized, we want variety, and the variety we want is a reflection of what we already know. But suppose that one rule covers all the same cases as another, in all its relevant variety, and also covers a host of other circumstances as well. This sort of relation is illustrated classically by the laws of terrestrial mechanics and the more inclusive laws of Newton. The more general laws are confirmed not only on Earth but in the heavens as well. What justifies them, according to Harrison's account, is not merely the fact that they "explain more," but the fact that they are better supported. The class of facts that supports them includes the facts that support the more special laws plus a host of significantly different ones as well.

The last step of Harrison's argument which concerns us concludes that the second main condition of judgment—that the rule which connects a direct judgment with one which confirms it must be general in application—is satisfied only by rules which apply to *physical* objects.[113] The nub of this argument is that for the rule in question to serve its primary role of confirming a direct judgment it must be potent enough to refute the denial of that judgment; but if so, then the fact that the subject made the wrong judgment at all is irrelevant. We may illustrate his argument with Hume's example. When hearing the creaking sound with his back to the door, Hume thought of the door

---

113. Harrison 1974, pp. 151–52.

as being there even while unperceived, not merely because he wanted to think of his auditory experience as the effect of something or other, but because he had actually witnessed the door making that sort of creaking sound on many other occasions. Similar effects, similar causes. Suppose we alter Hume's example so that instead of having his back to the door he is facing it and directly judges incorrectly the door to be a cloak hanging on the wall. Now suppose the door creaks and he realizes that he has been gazing at the door and not a cloak. The creaking sound that now emanates from there is similar to the kind of sound by which Hume inferred the existence of the door while unperceived; the occurrence of such a sound now is just what refutes his direct judgment that he sees a cloak. But if this judgment that the sound has occurred really is sufficient to refute his direct judgment that there is a cloak there—as it must be for the rule ("Creaking comes from the door") to be potent enough to refute this direct judgment—then the fact that he made the incorrect judgment in the first place, which he then retracts, is irrelevant. He could have made the same inference to the door even if, as in Hume's actual case, he had not made the mistaken judgment at all (since his backed was turned). This means that Harrison's second requirement—that the rule which enables a subject to infer a direct judgment from another confirming one be itself supported in many cases—is satisfied only if the rule applies to objects which are in fact *physical*. For the rule to be potent enough to refute a direct judgment it must support the negation of that judgment. But then the fact that original judgment is made is irrelevant. The rule itself is sufficient for inferring the negation of that judgment even when no judgment either way is made, that is to say, even when the object (about which the direct judgment would have been made) exists *unperceived*.

Although it was not Harrison's concern to specify exactly how the step to individuation was forced, we are now in position to see why and how that step must be made to satisfy his conditions of empirical judgment. In the last chapter we saw that this step from the feature-placing level requires above all the distinction of internal from external negation, which is to say in effect that to individuate one must think of some things as genuinely lacking properties. This requirement is now forced on us as we are forced to acknowledge physical objects. While unperceived such objects still have the capacity to be perceived. It is thus that we have reason for thinking of them. The rules of generality must be potent enough to predict a state of affairs that is actually unperceived but could have been perceived. If the subject had perceived them in this way the object perceived would have had certain properties which it actually lacks: the properties which indicate how it would have appeared now. While Hume's back is to the door and he hears the creaking sound, he knows that the door is there unperceived. He is justified in thinking this since the rule, "Creaking comes from the door," is sufficiently well-supported for him to infer from the sound the unperceived door. This inferred judgment is justified, however, because it is about some state of affairs that would have been judged directly if his attention had be focused differently. He is justified in thinking of an unperceived door only because it offers the "possibility of sensation." It thus has the power to affect our senses which it is not exercising while unperceived, and it is owing to this lack of exercise that it lacks certain properties.[114] For the thing to exist there with an unexercised power is more than for the thing just not to be there. The mere absence of such a thing would not support the direct judgment that would have been justified if it had been perceived, and which is justified by inference when it is unperceived. Hume is justified in thinking there is a door which he does not see because he hears the creaking sound and knows from past experience that this sort of sound comes from a door. The door lies out of view as something which could be seen even though it is not, and it is only because of this that it would have supported the direct judgment predicted by the rule, that there is a door there. The door is there *lacking* the property of being seen. This is different from its being false that there is a door there being seen, since this statement of external negation is true wherever there is simply no door there at all. But it is plain that the sheer absence of the door is not enough to yield that conclusion that it would look as if there were a door there if one's attention were so directed. This external negation is therefore too weak to make the prediction made by the rule pertaining to unperceived circumstances. We need the internal negation, describing the actual

---

114. Irwin explains how Aristotle makes a similar point against the Megarians, who failed to admit unactualized potentialities (see Irwin 1988, pp. 227–30).

presence of something which would have appeared a certain way, to describe adequately the prediction to the unperceived made by the rule in question. We need, therefore, genuinely to individuate that thing.

We saw in the second chapter that individuation terminates in self-awareness, in that one can individuate anything only if one is capable of having I-thoughts which relate the thing uniquely to oneself. It is clear how the need for self-awareness arises in our account of the step to individuation in general. We need to be able to individuate physical objects since the rules by which we confirm our direct empirical judgments must be potent enough to make predictions about them even while unperceived. These are predictions specifically about how it would appear if one's own attention were directly differently. To think of how it would so appear differently requires thoughts which involve that "pure" grasp of demonstratives described in the second chapter. One must be able to grasp such distinctions as between being here and there or being now and before *as such*. As we saw, this is made possible by thinking of oneself as a continuant capable of undergoing a certain change in perception or thought. There is, in fact, a clear sense in which the step to individuation is taken only when one is prepared to draw the distinction between appearance and reality. For in thinking of an object as unperceived we think of how things are other than what we can think on the basis of how they now appear. We saw in the last chapter that this is a condition of individuating continuants and thus of individuation in general. The creature who gives evidence of being aware of only what is perceptually present gives no evidence of individuating anything at all. One must show that one is capable of thinking now of states of affairs not evident from current perception. We have now seen, with the help of Harrison's account of judgment, why the ability to make empirical judgments requires the ability to individuate unperceived physical objects and thus to draw the distinction between appearance and reality. This may seem to involve a non-standard use of the distinction, since it is usually invoked to describe cases of non-veridical perception such as illusions and hallucinations. The possibility of this more standard use of the distinction is, however, implicit in his account of judgment. This is clear from our discussion of how the

131

account applies to Hume's example. Hume is able to infer the existence of the door from the creaking sound whether or not he is looking at the door. If he is looking at the door and misjudges, say, by thinking there is a cloak hanging there, when he hears the sound he will know that he misperceives the door: that things are not as they seem. But whether the subject correctly perceives something is a contingent fact about him; the possibility of misperception cannot be ruled out. Neither, then, can the possibility of misperceiving be ruled out in the circumstance in which he has already acquired sufficient information about how things go to realize that he has misperceived. Thus he must possess the conceptual resources for recording misperception in order to grasp the general rules which make empirical judgment possible. He must, therefore, be able to think that things appear to him other than the way they really are.

We have now seen that Hume's psychological account of why we think of "bodies" can be modified into an account of why we are justified in thinking of them and hence of why we are justified in applying the concept of identity in the first place. It is the latter, epistemological account, that supplies what I have called a "general rationale" for the concept of identity. Harrison argued that our direct empirical judgments must be confirmable by rules of general applicability that are potent enough to make predictions about the unperceived which might have been perceived. Hume's "bodies" can exist independently of perception and thus unperceived. Since they are sources of power to affect our senses, they might have been perceived even while they are not. And since we learn of the manner of their operation on our senses only by observing their effects on our senses on many occasions, we know of them only as things which create patterns in our direct judgments and thus comply with Harrison's rules of general applicability to these direct judgments. We have therefore found a deep justification for applying the concept of identity in the first place, for transcending the level of feature-placing. We need to apply the concept to physical objects at least implicitly, since we need to individuate them, to know which ones they are. This is because we need to be able to think of them not only when they are perceptually present but also when they lack the properties they would have if they were perceived. This is justified as a condition for applying the general rules which we need to confirm our direct empirical judgments. Since these direct judgments call for such rules, individuation is needed for empirical judgment itself.

It is important to appreciate what we have accomplished and how we will use these results in the following. It is easy to imagine physical objects which do not conform to the conception of physical objects found in Hume's and Harrison's accounts. Objects which exist in space but only for a moment would be "physical." So would be continuants which are entirely passive. Or we might imagine continuants which are quite active but never by having any effect on our experience. We might even imagine ones that can affect our experience but only by exerting their effect at a single moment and not through of succession of them that allows us to discern a pattern of effects. Our complaint against such objects is that they are not epistemically primary. It is not even that they are not knowable, since we might imagine also small entities known only through physics that would be "physical" but not among the things which we must individuate in order to individuate anything at all. We are concerned with physical objects which are epistemically primary because we know that we are among them. We now have a theory of what these are like. In the absence of a competitor which is established on such firm grounds we will assume that these are the *only* physical objects which are epistemically primary. And in light of previous arguments that we are among such objects we will assume that we conform to this conception of physical objects. In the next chapter we will use this theory to arrive at a conception of the kind of identity through time such objects have. Before we turn to this I want to explain how our possession of the concept of identity gives us an advantage over the brutes in anticipating the future. Besides being of interest in its own right, it might help us to see more clearly what kind of account this chapter claims to establish.

Our general rationale pertains to the issue of what *justifies* applying the concept of identity at all. This is different from the issue of what is the *purpose* of applying the concept. Dummett emphasizes that since concepts are used to mark distinctions which serve purposes of ours, no account of a concept is adequate which fails to explain how we put the concept to use.[115] This means however that for any concept of ours such an account should be possible. It does not follow, of course, that we have a right to use that concept. Just because some people use the concept of a miracle to explain certain events does not mean that there is good reason to think that miracles have really occurred. It is possible to be clear about one issue and not about the other. One may, for example, have a clear view of how moral concepts are used to resolve disagreement through reasoning, or of how theological concepts are used to guide one's life, while still being unsure what gives us a right so to use them. Or, as in the present case, one may see what is the ground that gives us a right to think of instances of the concept in question and still fail to see clearly what good it is to do so. Let us, then, address this question. To do so, it is just as important to have a clear and accurate view of what can be done *without* the concept of identity.

We have seen already that a creature who lacks the concept of identity may still be capable of feature-placing and thus of gaining from its experience reasons for its actions. Suppose once again that my dog, Argus, is such a creature and is quite familiar with the forest behind my house. Not being born with knowledge of this terrain, Argus displays knowledge gained from experience when he comes to negotiate the trees and bushes with ease. Much of this knowledge is expressible in the form of rules in accordance with which his expectations are created when various objects appear to him. By possessing a rich knowledge of such rules, even Argus has a whole "cognitive map" of the terrain. As a merely feature-placing creature, however, this map must be describable only in purely general terms. To represent what Argus knows, it can describe only such things as the general way something will look (or feel, and so forth), now that it looks (or feels, and so forth) a certain way. What Argus's map must leave out, therefore, is *particularity*. Argus's map must be applicable, in principle, to other terrains qualitatively similar to this one. He does not know that he is in *this* terrain or, for that matter, *which* dog he is. And yet for practical purposes, as this example shows, his map can serve him quite well. To appreciate just how the concept of identity gives us an advantage

---

115. Dummett 1978, p. 3.

we should not underestimate our feature-placing fellows.

When we consider how proficient Argus is while traveling through familiar terrain the fact that he is only feature-placing may seem not much of a disadvantage. Lacking the concept of identity, he will lack self-awareness, and thus not be aware of demonstrative distinctions as such. But, Why is this a disadvantage?, we may wonder. Since he knows how to get around so well, what does he miss? Is it just that if he became self-aware and could give reasons for empirical cognitions which he now makes that he would be able to offer reasons for what he already knows so well? I think we can begin to see what is wrong with this worry if we realize that Argus's knowledge of the rules in accordance with which he acts is only tacit. It is precisely because he lacks self-awareness and thus cannot distinguish different instances in which a pattern of experience has recurred that Argus lacks consciousness of the pattern as such. The patterns recur, we are supposing, and when Argus is in the condition described by the antecedent of the rule, he comes to be in the consequent condition. But as with Dretske's snail, all that this means is that he is aware of certain conditions in succession. He sees, for example, a bush of a certain shape on the left and expects a hole in front, which he also sees the next moment below when he jumps it. It does not mean that, seeing the bush, he infers that there is hole in front. To make this inference he would need to be conscious of the rule itself. But, as we have seen, to have the latter, more sophisticated, awareness would be to have knowledge of the rule which is explicit, and this knowledge shows itself only when exploited in novel projects. As Evans explained, a rat's knowledge that a substance is poisonous would be explicit if, for example, (without being conditioned to do so) it withheld the stuff from its family or served it to an enemy. The rule, "If this stuff is eaten, you get sick," expresses a reason, that eating this stuff is a reason for expecting sickness. Awareness of the reason as such is manifested in only such novel behavior. It is understandable, therefore, that the advantage of having the concept of identity will not show up in circumstances in which the creature is already well-conditioned to know what to expect. Argus negotiates the terrain behind my house well because his tacit knowledge of the rules which he has acquired through frequent encounters prepares him well, by creating many accurate

135

expectations upon which he successfully acts. When circumstances are this way, a self-aware creature can use the concept of identity to think of himself as having a certain perspective on the general scene which enables him to see the patterns of his expectations as such, as patterns which have recurred many times in the past. But then he is not really taking advantage of the concept because he is not taking advantage of his ability to make inferences. If we made inferences only to become conscious of states of affairs that we already correctly expect (due to past conditioning), then the consciousness of inference would be only an epiphenomenon. If we want to see clearly what good it does to have the concept of identity, the power of individuation, we should therefore look to examples like that of Evans's rat, in which (correct) expectations are created by inference alone, and not by past conditioning. Suppose the rat was not conditioned to expect the enemy to be harmed by feeding it this stuff, but it does know that this stuff is harmful through its own experience. Given enough other evidence about what the rat wants and recognizes in the present circumstance, it appears that its expectation must be created by inference. But this will require explicit awareness of rule in question, which in turns requires that perspective on one's scene which enables one to see a rule as having several instances. And this requires using the concept of identity.

In the last chapter we were content to establish that to show that one was individuating anything one would have to show that one individuated continuants. We are now in a better position to see how the power of individuation is manifested (an issue of considerable importance for the study of animals and artificial intelligence). We have seen that the concept of identity, when applied in the basic circumstance of re-identifying a continuant over time, will be especially advantageous when it enables a creature to gain explicit knowledge of rules, since it is such explicit knowledge (the mark of conscious rationality) which enables the creature to make inferences which create expectations beyond those that are created simply by the way in which it was conditioned. Although a creature may be individuating itself and other things in circumstances in which its behavior is predictable from the way it has been conditioned, this sort of behavior gives evidence of only tacit knowledge of the relevant rules, expressible in feature-placing terms. The fact that a creature such as Argus learns from its environment shows only that it is aware of its environment. But it may be consciously responding to only general features of it. To show that it is individuating things in this environment, it must exhibit self-awareness and a grasp of demonstrative distinctions themselves. The best evidence for the possession of such sophisticated concepts will be available when they are most advantageously put to use. According to the present account, this will only be when a creature reveals knowledge of the rules which is explicit.

No account of how we use the concept of identity would be complete without discussing what is considered its most distinctive principle, Leibniz's Law, which says that if *a* and *b* are identical any property of one is a property of the other.[116] By alluding to this principle Paul Grice used to say that the *point* of identity was to license a transfer of properties, and he would use this idea to argue in a certain way for or against various identity claims. He held, for example, that the fact that two things in the same place at the same time, such as a gold ring and the gold of the ring, are very similar would provide some reason to think of them as identical. The fact that so many properties could be "transferred" from one to the other seemed to him to be some evidence for the identity claim. He would also argue from this same idea that when we did not want to "transfer" properties, as in ascribing physical properties to mental entities, there was some reason to deny the identity claim. Now, I do not dispute the idea that identity is useful mainly because it allows us to "transfer" properties from *a* to *b* once we know they are identical. But, as I explained in the first and fourth chapters, I am strongly opposed to using the appearance of similarity as evidence of identity or the appearance of difference as evidence of distinctness. For this is the hallmark of that "Humean" metaphysics which construes change on the model of destruction and thus indirectly supports the "short" view of personal identity I want ultimately to refute. I have complained elsewhere about this sort of argument on the ground that what is said of identity can

---

116. Frege held that identity was needed in order to see that two ways of thinking of something were really ways of thinking of the same thing, which is in effect to see that the property corresponding to each way of thinking can be ascribed to the object thought of in the other way. See Frege 1966.

be said more generally of the relation of similarity: surely, the fact that an object and its surface share many properties is no evidence of their identity.[117] I want now to show that when we see how to apply the principle of substituting identicals in the basic case of our epistemically primary continuants, we will be disabused of supposing this supports a Humean metaphysics.

We have taken care already to distinguish an account of what justifies applying a concept at all from an account of how we put the concept to good use in serving purposes of ours. I have argued that what, most fundamentally, gives us good reason to use the concept of identity in the interpretation of experience is that this is necessary to make empirical judgments. By contrast, I have argued that the concept of identity gives us an advantage over creatures who are restricted to feature-placing by enabling us to gain explicit awareness of patterns in our experience and thus to exploit our power of inference. Without the concept of identity it is still possible, as we have seen when considering feature-placing creatures, to have many correct expectations created as a result of past conditioning. When restricted to feature-placing a creature can still recognize a general feature of its environment and as a result of past exposures to this feature correctly expect something of how things will be. Lacking the concept of identity, however, the creature will not be able to form a conception of how the thing was before which it can "transfer" to the present recognition. There are two ways in which this ability to 'transfer" properties in this basic application of the concept of identity gives us an advantage over feature-placing brutes. We use it both to correct and to augment expectations formed from past conditioning. For an example of the first, suppose that while a soldier I see someone in enemy uniform and expect trouble; but then I recognize that he is a friend in disguise. I "transfer" the properties of his past to the present and my apprehension vanishes. Notice that it is not merely that my expectations are altered by my past knowledge: they are *over-ridden*. Suppose that Argus, who lacks the concept of identity, is familiar with

---

117. See Doepke 1982. I mentioned this in the first chapter and will discuss these issues more fully in the seventh. I made this point first in my doctoral dissertation; Grice was the Chair of my dissertation committee while he and George Myro were working on these same issues. I discuss their ideas more in the seventh chapter.

my friend, and when exposed to him normally expects friendly treatment as well. Suppose further that, like me, he is normally afraid of people in the uniform of the enemy. When seeing my friend in plain light, in this uniform, Argus is now aware of features which together create a confused mixture of apprehension and security. The difference between him and me is that his expectation is merely a *resultant* of different conditioned responses.[118] (It is much like his behavior in real life when I return from the zoo: my normal scent mixes with that of strange animals, so that he is more cautious in approaching me but less cautious than he would be in approaching them.) But when *I* identify my friend I *discount* the feeling that arises from the perception of the enemy uniform. My knowledge of my friend's past "trumps" the belief that he is hostile now (because of his uniform).

Knowing a thing's past may also enable me to make predictions that simply augment those that arise from present perception. If I expect my friend to deliver a message as a result of remembering his promise to do so when we meet, there may be no expectation I have from present perception that conflicts with this. Argus may well have no expectations either way about what sounds or gestures my friend will make now that he is appearing in enemy uniform. But I do, since I use my knowledge of his past (the fact that he promised to give me a message) to predict how he will be now. By identifying the person now appearing as the friend who in the past promised me the message I now predict that he will give me this message, even though I am not conditioned to expect this behavior merely by the way he now appears.

If reality were so constructed that knowledge of a thing's past never provided more of a guide for judging its behavior than the way it appears in the present, we would, therefore, have no advantage in anticipating the future by being able to use the concept of identity to re-identify continuants over time. The concept of identity allows us to interpret different appearances as appearances of the same thing. For Argus, the brute who is restricted to feature-placing, there is no difference in kind between encountering the same thing again in a new

---

118. Dretske describes such resultant responses in Dretske 1988, Ch. 6, in order to show how his account of explanation by reasons can cover relatively sophisticated forms of behavior. I am describing a difference *in kind* with such behavior.

appearance and encountering a new thing. This is why he reacts to my friend in enemy uniform as if he were of a new kind, friend-in-enemy-uniform, whereas I am able to react to him merely as my friend, discounting the appearance of the uniform, and expecting him just to be friendly. Reality is so constructed that it contains continuants like my friend who behave the way they do not simply because of the way they appear (in the present) but because of their past—because, for example, they have changed clothes or have made promises. It is only in such a reality that we have an advantage in using the concept of identity to "transfer" the properties of a thing's past to exploit the knowledge which augments and corrects the expectations which arise from present perception alone.

We may perhaps see more clearly how we use the concept of identity in the basic application of re-identifying continuants over time if we connect our application of this concept with that of drawing the distinction between appearance and reality. By lacking the concept of identity Argus does not distinguish from the way things seem a conception of something with an objective nature by virtue of which it can appear otherwise, for example, which can be perceived from other perspectives. But we can use the concept of identity to transfer the properties attributed in our objective conception to the thing as it appears in current perception. I am not saying of course that we can individuate with one conception without the other. It is because Argus lacks an objective conception of what is appearing now that he only feature-places. But we who individuate an object of perception can distinguish between those currently manifest features (which can be "placed") and those properties in addition to these which we attribute to the object. In marking this distinction we draw a contrast between how the thing appears and how it is objectively. Now, a clear consequence is that this is a useful distinction to draw especially in cases in which our objective conception includes relatively much that does not describe how the thing appears. This is why the example above of my friend in uniform illustrated well how to use the concept of identity over time. There is relatively much in how I think of him that does not describe how he appears now and yet is useful in predicting how he will be now. His "reality" includes much beyond his present "appearance." By contrast, if we turn from the things which appear to us objectively and restrict our references to the appearances themselves—the various ways things appear now—there is no point in distinguishing the reality of the appearances from the way they appear and consequently no use for the concept of identity. This is why attempts to refer to "sense-data" alone are bound (by the argument of the last chapter) to collapse into feature-placing. The upshot of all this, I submit, is that when we see under what circumstances the concept of identity is most useful, at least when we apply it in the first instance to continuants, we discover something quite different from the lesson Grice tried to draw from the point of identity. Recall that he held that since the point of identity is to transfer properties (as suggested by Leibniz's Law) when we find that things, such as those in the same place at the same time, are very similar, we have some reason to identify them. But since the concept enables us to identify an object of perception by transferring to it properties from an objective conception, and since there is the most reason to do this when the transfer is the most *informative*, the concept of identity is most useful in this basic application when the object is thought of objectively as being very *different* from the way it currently appears.

Although we use the concept of identity to describe things of many different kinds, I have offered some account of its use, a partial account, by describing it in application to our epistemically primary continuants. It is not difficult to see how this account complements the one previously developed of why we are justified in applying the concept of identity in the first place. Harrison took pains to explain why a subject who made judgments in the face of experience must apply rules which are potent enough to refute a direct judgment. It is this same requirement which justifies our use of the concept of identity to discount certain expectations that arise from present perception. I use the concept in this way when I ignore my friend's uniform. The appearance of the uniform causes me (and Argus) to expect trouble. I might even initially judge directly that there is an enemy here. But this judgment would be retracted entirely by me on the strength of the rule that my friend is safe, which I apply consciously to the present circumstance. This is how I use the rule. What justifies my using it is that it is supported on many other occasions, and I need to use such rules of general applicability to make empirical judgments in general. And since the rules themselves are objects of judgment, when we apply a rule in a present case, we are conscious of the state of affairs predicted. When I interpret my present perception as that of seeing my friend who promised to give me a message, I make a prediction which augments any expectation that arises unconsciously from past conditioning. What justifies this use of the concept of identity is again that this rule is supported in many instances (e.g., my friend has proven he is trustworthy), and that such well-supported rules are, in general, required for empirical judgment.

Although I have used Hume's own account of bodies or continuants to an appreciable extent in this chapter, I want the main point of it to be, in a certain (unfair) sense, anti-Humean. Let us recall that Hume held there to be two distinct causes which lead us to believe in bodies: the similarity of successive momentary impressions and their apparent causal connectedness. When I shut my eyes for a moment I am supposed to believe that a body persists unperceived either because of the similarity of my earlier and later impressions or because the later impression appears to be causally connected with the former when I think, not merely that I have momentary impressions, but that I have been seeing the same body at both times. It was the latter sort of situation that was involved in the case of the door. When Hume hears the creaking noise with his back to the door he is led to think of the door anyway, not because the creaking sound resembles sounds which he has just been hearing, but because the supposition that it comes from the door lets him connect this impression with those of many past occasions in which he heard that sort of noise while observing the door. Now, whatever the merit of this as Hume intended it to be, a merely psychological account of why we think of continuants, what must be realized is that the only aspect of it for which we found justification is the second one. That is, we have justified applying the concept of identity to continuants, not because there is an appearance of similarity, but because the appearances conform to rules which enable us to confirm judgments. I call those metaphysicians "Humean" who see in Hume's psychology a ground for identifying objects in similarity alone, or conversely, a ground for denying identity in apparent difference. That there really are such philosophers and that it is important for the issue of personal identity was seen clearly in the last chapter. We saw that Parfit thought that in the case of the "Combined Spectrum" there were grounds for re-identifying persons because they were physically and psychologically very similar; and we saw Lewis saying that the great changes in personality in a long life like Methuselah's would mean a loss of personal identity. A similar view is expressed by Eli Hirsch in his theory of identity based on the minimization of change;[119] and we have just seen how Grice was attracted to such a view by reflecting on Leibniz's Law. The last chapter was "negative" in that it served to undermine this Humean metaphysics. I argued for the reality of permanence or persistence: we must apply the manifest properties of experience to things which genuinely persist through changes in them, so that manifest change is not itself evidence of distinctness of objects, as it would be if the stage ontology replaced the continuant ontology. Since the metaphysics which construes all change on the model of destruction is wrong, its counterpart, which finds in similarity alone a ground of persistence, is at least highly questionable. In the present chapter I have argued "positively" that rules such as those that apply to the creaking door really are what entitle us to think of such continuants. A rule may of course predict that a thing will continue to appear a certain way, but in such a case the identification of the future thing will be based on the rule and not on the fact of similarity itself. If a chameleon stays on a color what justifies re-identifying it is not that it looks the same but that the future chameleon results from the previous one by a rule that applies to chameleons.

The examples from Parfit, Lewis, and Grice showed how real philosophers are under the influence of the Humean metaphysics which considers similarity itself, even in the absence of causal connectedness, a ground of identity. We will see more of such examples in the next chapter. I called the description of this metaphysics "unfair" when attributed to Hume, since Hume himself was only trying to explain our beliefs and not, like these other philosophers, trying to justify them. In the first chapter I offered, as did Hume, an explanation of why qualitatively indistinguishable things in temporal succession which are

---

119. Hirsch 1982, p. 81ff. In fairness to Hirsch I should say that, like Hume, he regards his "change-minimizing" account of identity over time as merely descriptive of how we actually individuate.

causally unconnected may easily seem identical. The intuition of their identity is easily produced by the merely subjective phenomenon of ignoring the lack of causal connection. Hume himself seemed to have such an explanation in mind when he spoke of the "easy transition" permitted the imagination by the succession of similar impressions. It is ironic that Hume's own explanation of why we are inclined to identify in such cases is discrediting. To explain our intuition of identity as due to purely subjective factors is in effect to show that in themselves they carry no epistemic weight and so must be justified or ignored. Of course, Hume offered a similar subjective explanation for the intuition that causal connectedness is evidence of identity.[120] But we should not ignore this intuition because, following Kant, we have found through transcendental argument that it can be deeply grounded.

The present chapter has arrived at an account of what justifies applying the concept of identity in the first place and a complementary account of how we make good use of the concept when we do so apply it. What gives us the right to apply the concept in the face of experience, to report it not merely in feature-placing terms but by individuating objects which appear to us, is that the concept is necessary for empirical judgment. Harrison had defined a notion of judgment as requiring a conscious selection of a proposition over its negation. He argued that to appear non-arbitrary the subject who made judgments would have to think there are reasons for them, themselves expressible in judgments. For these further reasons to confirm our first direct judgments they must report states of affairs causally connected with those of our first judgments. And these states of affairs must be seen as conforming to rules of general applicability. For it is only by gaining support in many other instances that the rule itself can be applied to retract a mistaken judgment, and without this power the rule would be useless in supporting a direct judgment. But then the rule must predict how things will be whether or not that judgment is

---

120. In saying that Hume "discredits" our intuitions I do not mean to imply that he thinks we are not really entitled to talk of causes and the like. What is discredited is the conception of causality as an objective phenomenon. But this is important, since this lack of objectivity is what has seemed to Kant and others to give rise to skeptical problems such as the problem of induction. It is this objective conception which is in effect recognized by Harrison's account of judgment, since the need to confirm our corrigible direct empirical judgments would evidently not be satisfied by causal predictions as conceived by Hume.

made and thus even if it is not actually made. It must therefore make predictions about things unperceived, which have the power to be perceived. While unperceived they lack the properties they would have if perceived. Since to think of things as genuinely lacking properties is the hallmark of individuation, empirical judgment requires that we individuate physical objects. These objects conform to Hume's conception of "bodies," since they not only have the power to affect our senses, but reveal their powers only in the particular manner in which they create patterns in our direct judgments. The general rationale for applying the concept of identity in the first place is that it allows us to individuate objects which comply with Harrison's rules of confirming our direct empirical judgment and thus to make empirical judgments in the first place. Moreover, we know that this general rationale will apply to us. From the second chapter we know that individuation in general is possible only if the individuation of self-awareness is possible. We must, therefore, be among the things to which the concept of identity is first applied (if only implicitly) since we must be among the first things individuated. From Kant's lesson of the billiard balls we know that we will be able to individuate ourselves only if we know ourselves as members of the physical world. We now see more clearly how this requirement will justifiably be met. For we must individuate above all things which can be perceived but which are not. To think of them as such is to think of how they would appear to oneself if circumstances were different. But this is to think of oneself as having an objective nature, and thus presumably a physical nature, a spatial location. One thinks of the unperceived object as existing now but lacking properties it would have if perceived now. This is to think of oneself as standing in a certain relation to that object not revealed by present perception. Following Kant, we have presumed that such objective relations are spatial. Empirical judgment thus requires that we acknowledge that we are physical objects, and the present account establishes that we are "bodies" in Hume's sense. We also saw how individuating such physical objects gives us an advantage over creatures confined to feature-placing. By gaining explicit awareness of the rules which confirm our empirical judgments we are able to use them to make inferences. By interpreting present experience as revealing a thing with a past, we "transfer" with the concept of identity properties from the past to correct or augment those expectations of ours which arise from present perception and past conditioning. But the right to use the concept of identity in the first place is, according to our account, based on our bedrock assumption that we are entitled to make any empirical judgments at all. I call the arguments leading to this first account "transcendental" because of the unavoidability of making such judgments. I take it that it is this feature which is supposed to make them effective against traditional forms of skepticism. If a skeptic who doubts the existence of the external world were stuck with a pin he would no doubt find it impossible not to make some empirical judgment. Arguments such as we have reconstructed, if successful, should thereby lead him to acknowledge the external world. Whether this is an adequate reply to the skeptic, however, is controversial and not our concern. Instead I acknowledge that our assumption of the legitimacy of making empirical judgments is bedrock. But this is sufficient for our purpose of adopting a starting point that will be shared by a revisionist who wants, not to question whether we are entitled to interpret the empirical world at all, but rather to interpret it differently than we ordinarily do. Our account of what justifies applying the concept of identity in the first place may be pictured as follows: although the feature-placing brute has expectations that accord with rules to which his experiences conform, *awareness* of such rules, and of reasons as such, emerges only when they are applied to oneself and other things. The theory favors in effect only half of Hume's account of bodies, acknowledging the need for causal connectedness in judgments of identity and finding no reason for allowing that apparent similarity itself is also a ground. This theory does not in itself provide a general conception of the identity criteria for epistemically primary continuants, but it offers a basis for creating such a conception. The purpose of the next chapter is to establish that conception and show that it is not vacuous in settling questions of ontology.

6

Essence As Activity

We commonly think of objects which undergo changes or remain unchanged in regular patterns revealed to us in experience. Taken together the last two chapters have sought deep justifications for this commonsense ontology. The admission that there are continuants which occupy space and genuinely persist through time, complying with laws, nevertheless leaves open many questions about what determines the identity through time of those continuants. I hope to answer a number of these in the present chapter by developing the account given in the last chapter of what justifies applying the concept of identity in the first place. Kant had said that although all things in nature act in accordance with laws, only a rational being acts in accordance with a conception of laws. I pointed out in effect that among the laws with which a conscious though non-individuating creature may accord are those which describe how its expectations are created from past experiences. This is, however, very different from being actually aware of such rules. What I argued was that the concept of identity must be applied for this awareness. This provided a deep justification for the concept in light of Harrison's demonstration that this awareness is required for making empirical judgments. But it is not yet clear how this general rationale for the concept translates into a conception of the kinds of epistemically primary things which we are justified in thinking there are. It does seem clearly enough to demand that causal connectedness (and not similarity alone) be involved in re-identifying continuants, since the rules in question, in being rules of confirmation, describe causal relations of some sort. But as we will see, there are many attempts to re-identify continuants over time on a causal basis that are objectionable. What I want to show first in this chapter is that the very general rationale defended in the last chapter leads to a rather specific conception of identity over time. Since this conception is recognizably Aristotelian, my argument is meant to show that "Kantian" epistemology leads to "Aristotelian" metaphysics (in senses of these terms which are not broad). Although I try to show that this conception is not vacuous in settling some questions of identity, there are other questions which require more elaboration of our metaphysics and which we need to see how to settle before we have an ontology sharp enough to address the question of our own identity. The next two chapters will be devoted to this task of developing further our more general ontology.

Let me paint the general outline before showing how our previous results support it. Aristotle held that in some cases the "formal" cause of a thing corresponds to its "final" cause. In these cases what the thing *is* is a matter of what it is striving to *become*. A classic case is the acorn which is striving to become an oak tree. We say what the acorn is by saying how, in favorable conditions, it will develop. Now, if we are to take seriously the claim that this is the formal cause of the acorn, then the point is not merely that the acorn has a tendency to develop in this way; it is that this tendency indicates "what it is." It is crucial to realize that this is not merely the weaker *de dicto* claim that "as" an acorn it has this tendency. For the *de dicto* claim is consistent with the claim that being an acorn is only an accident of the acorn, just as being a golfer would seem to be only an accident of a golfer. It must be the stronger *de re* claim that this tendency determines the identity of an acorn. The future oak tree is identical with the present acorn because the acorn just is the sort of thing which develops in this way. A point to emphasize is that the identity of the acorn is determined by something that is done by the acorn alone. It is the acorn which is responsible for its own future state; and it is identical with the thing in that future state because it alone brought about that state. To say that it brought about this state "alone" is not to deny that it needed support from other things. Of course the acorn needed water, air, and minerals in its surroundings to become the oak tree. But the acorn took these materials and made itself into an oak tree. To say this is to describe its own distinctive contribution to the process. It is to attribute to the acorn a form of "activity," in the sense that reference to the acorn is necessary to explain how the whole process took place. This activity on the part of the acorn explains a change which takes place in it for which it alone is responsible. And to equate its formal with its final cause is to hold that its identity is determined by the very fact that, in a certain way, it contributes to the creation of its own future states.

Although the acorn vividly illustrates the generic conception of identity criteria I wish to defend, I want to point out that quite different things also fit the general picture. The acorn has an essential tendency to bring about in itself a certain kind of change. But the identity of some things is determined by a tendency to remain the same. For example, quantities of stuff like this water or the gold of that ring are identified over time on the basis of the fact that they neither lose nor gain any amount of the stuff of which they are quantities. Let us suppose that this water is five ounces of water. Then the fact that there continues to be something of that exact amount is explained by the fact the thing in question is a quantity of water of that amount and that it is the same thing which has been there all along. If the water is divided into parts the fact that the parts together equal five ounces is explained by the fact that they are really just this same old water and that it cannot vary in amount. Organisms like acorns present vivid examples of things "striving" to become certain ways since they actually consume and expend expend energy in these processes. Perhaps only this makes the term "striving" literally correct. But, as with the acorn, the future state of the water is explained by reference to it in the earlier state and by the fact that it has a certain essential tendency. The water, like the acorn, is "responsible" for its own future state in the sense that it is by reference to it alone at the earlier time that we explain this future state.

As Wiggins clearly explains, the ideal examples of such things are the substances of Leibniz.[121] Although God creates the monads, and is thus responsible for their existence, they themselves are responsible for *all* their future states.[122] Since their interaction with other things is only apparent, the fact that a monad becomes a certain way is due only to its own internal activity. Moreover, its future identity is determined entirely by the way it unfolds itself. Once we break with Leibniz and admit the reality of interaction, things can be seen only to approach Leibniz's ideal more or less. Greater degrees of approach will explain the intuition that some things are more "substantial" than others. Organisms will thus appear highly substantial by showing a relatively high degree of independence from their surroundings. They emerge from their environment in high relief because of the preponderance of their own states whose possession is explained by references to themselves. They approach relatively well the ideal of the "perfect" substance which is entirely "self-sufficient."

The ontology of epistemically primary continuants which I support acknowledges *only* such continuants as I have been describing. Although continuants like organisms are understandably our favorite examples (as they were for Aristotle), we will find room for far more humble things, such as artifacts and even lumps of stuff. To speak of the "things" we admit is, however, a bit misleading. The real question is what are the principles of identity to admit. The question is not so much whether there are artifacts, lumps of stuff or golfers, but what these things *are*. Again, what is wanted is not an analysis of these notions, but a way of seeing which notions describe the essence and identity of the things to which they apply. Our ontology of (epistemically primary) continuants will include only those things whose identity is determined by their own internal activity. Although organisms catch our attention, we will admit anything which exhibits any degree of independence from its environment.

In an incisive analysis of the notion of behavior, Dretske encourages us to see this notion as having a broad range of application, so that even simple things like thermostats "behave" by doing things

---

121. Wiggins 1980, pp. 76–86.
122. For the sake of illustration I am ignoring the fact that for Leibniz time also belongs only to appearance.

like turning off furnaces.[123] Since behavior, for Dretske, is the process of an internal condition or event bringing about the change in question, a thing "behaves" whenever the condition or event which is the cause is within the thing. Like us, Dretske wants to preserve the distinction between the active and the passive, thus pointing out that such events as breaking, rusting, and getting repaired are things that happen to things (the causes of these events are not within those things). But even Dretske was unwilling to allow that all continuants "behave" in his extended sense. When a stone is put in water, it sinks. But is this something it does or something that happens to it? Failing to see an answer, Dretske suggested that the active-passive distinction applies only to things with an articulated internal composition. If Dretske was right, then I am committed to denying such things to our ontology. More precisely, the notion of a stone will not be associated with a distinctive principle of identity that we will acknowledge. Stones will exist, but to say what they are we will need to "reduce" them, by offering a different concept, such as one which describes the chemicals of which they are composed. I believe, however, that our ontology is more liberal. Suppose that to be a stone is to have a tendency to preserve a certain shape (in a certain kind of material stuff). This is different from merely being in that shape. If some ground up stone stuff were thrown in the air and momentarily happened to assume that shape there would be no "stone" there. I claim that this characterization of the stone helps to see how it enjoys a modicum of "activity," in our sense. When the stone sinks in water, what it "does" is to preserve its shape. This explains, not the fact that it sinks, but that it sinks as it does. The stone interacts with the water in such a way that requires explanation by reference to the stone as such. It is only because of its tendency to retain its shape that it sinks in such a steady path. After putting this case to Dretske, he himself suggested that the glass before him was responsible for holding a martini. This is so, I submit, because, like the stone, it tends to retain its shape.

Wiggins places in the center of his ontology those continuants whose identities are determined by their own internal activity. They occupy this place for him because their identities are relatively clear

---

123. Dretske 1988, pp. 9-11

and determinate. Their identities are determinate in the sense that they are not up to us to decide. Because the thing itself brings about its own future state its identity is a matter of discovery and not invention. He is disturbed by the idea that our identity might be up to others to decide and suggests that we belong to the favored class of continuants. This leads him to identify us as human organisms, which is to say in effect that Locke was wrong: being the same person *is* (for us humans) a matter of being the same human. But he admits that he does not know how to show this.[124] What causes special problems for him is his admission that there are continuants, such as artifacts, whose identities are governed by quite different principles of "function" or "operation." This is based on the idea that artifact terms like "ship" or "watch" indicate only what is the purpose of the thing, and do not, like "horse" or "tree," indicate a distinctive kind of natural development. It is because of this that he thinks that their identity is relatively indeterminate and so up to us to decide. But once he allows such things into his ontology he creates the problem of allowing that our identity, like that of his artifacts, might also be somewhat conventional.[125]

The chief difference between Wiggins's ontology and mine is methodological. Wiggins admits kinds of things when he thinks that they reflect ordinary ways of thinking and speaking, provided these are coherent. But we have adopted more stringent standards of justification, on the ground that the coherence of ordinary speech shows only that its kinds of things are possible, not that they are real. This stance of ours was adopted on the conviction that revisionist alternatives are to be taken seriously. I realize that many philosophers have a dimmer view of these. But what specially motivated our stance was that we do not want to beg questions against views of personal identity like Hume's and Parfit's which are themselves revisionist. What I now want to show is that the method we have followed will countenance only those continuants (as epistemically primary) that Wiggins accorded a central place. This will mean, among other things, that none of our (primary) continuants will have relatively indeterminate identities such as Wiggins's artifacts. And since we are among the

---

124. Wiggins 1980, p. 178.
125. I discuss this at more length in Doepke 1987.

continuants which are justified as epistemically primary, it will follow, as Wiggins wanted to show, that our identity is not up to others to decide.

In the last chapter we made a substantive assumption. We assumed that the *only* physical objects which are epistemically primary (in our sense of being the sort of things which must be individuated to individuate anything) are those which conform to the specific conception of physical objects that we found both in Hume's psychological account and in Harrison's account of judgment. It was only on this assumption that we were able to conclude that this conception characterizes ourselves insofar as we are physical objects. Our reason for making this assumption was simple: these are the only physical objects which are acknowledged by our account of what entitles us to apply the concept of identity in the first place. To see how our "Kantian" method of justification leads to the "Aristotelian" ontology described above we will make a similar assumption. I will first show how the conception of physical objects of our previous account *can* be used to define the conditions of identity over time of these objects. Then we will assume that it *does*. This is analogous to the previous assumption. We will see how our general rationale for applying the concept of identity supplies a generic conception of the things to which we first apply the concept. In the absence of an alternative rationale with such deep justification, the idea that there is perhaps is one, supporting a very different generic conception, presents a merely abstract possibility. We will accordingly consider ourselves justified in thinking that our generic conception is the one which describes the identity conditions over time of the things, including ourselves, which we first individuate.

Our general rationale shows that we are justified in individuating physical objects, including ourselves, that are sources of activity, capable of affecting how things appear to us by acting in accordance with general rules which we can see exhibited repeatedly in our perception of these objects. To say this much is only to describe what they are like, and not yet to say what kinds of things they are. It does not say what is essential to these things, what determines the conditions of their identity. To make this step, let us distinguish the circumstances in which we apply such rules into two kinds. In some cases the rule describes how one thing affects another; in others the rule describes how the thing itself is responsible for how it becomes. Let us call rules of the first kind, "rules of interaction," and rules of the second kind, "rules of activity." Recall that at the heart of our general rationale is the idea that we need to apply Harrison's rules to continuants (of a certain physical conception). For this general rationale to supply a generic conception of identity conditions, our epistemically primary things must be identified over time as the compliants of such rules. The rules themselves must somehow provide their identity conditions, and since these are identity conditions of continuants, they must determine their identity through time. The question is whether this need to apply such rules *can* determine the identity over time of continuants. It is clear that of the two kinds of rules just distinguished, it is rules of the second kind alone which are able to indicate conditions of persistence. A rule of interaction enables us to link judgments pertaining to how one thing affects another, and thus to link a succession of states of affairs in distinct things. They tell us that when one thing is a certain way another thing will become a certain way. Plainly, this in itself will tell us nothing about how either persists through time. Rules of activity, on the other hand, tell us how a thing is responsible for a future state of its own and thus have a content that can be used for re-identifying a continuant over time. We thus see how, in outline form, the general rationale is adequate for supplying a generic conception of identity conditions for continuants. By acknowledging that some of the rules which we need to apply by Harrison's account are rules of activity, we see to some extent how to re-identify the continuants to which they apply. Whenever we apply a rule of activity we know that if things come out as the rule describes, the continuants persists *at least* this long. We may discover, or already know, that the thing complies with rules of activity that predict much longer durations of persistence. But whatever the extent of persistence we know, this will be determined by our knowing that an appropriate rule of activity is applicable. This is because it is the applicability of such rules which both justifies and enables us to re-identify such things in the first place.

We have established by this point that some of Harrison's rules must be acknowledged as rules of activity, enabling us to trace continuants through time. But until we know which rules are so to count, we do not know what kinds of things we are encountering in experience. Our epistemically primary things divide into different "kinds" depending on the conditions of identity they satisfy. We have seen that these kinds will be determined specifically by rules of activity, so that objects which comply with different rules of activity belong to different kinds. But the rules in general may consist of both rules of interaction and of activity. There must be rules of the second kind to trace the continuants through time and there must be rules of first kind to describe how these physical objects act upon one another. At the feature-placing level the difference between the rules does not emerge, since all that appears at this level are patterns in our direct empirical judgments. The question is in effect to determine which of these patterns reveal the persistence of a thing and which reveal an action of one upon another. The answer to this crucial question, I submit, is that we should *presume* that such a pattern corresponds to a rule of activity, so that to recognize a rule of interaction we must defeat this presumption with special considerations. If it is the rules themselves which tell us *which* things we are entitled to individuate, then we must make this presumption. If all of the rules were rules of interaction, whenever we applied any one of them, since the rule itself would describe how one thing affects another, we would need something other than the rule to describe the identities over time of the objects involved and thus say what *kinds* of things were involved. Put another way, if in applying a rule we always assumed that it described one thing affecting another then we would need something other than such rules to tell us of what kinds of things we were thinking, which is just what we are denying. Suppose, for example, that we find some strange green object that, whenever held up to light, is immediately succeeded by an object of a different shape, color and texture. I am claiming that in the absence of any other data by which we could judge the objects distinct, we have presumptive evidence that there is a single object undergoing dramatic changes. Of course we could be wrong. We might find out that our ever-busy distant scientists are causing by remote control the destruction of the first object and its immediate replacement by the second. But the whole reason for applying the concept of identity in the first place to physical objects is to be able to link our direct empirical judgments, and we do this in basic cases in which we perceive such objects only by individuating continuants. If, as we are assuming, this *enables* us to re-identify continuants, when we do, the identity of the continuant will be determined by how it is responsible for the way it becomes according to the rule in question.

It may seem that our account leads to a vicious regress. When we do re-identify a continuant in accordance with our account on the basis of current observation, it is only because we see it complying with a certain kind of rule which must be supported by many other instances. I have reason to think that the green object is undergoing the dramatic change only if I know this sort of change has occurred many times before. But if I must think of the change as involving a continuant which I can re-identify in one case only by knowing that things of its kind typically undergo such changes, how can I re-identify one in the first place? There would be no problem if I could refer to other things for reference points. I might wonder when first presented with the strange green object how "the thing in my hand" will behave. But since our theory concerns how to justify applying the concept of identity in the first place, it cannot suppose that we always have such crutches. The reason why our account is not viciously regressive may be seen by referring to the picture I offered in the last chapter: although a feature-placing brute will have perceptions and expectations that accord with rules, awareness of such rules emerges hand in hand with individuation. We can first be in the position of the brute (for instance, in infancy), learning a good deal about how the world around us works, but having this knowledge only by a grasp of the rules which is tacit (as discussed in the last chapter); with an explicit grasp, according to our theory, we begin to see a world of continuants which have been complying with these rules.

I have argued that our general rationale for applying the concept of identity in the first place requires that we see our epistemically primary continuants as being responsible to a certain extent for the way they become. I have not said that every such tendency to create one's own future is what determines the full identity of the things which have that tendency. Golfers are disposed to sink balls in cups, and ascribing this disposition to golfers in the appropriate circumstances allows us to see how to determine to some extent where they will be and what they will be doing. But if this disposition fully determined the identity of golfers, when they lost it they would cease to exist altogether. The sort of activity in which one engages to be a golfer does not determine the full identity of golfers if, as we normally think, being a golfer is merely an accident of golfers. In the next two chapters we will try to discover how to tell if a tendency to create one's future is one which fully determines the identity of things which have it and thereby comprises its essence. The present chapter is concerned to establish and illustrate the point that the identities of the continuants of our metaphysics will be determined in this general way.

I say that the identities of our continuants are determined by "tendencies" to create their own future to emphasize two points. First, since there is no reason to think that any one we discover could not cease to exist, we want to allow the possibility that one will not become the way it is supposed to become; this happens just when it does not survive the transition it was meant to undergo. So, I say only that it "tends" to become a certain way. Acorns tend to grow into oak trees, and they will in favorable conditions. Second, if the identity of the thing is determined not only by how it becomes but because it is alone responsible for this, then to attribute to the thing a tendency makes clear that it is the source of the future state. If a tendency of a thing to create its own future is what determines it identity, then all that is needed to see why it came to be a certain way is to know that it persists and that it belongs to the kind of thing whose identity is determined in this way.[126]

When Hume was concerned to explain why we think of "bodies" he was not concerned with the question of what determined, for any one of these, its identity over time. True, it must persist through time retaining a power to affect our senses which can be repeatedly exercised. But this much could be said of physical objects of many different kinds. When Locke, on the other hand, emphasized how much ideas of such powers comprised our ideas of "sorts" of material

---

126. Our "tendencies" are thus meant to match the "potencies" which characterize the essences of Aristotle's primary substances in the Metaphysics. Irwin has an excellent discussion relevant to our own on how the notion of a potency is richer than the notion of a possibility in being an explanatory notion (see Irwin 1988, pp. 227–30).

substances it was this question of identity conditions that he meant to address. His point was not merely that material substances have certain powers, realized in an underlying structure, which cause those substances to appear as they do. It was that we *use* our ideas of these powers to think of what they *are*. We find in our experience that certain manifest properties regularly go together. We find in certain circumstances that where it appears yellow, it also feels solid, soft and malleable. We ascribe these properties to the same material substance, "gold," not simply because we want to find a "bearer" for them (why then ascribe them to the *same* substance?), but because we suppose that there is, in Locke's terms, a "cause of their union." It is clear, I think, that our primary physical objects nicely fit Locke's conception of material substances. They divide into kinds by virtue of satisfying different identity conditions, and their identity over time is determined by their having essentially certain "powers" (to contribute to their own futures) distinctive of their kind. But we break from Locke on an important point: since, following Kant, we think of *ourselves* as material substances, our own identity over time will be determined by the exercise of some "power," presumably realized in an underlying structure or "real essence." This stands in sharp contrast with Locke's own view of our identity, in which our identity over time is, so to speak, a "surface" phenomenon, transparent to consciousness, in particular, by linking stages of life through conscious recall. (We will return to this difference in the last chapter.)

Although I will not try to say more specifically what we are until the last chapter, it might help to see how it is even possible for our generic conception of identity criteria to apply to our own identity over time. This is not difficult, since we seem to present very clear examples of entities which determine to a large extent how we become. Whenever we make inferences or form intentions, for example, we seem clearly to display a form of activity that belongs to us alone and by which we determine how we become. But since this much can be admitted by those who hold very different views of our identity, we need to develop our theory beyond our generic conception in order to decide between them.

I have tried to show in this chapter so far that our Kantian epistemology has lead to a definite conception of the identities of continuants, including ourselves. We were reminded of Aristotle in seeing their identities as determined by their own activity to make themselves become certain ways. Now it might be thought that, on reflection, this is an entirely vacuous conception, one that can be applied to virtually any ontology of continuants. Suppose, for example, that an object is annihilated and by sheer accident an exact duplicate takes its place. We can write a rule to just that effect which says that the duplicate is identical with the first thing. That being so, why can we not say that the first thing is "responsible" for the original state of the duplicate and other ones thereafter, and that this "determines" its identity? Again, suppose that we give a name to that "one thing" which first was Caesar and then Betsy the cow. Could we not adopt the Aristotelian language (to no real purpose) and say that Caesar is identical with Betsy because of his "production" of future states of Betsy? The form of this objection is clear. Since any statement of the conditions of identity over time of a continuant takes the form of a rule, it is supposed that the language that we used in describing our rules applies to any such rule. By seeing how it does not, we will see how our metaphysics has already developed a bit of an edge.

Let us start with the first example just mentioned, the case in which something is annihilated and duplicated by sheer accident. The fact that the duplication happens by "sheer accident" makes it especially easy to see how our account rules it out. Presumably the whole import of this is to deny that the creation of the duplicate or its initial states depends upon the way the first thing was at its end. The duplicate would have come into existence, the way is was, even if the first thing had never existed. Because of this, the first thing cannot be "responsible" for the way the duplicate is. Reference to the first thing is entirely irrelevant in explaining the creation of the duplicate. And because of this, judgments about the duplicate at its creation confirm no judgments about the way the first thing was at its annihilation.

Our first example presents an extreme case which lacks the requisite causal connectedness for re-identifying a continuant. Just this sort of case has been urged by Daniel Kolak and Raymond Martin as showing that personal identity requires no causal connection.[127] They claim

---

127. Kolak 1987.

that if the body of a person were annihilated and perfectly replicated the person would continue to exist even though the switch occurred by sheer accident. They support this claim by their expressed conviction that the switch would be of no practical or emotional significance. The replicated person should, for example, not be fired from his job nor should his wife ignore him. It is from this alleged fact that we are supposed to be entitled to infer personal identity. There is much to say about this whole line of argument. First, it ignores the challenges of Wiggins and Parfit concerning the practical importance of personal identity. As we saw in the third chapter, Parfit would say that personal identity does "not matter" in survival, so that the wife should care for the replica even if he is not the same man; if Parfit is right, the transfer of concern would not signal a transfer of identity. Wiggins denied that one could "evade responsibility" by contriving his own fission; since he believes that this involves a loss of identity he is saying that responsibility can be transferred without identity; presumably he would say the same of rights, so that the new man should keep the job even if he is new. I, on the other hand, argued for the importance of personal identity. This does not mean that replicas are of no importance. Kolak and Martin point out that the new man should not be treated like a stranger. But this presents a false alternative. Since the new man is a replica, having him can be regarded as much better than simply losing the first man, but not as good as having this first man instead. This is my position. My main objection to their argument is that it turns things upside down. We cannot first decide all of the attitudes we have and then infer from this whether we have the same person; whether it is the same person ought to shape our attitudes in certain ways. As I argued, the new man will not really satisfy the self-involved desires of the first, nor will he really fulfill his intentions. And even if there is a loss of identity in such a case, as I have claimed there is, the fact that the new man is a perfect replica can still explain why we would not treat him as a stranger. Assuming that he is not deeply disturbed by the realization of who he is (a very artificial assumption!), it is obvious why he might be retained on the job. Assuming that he might carry on the concerns of the first man, a transfer of rights might be explained as licensed by the dispositional consent of the first man: it might be reasonable to suppose that this is

160

what the first would wish. The point is that even if we can make some judgment about what our attitudes would be in this case independently of knowing whether it is the same person, there are alternative explanations of these, consistent with non-identity, so that identity cannot be inferred from them. But to suppose that there would be no difference in attitude which hinges on a prior conviction of identity is both question-begging and implausible. As Grice once said to me, although we may not care whether our accountant is a mere replica, we certainly do care in the case of a spouse. (The argument of the third chapter defended this opposite intuition.)

My second sort of case is really very similar to the first. Locke held that an object could not begin to exist at different times.[128] Reid defended Locke by claiming that the idea was self contradictory: a thing cannot exist after it exists or before it is produced.[129] It does not take much reflection to see that Reid's defense is question-begging. One might as well say that a thing cannot be composed of two spatially separated parts, since then it will exist past where it has stopped existing and exist outside itself. Just as this shows only that the parts are spatially separated, Reid shows only that the object would have temporally separated periods of existence, not that this is impossible. I submit that this is just one more example of how little can be done in metaphysics on purely logical grounds, which is why we followed Kant in adopting the transcendental method. In taking this path we are not going to allow kinds of things just because we can make up words for them and "find" examples of them in experience. This is why I cannot go along with Peter Simons, who gives as an example of an "intermittent" object the fist which comes into existence twice when he closes his hands twice in succession.[130] This seems to me to be just like the previous case in that the fact that the second fist comes into existence, as it does, is entirely independent of how the first fist was at its end. I am supposing, for example, that the second fist was not made by deliberating copying the first. (We will discuss copying shortly.) The second fist would have been made, just as it was, even if the first had not been made. So, nothing is explained about the second

128. Locke 1975, p. 328.
129. Reid 1975, Ch. 4.
130. Simons 1987, pp. 204–05.

by reference to the first, and nothing about the first is confirmed by reference to the second. By our theory we have no reason to identify them; lacking any apparent justification, we ought not to.

I said that this second example was much like our first. Both violate our theory by identifying despite a lack of dependency of future states upon previous ones. They differ, however, in that there is a kind of material continuity in the second but not in the first. Many philosophers feel that this is a relevant difference. In the first case, it is clearly just an accident that no more than one replica was made. In a famous discussion, Williams argued that the mere possibility of duplication in replicas rules out identity.[131] (We will return to this argument soon.) But in our second example, the fact that the fist is made with the same hand rules out this possibility of duplication. There are many examples like this, in which something is constructed from materials, then apparently destroyed after altering the materials, and then something of the same kind is constructed from the same materials. A child may, for example, build a favorite house or boat repeatedly from the same construction toys. It is very tempting to many philosophers to allow that the same toy reappears in such cases. And as Simons explains, the reason why this seems to be more like a reappearance and not a case in which the object exists in a disassembled state is that if the toy is not reconstructed there is no temptation to admit disassembled existence; but whether this happens is purely accidental.[132] It seems clear to me, however, that our theory takes a hard line on these examples, thus supporting Locke in his denial of intermittent existence. Although my final position on artifact identity will not be fully disclosed until the eighth chapter, what I am committed to saying now is that if the case really is as I describe it, as one in which the second comings are not at all dependent on the state of the first object at its end, then I see no reason to identify. I simply see no reason to allow that the fact that continuity of the same matter prevents duplication is sufficient for identity. I realize that this goes against the intuitions of many, but our whole stance in this project is to question intuitions so as to develop a justification deep enough to rebut even revisionist ontologies. It should not be surprising that some intuitions will not

131. Williams 1973, pp. 8–10.
132. Simons 1987, pp. 195–99.

pass muster when the justification must be deep. Of course, as philosophers, we always want to explain these intuitions, or "explain them away." This is what I did in the first example, by showing how a transfer of rights or responsibilities could be explained without assuming personal identity. In the present case, we must explain the intuition that an object exists intermittently when objects of the same kind are constructed at different times from the same matter. Now, one thing that would explain this intuition is adoption of the Humean metaphysics which finds grounds for identifying when things are similar despite a lack of causal connection. The second object is very similar to the first, sharing exactly its same matter and being of the same form. We saw in the first chapter that this intuition (that similarity itself is evidence of identity) can be explained by the fact that very similar things can easily seem identical: just ignore the relatively few differences. This explains the intuition, or rather "explains it away," for we have seen no reason to adopt the Humean metaphysics. There is also the fact, mentioned by Wiggins, that with artifacts, we often simply do not care whether it is the same, so that denying identity in ordinary affairs often seems pointless. Finally, there is the possibility, which we will examine critically in the eighth chapter, that the object should be "reduced" to its matter, so that the reason why there seems to be the same object at both times is that the object is really identical with the matter which persists throughout.

I have argued that just because the same materials are given the same form at different times there is no reason to identify an intermittent object essentially of that form. And I concluded from this that we ought not to identify, which means that we ought to think of them as distinct. But why think of them as distinct? With reference to just these sorts of examples, Michael Burke argues that in the absence of special reasons for distinguishing objects we ought to identify them.[133] The continuity of matter ensures that "branching" cannot occur, that there cannot be competitors for identity with the original object. So why not identify, he asks, when we can? A similar stance toward questions of identity is taken by Robert Nozick with his "closest continuer" theory.[134] Although Nozick demands both similarity and some causal

---

133. Burke 1980.
134. Nozick 1981, pp. 29–70.

connectedness for persistence, he is liberal in what counts as enough of these, since the root idea is that there is a presumption that a thing persists, which has to be defeated by enough reasons. My position with regard to questions of identity is the opposite. Claims of identity have to be specially justified, and I have given a theory for when these conditions obtain. But to these philosophers my position may well appear arbitrary. Why not demand that claims of distinctness are what need special justification, so that when these conditions are not met we ought to identify?

My response to this objection is to remind ourselves of the whole way in which I have argued for how to apply the concept of identity (to primary continuants). I did not start off with the assumption that in any pair of manifest circumstances we must either assert or deny identity. If I had, I really would be open to the objection in question, that it is arbitrary to demand that it is the assertions of identity and not the denials that need special justification. I started off with the assumption that feature-placing or universal recognition is an intelligible alternative to making either assertions or denials of identity. Because of this, I do not really infer from only the fact that there is no reason to identify that we ought to assert distinctness. With the feature-placing or universal recognition alternative in mind, we were prepared to do neither. I can, accordingly, question Burke's strategy of asserting identity in the absence of special reasons for distinguishing objects, just as I would question the strategy of asserting distinctness *merely* from the absence of special reasons for identifying objects. By "descending" to the "level" of feature-placing or universal recognition we can demand justification for both the assertions of identity and of distinctness. But there is a clear sense in which the justifications of the assertions of identity are basic. Whenever we judge that that there are two objects and not one we still need to individuate each of the objects; and to justify this judgment we will have to justify how the concept of identity is to apply to each. It is true, as we have allowed, that our primary continuants will need to be distinguished from each other in a system. But the fact that we need to distinguish objects from one another does not tell us what *kinds* of objects are to be distinguished. Assertions of identity are what are needed to indicate the kinds of things which form the system in question. It is their peculiar identity conditions which determine the sorts of relationships they bear to one another which we indicate when we distinguish them from one another. For example, we know that the fact that Argus is over here now makes him a distinct object from the food bowl over there now because Argus and the bowl have identity conditions that do not permit them to be simultaneously in two places. Without this knowledge of which identity criteria to use in the interpretation of experience we would be in no position to make judgments of distinctness. This is why I asked, from the "level" of feature-placing or universal recognition, what justified asserting (and not denying) identity. We need to see what kinds of pieces we have on the board before we can see how they are related.

I have argued that we ought not to admit objects that exist intermittently, even when they are composed of the same matter. Simons offers a novel solution to the famous problem of the ship of Theseus that depends upon his acceptance of intermittent existence.[135] It seems that the parts of a ship can be gradually replaced throughout a journey; but if the original parts are used to create a ship just like the first at a time in which the ship with the new parts still exists, the question arises of which of the two later ships is identical with the first. Simons rejects the assumption of the question, that there is only one ship at first, and says that there are really two ships there, one which can survive replacement of its parts and one which exists whenever the original parts are in the shape of the ship. The two ships at the end of the story are thus not competitors, since they both coexisted at the beginning. His argument for this is that it respects the intuitions of both camps: those who favor preservation of form and those who favor preservation of matter. But we have already opposed the intuition of those who favor the new ship with the old parts. Simons has criticized me for ignoring his argument.[136] Perhaps a fair statement would be this. Simons is working within our common metaphysics, so that there is a strong presumption that intuitions are true. (Recall our discussion of the method of cases in the first chapter.) Within this framework—which is the framework of many—he offers good reason

---

135. Simons 1987, pp. 199–04.

136. This criticism was made in correspondence pertaining to my review of his book in *Nous*, June 1991.

to accept both ships. To take revisionist alternatives seriously, however, we stand outside this framework and accept its elements only piecemeal, by demanding that they meet a stringent standard of justification, revealed by transcendental argument. From this standpoint, the intermittent ship with the same old parts is not admitted into our ontology.

A third example, similar to the first two, is provided by Shoemaker.[137] Suppose that in a certain house there is a table in the living room and one in the kitchen. And now suppose that a "klable" shares the history of one table for half the day and the history of the other table for the other half, so that it suddenly "jumps" from one room to the other twice a day. This case certainly looks like the previous cases, for the state of the klable just after a "jump" seems in no way dependent upon the state of the klable before one. This is of course because of the apparent lack of dependency of the states of either table upon those of the other. But suppose it is pointed out that, being a klable, there are certain "rules" that enable us to predict how the klable will "jump," so that when it does "jump" this way, the way it ends up confirms judgments about how it was before the "jump." We might say, for example, that at noon we expect the klable in the living room to disappear and reappear in the kitchen. It would then be claimed that our judgment that a klable does indeed exist in the kitchen at noon would confirm our judgment that we were not hallucinating when we thought there was a klable in the living room a moment before. What rescues us from admitting such objects is Harrison's observation (discussed in the last chapter) that our rules link judgments which are logically independent. The problem with the klable is that the only way that we can judge at noon that it is a klable before us is to know already that it was in the living room before noon. But then the later judgment will not allow us to confirm the former judgment, owing to circularity. This shows an important difference between the concept of a klable and the ordinary concept of a table. Although both concepts incorporate certain criteria of identity, they have quite different sorts of criteria of application. Ordinary sortal concepts not only tell us how to re-identify things, they can be applied on the basis

---

137. Shoemaker 1984, pp. 256–59.

of current experience. Tables look and feel a certain way, so that we can make judgments about their presence directly on the basis of current experience. Only this enables us to make another direct contact with the world to confirm our corrigible judgments about them. Since klables are recognized not merely by how they appear but also by knowing how they were before, we do not know they are present without already knowing their past. But then we cannot use our present judgment to confirm our past judgment since the latter must already be known in order to know the former. Since judgments about how they are now do not, therefore, confirm judgments about how they were then, our theory rejects them. It might be said further that our theory *explains* the intuition that they are bogus. Since the admission of their existence offers no support for our judgments it has an air of arbitrariness about it.

Our fourth sort of example will be somewhat trickier. We are now to imagine that an object is annihilated and that an exact copy is made. I now call this a "copy" to indicate the fact that the exact similarity of the new thing with the old thing is no accident, but comes about by some sort of design, perhaps by machine, advanced scientists, or God. Unlike the second case, however, we are supposing that there is no material continuity, so that the fact that two or more copies are not made is merely contingent. Williams denied identity in such cases.[138] His reason was that the original would be related to the copy in the same way as it would be to each of both copies in the non-actual situation in which two copies are made. Since identity is one-to-one, this one-to-many relation could not be what grounds identity, and so it would be arbitrary to claim that they are identical rather than only similar. This appeal to the "way" in which the objects are related was too vague to satisfy all parties. After all, the uniqueness of the copying in the actual situation is a "way" in which the objects are related which separates this case from the duplication case. Essentially this tack has been taken by many philosophers. I believe, however, that Williams was on the right track. I want now to argue against such copying in a way that perhaps develops his point.

Parfit's own criterion of personal identity, non-branching

---

138. Williams 1973, pp. 8–10.

psychological continuity, is an example of the sort of thing that Williams denied. Such continuity obtains whenever there is overlapping psychological connectedness, as when a belief or desire is retained or an intention is carried out. Since Parfit thinks that a person would be psychologically continuous with any number of copies, such as offshoots of fission or artificially made replicas, he holds that when there is only one copy the original person continues to exist as the copy. (In the third chapter I argued that branching is not as benign as Parfit would have us think, since the duplicate copies would not be psychologically continuous with the original person; but let us waive this point now.) Parfit agrees with Williams that since identity is one-to-one, the basis of it cannot be one-to-many. But he ensures that his basis is one-to-one by the simple expedient of stipulating that the psychological continuity not "branch" into two or more streams. In effect he is "constructing" a new relation from one which permits branching by stipulating that it not branch. Psychological continuity supposedly permits branching, but non-branching psychological continuity, by definition, does not.

Williams's point was not restricted to personal identity; it was a general point about the basis for a claim of identity over time. I want to show that there is something clearly right about his point when it pertains to continuants which are epistemically primary. I will not now be restricting my attention to those "Aristotelian" things which comprise our ontology, but will discuss more generally continuants which can be individuated non-parasitically. In the fourth chapter I allowed that there might be such things as momentarily existing stages which can be individuated by reference to things already picked out, but they contrast with the epistemically primary things such as ourselves and objects which we pick out in perception. Now, any continuant, primary or secondary, will have some criterion of identity that describes correctly what determines its identity over time. Assuming, as we have been doing, that this is a criterion which we can know and use, the correct criterion of identity for a primary thing is one which will allow it to be picked out in the first place, without having first to individuate other things and then to individuate it in relation to these. I am not saying that this is the only way we can individuate these things. After all, the whole problem of personal identity is that of discovering which criterion correctly describes the identity of beings like ourselves. In putting the problem this way it is assumed that we can speak and think of ourselves without knowing exactly what kinds of things we are. Similar problems arise for continuants of other kinds. While apparently talking about the same watch or ship, we might disagree about whether it is the kind of thing that survives disassembly. In both sorts of cases we agree to some extent how to re-identify the continuant in question. All who wonder about personal identity will agree at a minimum that I am the same person who now seems to see and touch a computer and to feel myself in an upright position. I know at least this much about how to re-identify myself from one predication to another. The question of personal identity is in effect to supply a rule which applies to these states and shows informatively how to extend the re-identification of myself to other, controversial cases. Similarly, all who wonder about the identity of artifacts will agree, for example, that it is the same ship when there is no replacement of parts and the parts are not disassembled; the question is how to continue the re-identification of a ship in cases like the ship of Theseus in which these conditions fail to obtain. This shows that while the individuation of a thing is possible only with some minimal commitment to its identity conditions, the full conditions may be unknown, or at least not consciously known. Nevertheless, if we were in possession of the fully correct criterion of identity for a primary thing, it is clear that it could be used to individuate something non-parasitically. Given, for example, the correct criterion for persons, we could ostend a person and refer to "that thing" which satisfies this criterion, and would surely if ever be individuating that person. What I want to show is that such criteria cannot be relations, such as Parfit's criterion of personal identity, which are constructed from branching relations by adding the stipulation that branching has not occurred.

In general, the reason is this. The constructed relations in question differ from their branching counterparts (for example, being copied) only in stipulating that the branching actually not occur (for example, being uniquely copied). To tell that such a constructed relation obtains, we first have to tell that the relation which permits branching obtains and that, as a matter of contingent fact, there is no branching. But since the branching relation itself will not enable us to re-identify

169

anything (as even Parfit would admit), this means that to individuate the thing by its correct criterion we will have to be using some *other* relation. And this means that even if we can then go on to individuate something with the constructed relation, it will be only by differentiating this thing from an epistemically primary one. But then thing in question will not itself be primary.

To illustrate this point, consider a stone path. Let us suppose that a stone path exists whenever some stones are in a single line. The relation between the stones of a path is one of our "constructed" ones. The stones form the path when there is a series of them on the ground and there is no branching, so that they form a single line of stones. But to tell whether a stone path, in this sense, exists, we first have to tell that there is one stone after another on the ground and that there are no competitors for being "the next one" in the series. As this example illustrates, a stone path is not a primary thing, since we have to individuate the individual stones before we can individuate the path itself. It is by only by examining the stones and how they are actually related that we are in a position to see that there is a stone path there. This is because to tell that there is only one stone next to the previous one we first have to tell that there is at least one nearby and that there are no others. There could have been two nearby and we had to rule this out by looking at the stones. The relation of being nearby is the branching one. To discern that the non-branching one obtains we have to see that the branching one obtains and that branching has not occurred. But then we cannot be using the non-branching relation to pick out a primary thing in the first place.

This argument clearly applies to ourselves on the assumption, argued for in the second chapter, that we are epistemically primary. Consider, for example, Parfit's criterion of personal identity. To see that it obtains we must first see that psychological continuity obtains and that as a matter of fact branching has not occurred. This requires that we be able to individuate the states or events which are psychologically connected, as we individuate the stones of a stone path, before we can apply the criterion which says there is a single person persisting throughout. And this means that the criterion could not be used to pick out a person in the first place.

Many accounts of personal identity are subject to this criticism. In a self-conscious attempt to generalize Parfit's criterion of personal identity to describe continuants of other kinds, Brennan describes a "survival" relation which requires that an earlier thing be structurally similar to and "play a significant role in the production of" the later thing; a sufficient condition of survival is achieved if in addition the later thing be composed of the same kind of matter.[139] Survival itself is clearly a branching relation which obtains, for example, whenever any number of copies are produced. The survival relation is offered by Brennan to illuminate the identity conditions of the ordinary continuants around us: they persist when survival obtains and does not actually branch. We have seen, however, that no such notion will correctly describe the identities of those very ordinary continuants, including ourselves, which we first encounter in experience. A similar problem occurs in Unger's account. Although he favors a physical approach to our identity, this is described by reference to the "sufficiently continuous realization of the core psychology," which, like psychological continuity, would seem to permit branching, thus leading him to stipulate that there should "probably [be]... some suitable clause for ruling out unwanted cases of branching."[140]

Having laid down a new requirement for epistemically primary continuants I want now to show how our "Aristotelian" conception meets this by ruling out even the possibility of branching. According to our theory, the identity of each primary continuant is a matter of how that thing contributes to its own future states. Although none of our things are Leibnizian monads, they nevertheless make a distinctive contribution to the way they become and this is precisely what determines their identity in the future. The acorn gathers air, water and minerals and makes itself into a tree; and the presence of the oak confirms the past presence of the acorn. Now suppose that we admit among this class of primary things those which result by copying something previously annihilated. What is somewhat trickier about this case is that the copy really does depend upon the way the earlier thing was, simply because it is a copy of it. It was made to be the way it is only because the earlier thing was the way it was. But

---

139. Brennan 1988, pp. 26–27.
140. Unger 1990, p. 109.

even though this is so, what is crucially missing is the requirement that it is the earlier thing *alone* which makes the copy the way it is. It is only because this requirement is missing that branching is possible. Whether the copy is made at all is up to the copying agent—a machine, advanced scientists or God. It is only because of the intervention in the process by such an external agent that the possibility opens up that He, they or it might have done it twice or more. But then it is not the thing itself which is producing itself in the future. For no such thing could produce itself by making two copies of itself. This is not to say that nothing could be naturally cloned like an amoeba. But this would be, not a case in which something made itself a certain way, but one in which the parts naturally separate, thus destroying the original. The whole idea of our theory is that the identity of the thing is determined by how it creates itself. This cannot be a process in which two or more things could be produced, thus resulting in non-identity with any of them. For if the process does not *ensure* identity, whether one or more things are produced as a result of it will depend on the influence of other things and it will not be the process itself which is determining the thing's identity. Williams's intuition that even the possibility of duplication rules out identity is thus supported, but only by accepting a theory like ours.

We have seen that we must reject Parfit's criterion, as it stands. This is not of course to show something so grand as that the "long" view of identity that Rawls associated with Kant is now established over any "short" view that could be associated with Parfit or Hume. All it means is that Parfit's "short" criterion must be somehow accommodated within our "Aristotelian" framework. It must be modified so as to describe a natural tendency of a person to contribute to his or her own future, a tendency which is expressed only by ruling out even the possibility of branching. This will be a substantive modification, to be sure, since it will rule out persistence by unique copying, which Parfit wants. But our general metaphysical account is not yet sufficiently developed to rule out any "short" view that would be significantly similar to Parfit's. Now, the most straightforward way of modifying Parfit's criterion would be to say that personal identity is determined by a natural tendency to preserve one's current mental states. This would have to be understood in a weak enough sense that personal identity would not be simply destroyed by the first psychological disconnection, such as a change in belief or desire; but such a change would have to "erode" the basis of identity, as Parfit maintains. The important point would be that my current mental characteristics determine which person is here now: this person is striving to preserve these states and not some very different ones possessed later on. Only the essential reference to how my mind is now will make the view significantly "short." This will keep it within the Humean framework in which judgments of identity over longer stretches of time become increasingly arbitrary and trivial. We might modify the criterion further along lines which Parfit suggests. In many examples he suggests that with losses of deep affections and ideals, it is especially trivial to insist that personal identity is preserved. We might accordingly see personal identity as determined especially by a natural tendency to strive to preserve currently held values. We see what a person *is* by seeing what he (now) *values* most deeply. I take it that this view has serious appeal to many. We will discuss it in depth in the last chapter.

Ruling out copying gets even trickier when we return to an example like that of Simons's fist in which continuity of the same matter—in this case, the same hand—by itself rules out the possibility of branching. We denied Simons's intermittently existing fist before on the supposition that the occurrence of the second clenched hand was not dependent on the first. But what if Simons deliberately makes his second fist look just like the first? What if a child deliberately makes a favorite toy from the same parts owing to fond memories of his first construction? The second thing will be like the first because of the way the first thing was, and since there is the same matter throughout, no second copy can be made by the same process. Even so, I think it is clear that the same general objection applies to cases of this sort. After all, what brings it about that the second fist or toy is made is not something done by the first fist or toy, but by the fact—as stated—that the person in question made it that way. It is true that we need to refer to the first fist or toy to explain the production of the second. That is what makes the case tricky for us to rule out. But we do not explain the production of the second in the same simple way that we do when it is a case of identity within our theory. It is essential to the idea of copying, whether or not branching is possible, that the thing itself is somewhat passive to the extent that it does not alone bring about its future, but requires the additional action of the copying agent. The first fist does not take Simons and make him close his hand again the way that the acorn literally takes up materials from its surroundings and shapes them according to its own design. The whole point of re-identifying a continuant, according to our theory, is to enable us to make connections that are due to that continuant alone. When the connection itself is due to something else we have reason to re-identify that something else and not the thing which is merely passive.

I have denied that creating a unique copy, even with the same matter, is sufficient for preserving identity. Since I realize that many will find this counterintuitive I feel obliged to explain their intuition. Once again, however, this is easy to do and our own theory provides the materials. According to our theory a thing persists just when it contributes to its own future in that way which is distinctive of its kind. Whenever this really happens the future thing is dependent upon the previous one, so that we explain the way it becomes by describing the way it was. Now, this is just what happens when a thing is copied. And when only one is made, so that there is no competitor distracting us, it looks a great deal like it does in a genuine case of identity. The only difference is the presence of the copying agent. By ignoring this, it looks exactly like identity. I think this is part of the charm of science fiction examples like "beaming down" on Star Trek. The way in which a person's particles are disassembled and reassembled is not at all highlighted: it "just happens"! So it seems as if the persons themselves are merely undergoing a change. I suggest that if a good deal of attention were paid to how the machinery actually took apart the particles and put them together we would be less sanguine about making the journey. Of course a very important part of the "beaming down" case is that it is part of the story that identity is preserved; it is clear that everyone involved thinks it is.[141] In the same way, we get carried along in stories of time travel; but that hardly lends credibility to the idea. One last point is that "beaming down" is even easier to imagine if we are influenced by the Cartesian idea that we are not bodies but only

141. Unger makes this point and other useful ones to diminish the force of such science fiction examples in Unger 1990, pp. 83–87.

associated with them, so that the Cartesian soul needs only to travel with the particles.

The last example I wish to discuss is harder to imagine than the others but raises a theoretically important point. Suppose the cue ball hits the eight ball. Then the way the eight ball is after the contact depends upon the way the cue ball was before. Why not identify on this basis? Why not say that there was a certain ball which started off white and ended up black? After all, the motion of the eight ball certainly confirms the previous presence of the cue ball. If we are justified in re-identifying a continuant in order confirm judgments that we make about it, why not say that there is one ball which switches color rather than that two balls interact? Of course, no one wants to say this. I take this to represent an arbitrary case in which the rule in question links the states of two things rather than of the same thing. We have been concentrating on rules involving the same thing because of their importance in applying the concept of identity in the first case. But perhaps we may test the resources of our theory developed so far to see if we can discount this strange suggestion. The serious theoretical question is how to distinguish, with good reason, cases in which it is the same thing persisting from cases in which one thing is acting upon another. How can we defeat the presumption that the rule which describes the effect of the cue ball on the eight ball is a rule of activity, so that we can count it as a rule of interaction?

What makes this look like a case involving two balls is, of course, that after the contact a white ball remains at the spot and before the contact there was a black ball sitting there. Let us see what is the relevance of all this. After all, if this were not true it really would look as if the cue ball had turned into the eight ball. Now, the only thing going for the claim of identity in question is that it would enable us to link the two states of affairs, the state of the cue ball before the click and the state of the eight ball after the click. If we did identify in this strange way then it must be admitted that we could say that the later state of this one thing would confirm the earlier state. We could also point to the fact that this "transformation" was repeatable, so that the rule in accordance with which we re-identified did indeed have general applicability. This is an important point, for we saw in the last chapter that Harrison had shown that our rules must have this quality in order to serve us in the confirmation of judgments. We also saw, however, that rules of greater generality were preferable. This was because the rules themselves must be supported and more general ones reach out to more instances and can thereby find more support. We can accordingly support our ordinary judgment that there are two balls which make contact if we can show that this involves accepting rules of greater generality.

Let us say that the identities of billiard balls—ordinary ones, that is—are determined by the fact that they tend to preserve their spherical shape. This is not to say that they cannot lose this shape at all, but that as they lose this shape (slightly) there is a tendency to return to it. Actually, the identities of many of our continuants seem to be like this. What many of them tend to preserve over time is not a static state like an amount of water but a tendency to return to and maintain a certain state or kind of activity. Their identity seems to be due to a kind of double tendency: the tendency to preserve a tendency. Now, in the case of billiard balls this enables us to explain many things about them. It explains, for example, why when one hits another, so that both are compressed, they do not merely collapse like lumps of dough, but spring apart; it also explains why a ball sitting on a table does not collapse into a puddle. The identities of ordinary billiard balls enable us to explain all the same circumstances that would be explained by admitting instead the "extraordinary" billiard balls that "transform" themselves instead of interacting. This means that by thinking of ordinary billiard balls interacting in these situations there is no loss in the support that we have for our judgments. The fact that the ordinary eight ball takes off, for example, is at least as well-supported by the fact that it was hit by another ball as is the "fact" that the extraordinary eight ball was previously in the form of a cue ball heading in that direction. The extraordinary billiard balls must have a different kind of identity in order to be distinguished from ordinary ones. They do not simply tend to preserve their spherical shapes, but in certain circumstances radically "transform" themselves. These "transformations" are supported, however, only in those special circumstances in which one ball strikes another. Because the identity of ordinary balls is simply that they tend to preserve their spherical shape, they comply with a rule which has greater generality. If we trace the path of each ordinary ball we can see it in every instance as complying with the rule that says that it will tend to maintain or return to its spherical shape. Since this will include those occasions in which it impacts other balls, the rule which covers these impacts is the same which covers all the other situations involving the ball, such as when it is sitting on the table or bounding off its side. Since both of the ordinary balls are of the same kind, this same rule really covers all of the situations of both balls and thus attains the limits of generality that can be reached when confined to such things as ordinary balls. This makes clear what is wrong with acknowledging the extraordinary balls. It necessarily involves applying new rules to cover those special occasions we would otherwise count as mere interactions. We must now say such things as that when one ball approaches another and is not stopped, it keeps on going while switching colors and other characteristics of it. Why this happens is a brute fact about extraordinary balls. They do not in these circumstances simply compress and spring back as ordinary balls do, but in these cases alone compress and then switch places with the other ball. Even though these rules are repeatable, I hope it is clear how their admission is epistemically inferior. The alternative of admitting ordinary balls is to acknowledge a rule which is supported in far more cases. It is in such situations, I submit, that we know that one thing (epistemically primary thing) acts upon another.

I have spoken of a difference of having one rule which covers all the cases and having different rules covering different cases. There is a kind of skepticism which calls into question our ability to make this distinction. It takes what I am calling different rules and simply sticks them together into one. The extraordinary balls thereby comply with the "one rule" which says that they tend to preserve a spherical shape unless approaching without obstacle another one in which case they compress and switch places, colors and so forth. This looks to us a good deal more "complicated," so that we are inclined to think of it as a complex of rules rather than a single one. It is clear, however, that we intuitively agree about which is simpler even if we lack the theoretical resources for explaining the difference. I am relying on this intuitive ability. It is important to realize, however, that we must be able to exercise this ability. Harrison also explained why this is so.[142] Since for any sequence of judgments there is some rule with which they conform, there must be some basis for distinguishing those which are "right" and those which are not. Without this we would not understand what it would be to be in a position in which we ought to reject a judgment because it fails to conform to the right rule and would thus not be consciously selecting any judgments as true. The rules we prefer are those that strike us as "simpler." Since we need to be struck in this way, and since it is obvious that this is how we are struck in the case of ordinary balls, we are justified in thinking of them and their genuine interaction.

I hope our discussion of these more or less bizarre examples has shown that our theory of justification is not entirely vacuous in settling questions of identity. I want to show now, however, that there is a kind of question for which we need more development of our theory. So far we have taken the Aristotelian idea that the identity of a thing is determined by its having a certain tendency to influence its own future. When supported by Harrison's account of judgment this has enabled us to decide a number of questions of identity. In the easiest cases, there was no dependency at all of a future thing upon an earlier thing. In trickier cases, there was dependency but not the right kind. In cases of copying, this was due to the failure of the thing in question to be responsible for its own future. In cases of interaction, this was due to the gratuitous complexity of the rules. But what happens when the same thing has different tendencies to affect itself? How do we decide when a tendency to become a certain way is the one which determines its identity?

As obvious as this question is on reflection, the point of it is not always appreciated. For an excellent example of this, consider Shoemaker's otherwise interesting discussion of causality and personal identity.[143] Shoemaker points out that to attribute a causal property to a thing is implicitly to say how it will be over time. To say that something is rigid is not merely to say how it is now but to say how it would be in the future, given, for example, that one attempts to bend it. Shoemaker adds that mental properties are really causal. To say

142. Harrison 1974, pp. 73–75.
143. Shoemaker 1984, pp. 253ff.

that I believe that there is a hole in front of me is to say what will happen to me given other conditions. If I want to walk and avoid pain I will change my way. My belief in the hole is a cause of my behavior, since my change in step certainly depends on it. Shoemaker now spells out what he takes to be the relevance of this for personal identity: since "The most important properties of persons are mental or psychological . . . an understanding of what particular mental properties are . . . will intimately involve an understanding of the identity conditions for the subjects of such properties."[144] But what entitles us to say that mental or psychological properties are "the most important properties of persons"? Even if they are the most important for the property of being a person, this is just to make a *de dicto* claim. As we saw in the first chapter, it simply begs the whole question to suppose that the psychological concept of being a person, however "dispositional" in content it may be, is the concept which describes the essence or identity of the things (the persons) to which it applies. We might as well say that being concerned with sinking balls is "the most important property of golfers." And as we saw, this is no moot point. Wiggins, for example, identifies persons even after all the causal states of belief, desire and so forth are wiped away. And Parfit would say that even when the causal powers of beliefs, desires, and whatnot, create a series of causal links, and thus psychological continuity, with breakings of these individual links, claims of identity would be relatively trivial. The problem is that even if, as "persons" (in Locke's psychological sense), we have a tendency to become a certain way, owing to our state of mind, the question still remains whether this sort of tendency is the one that determines our identity. And no analysis of the causal nature of our mental states will answer that question.

I began this chapter by clarifying a general "Aristotelian" conception of continuants in which the identity of each is determined by a tendency, distinctive of its kind, to contribute to the way in which it becomes. And I argued that our "Kantian" epistemology of previous chapters lead to this "Aristotelian" metaphysics. The general rationale for applying the concept of identity in the first place had been shown to be our need to apply it in becoming aware of rules by which

---

144. Ibid., p. 259.

we confirm our direct judgments. These rules describe connections between directly observable states of affairs. Since we had seen that we must regard these rules as applying to physical continuants, the general rationale reveals at least some of them as sources of activity. But this rationale can be adequate only if it enables us to re-identify these continuants over time. And it does this only if we presume that the connections in question involve the same thing being responsible for how it becomes. On the assumption that our general rationale is the one which shows how to apply the concept of identity, the reason for re-identifying a continuant is to ascribe to it a tendency to be responsible for certain of its own future states. Although only a "generic" conception of the identities of the primary things of our ontology, it allows us to take a number of definite stands. These were based on the idea that not only is some form of causal connectedness required for persistence, but that it must be a form of connectedness, distinctive of the kind of thing involved, which rules out even the possibility of branching. But since the same thing may have different tendencies which fit our generic conception of identity criteria, we need to develop our metaphysics to determine to which kind a thing really belongs. The purpose of the next two chapters is to achieve this for primary continuants in general so that the more elaborate account can be applied to ourselves in the final chapter.

7

The Constitution Relation

The transcendental method of Kant has led to an Aristotelian metaphysics, idealized by Leibniz. By starting with the assumption that we have empirical knowledge expressed in judgments of ours, we found good reason to re-identify continuants, including ourselves, on the general basis that they have tendencies, distinctive of their kind, to determine some of their own future states. But given any such continuant, how do we know which tendency so characterized is the one that really determines its identity? In this chapter and the next our theory will be developed to answer this question for epistemically primary continuants in general. Although the question is of central importance in metaphysics, it also pertains specifically to an interesting question of personal identity. In the final chapter we will be concerned primarily to decide between what Rawls distinguished as the "short" view of personal identity associated with Hume and defended by Parfit and the "long" view associated with Kant (and common sense). What we need to realize at this point is that both views can be accommodated, even plausibly, within the general metaphysical framework we have developed so far. For the "Humean," in Rawls's sense, and as explained so well by Parfit, our deeper affections and ideals are somewhat essential to us, so that when we lose them, in an important sense it is as if a different person exists. Within our "Aristotelian" framework, the Humean might say that *what we are* is largely a matter of what is *important* to us: when we see what values a person holds most deeply, we see what, above all, he or she is striving to become, and to lose these values is much like dying. By contrast, the "Kantian" will say that however important these values are to us, we still possess them only accidentally in the sense that when we lose them it is not at all trivial to say that we continue to exist as the very same person. This is what makes the "Kantian" view relatively "long." To accommodate this view within our general framework we need to find a different tendency to determine our identity. What I will eventually argue is that our essential tendency is to make decisions supportable with reasons. This will mean in effect that what we are essentially is what I called (in Chapter 5, following Kant), "consciously" rational beings: those who are conscious of reasons as such. The idea will be that our identity is relatively "long" since it is determined by the fact that we are striving to be rational in this sense, so that our current attachment to certain values is merely a way in which our essential activity is expressed. I take it that both views are appealing. Since they are both clearly accommodated within our metaphysics so far, we need to sharpen our account.

What we want to know, more generally, is how to tell (without relying on the metaphysics of ordinary talk and thought) whether a property of a thing is what determines its identity. It will help to understand our question better to compare it with others of traditional concern. When Aristotle explained the nature of metaphysics, understood as the "science of being qua being," he offered, as an example of a question which belonged to this discipline alone, that of whether Socrates and Socrates-seated are identical.[145] Since we ordinarily think that when Socrates sits, no new thing called "Socrates-seated" comes into existence, Aristotle, in his paradigm of metaphysics, is asking, as we are, how to apply the concept of identity over time. And, also as we are, he is wondering how our ordinary way of identifying things could be justified. Another way of putting his question is to ask how to justify the claim that a change is a mere alteration and not a case of

---

145. Aristotle 1941a, Bk. 4, Ch. 2, 1004b.

substantial change. We ordinarily think of Socrates's sitting as a mere alteration because no new thing is thereby created or destroyed: Socrates merely undergoes a change. If Socrates-seated were not identical with Socrates, as Aristotle considers, then this would be a genuine case of creation. This is really just our kind of question, for the issue is whether being seated is a property which determines the identity of anything real. For if it is, then when this property comes to be instantiated a new thing comes into existence and when it is lost this new thing passes out of existence. So, the question of whether a property determines identity, when restricted to continuants, is tantamount to the question of how to distinguish conditions of alteration from those in which the continuants come into or pass out of existence.

The next chapter will be devoted to the question of how to justify making these decisions. The present chapter is preliminary to that. For there is a host of problems that surround the notion of substantial change with which we need to deal first. What I want in this chapter is to provide a conceptual structure for thinking generally of the difference between substantial change and mere alteration. We will not, therefore, be concerned to decide whether a particular case is really one kind of change or the other. Now we will ask such questions as, What if the sitting of Socrates is substantial? How should we think of it? Is it, for example, a case in which one thing, Socrates, "turns into" another thing, Socrates-seated? And what would this mean? Would Socrates cease to exist and be replaced somehow by Socrates-seated? Or would Socrates still exist, so that he and Socrates-seated would be in the same place at the same time that Socrates-seated comes into existence? If they spatially coincide in this way, how are they related at that time? Why are they so similar if they are really two objects? If this example seems silly, we should remind ourselves of more familiar examples. When some gold is given the shape of a statue, does not the gold still exist when the statue first exists? How, then, should we conceive of the relation between the statue and the gold, or what Aristotle would call the thing and its "matter"?

I want first to argue that in creation the "matter" which begins the change really does end up in spatial coincidence with the new thing. (Similarly, in destruction the matter begins in spatial coincidence with the old thing.) The alternative is to suppose that there is simply one thing going out of existence and being immediately replaced by another: they replace each other in time like beads on a string. This view may seem initially attractive, since it avoids the conclusion that two things would be in the same place at the same time. A plausible example would be a lump of gold which, when properly hammered, "turns into" a statue. First there is a lump and then a statue and at no time is there both. But is there not something else which underwent the whole change? Did not the gold of the lump become the gold of the statue? The only way to avoid this conclusion would be to say that the gold which begins this change ceases to exist with the lump. But this would mean that a different quantity of gold would spring into existence with the statue. This very idea is defended by Burke.[146] He embraces it to avoid the "counterintuitive" idea that two things can occupy the same place at the same time and also to avoid multiplying objects unnecessarily in the place in question.

I have already dealt with the first sort of objection before (in the first chapter). We really should be suspicious of appeals to intuition in applying the concept of identity. Burke is impressed by the fact that most folks with whom he discusses the issue, such as his students, balk at the idea that two things can occupy the same place at the same time. I said before that all that it takes to produce an intuition of identity is to ignore differences between things. This is especially easy to do in the present sort of case because the things in question *appear* the same. I share the intuition of Burke and his students but since I think it is entirely plausible that it has a merely subjective source I think it should be given not the slightest evidential weight.

I also deny that "multiplying objects" in the same place is really a violation of Occam's Razor. (Burke has conceded some force to the point I am about to express.) I think that, in general, Occam's Razor has been misapplied a great deal in modern metaphysics. I believe that what it really means, what it means in the only sense in which it is respectable, is that in constructing a theory one should minimize *assumptions*, that is, one should not make any assumptions that fail to contribute to the explanation in question. This is respectable, since the assumptions are justified only insofar as they contribute to the

---

146. Burke 1980. Burke defends on similar grounds the claim that if a person lost all but his head he would not end up with the same head.

explanation. But I do not see at all how the idea of "multiplying objects" in a given place illustrates this problem of making gratuitous assumptions. After all, there are still the same *kinds* of things: there are, for example, still statues and quantities of gold. And when we count the objects, not at a single time, but over time, there is not even an increase in objects by admitting two things in the same place. So, what is so special about counting them at a single time?

There is certainly something strange in the idea that just because something new, such as a statue, comes into existence when some gold is hammered, this is enough to think that one quantity of gold is destroyed and replaced by another. Wiggins once complained of my suggestion that this was even possible that it was just wrong: quantities of gold are just things which persist in such situations in which no gold is lost or gained, and this is what happens when a gold statue is made by reshaping some gold.[147] Wiggins is right about quantities of gold as we ordinarily think of them. But suppose we allow that Burke's entities are "extraordinary" quantities of gold which persist like ordinary quantities in non-substantial changes but cease to exist and replace themselves in substantial changes such as the creation of the statue. Since extraordinary quantities of gold have different persistence conditions, the idea that they are involved in substantial change instead of ordinary ones is revisionist, involving a change in ontology. Since we are taking revisionist alternatives seriously, we cannot simply dismiss this proposal. It might be thought that the strangeness of admitting that that there are two extraordinary quantities in the creation of the statue (one of which succeeds the other) is due to the fact that they are so similar. The gold which begins the change will be just like the gold which ends the change except for the change in shape. Our revisionist will presumably have to say that this is a brute fact about the two extraordinary quantities of gold. We should realize, however, that by allowing one (ordinary) quantity to persist throughout the creation of the statue, although we have avoided the problem of why the gold at the end is so much like the gold at the beginning (because it is the same gold just undergoing a change in shape),

---

147. In Doepke 1982, for which Wiggins was the referee, I called this the Dichronic View ("Dichronic" and not "Diachronic" because it pertains to distinct times rather than identity through time).

essentially the same problem pops up with respect to the relation of the gold to the statue. Why are *they* so similar? I will deal that question shortly. First, I want to use our previously constructed theory to deal decisively with the issue of whether to admit the same thing—"the matter"—throughout substantial change. (This does not have to be a single thing but could be a plurality of things persisting throughout.)

The key to my argument will be once again Harrison's idea that we should prefer laws of greater generality. His point was not simply that they "explain more." It was deeper: because laws are supported by their instances, those of greater generality have the potential of being supported by more judgments (the judgments which would report the individual instances themselves). Now, as with the "extraordinary" billiard balls that were discussed in the last chapter, it is not difficult to see that extraordinary quantities are governed by rules of identity of lesser generality. The fact that ordinary quantities of gold persist is supported in all those many non-substantial changes in which the amount of gold in question is preserved. The rule which says that if no quantity of gold is gained or lost the same quantity of gold persists is supported in at least all these cases. What is really strange is the idea that we should not also apply this same rule in the case of substantial change. It seems utterly arbitrary to stop simply because something new is coming into or passing out of existence. What is wrong with stopping is that it prevents the rule which governs non-substantial changes to reach out and find greater confirmation in the substantial changes as well. In the creation of the gold statue we see a certain amount of gold being preserved just as surely as we did in all the many alterations in a single quantity of gold leading up to the creation. Why not say that a certain rule, describing the tendency to preserve this amount of gold, is simply continuing to be instanced? After all, as Harrison pointed out, the rules themselves are things which we judge to be true. Our judgment that the rule for ordinary quantities of gold applies in the world is therefore better supported than the one for extraordinary quantities. This is why our ordinary ontology is, with regard to quantities, more justified than the revisionist alternative.

I have argued that in substantial change there is one thing (or one plurality) which persists throughout the whole change so that it ends up with a newly created thing or begins with the destroyed thing. The thing which undergoes the substantial change will thereby be at one point of the change in the same place at the same time with the thing created or destroyed. No one has done more than Wiggins to bring these cases to our attention.[148] And Wiggins has argued that they show that two things really can occupy the same place at the same time. The reason is simple. Since according to what seems to be the truism of Leibniz's Law, that if a and b are identical they share all the same properties, if there is any difference at all, the things in question must be two things. But the "matter" which persists throughout exists at a time in which the thing created or destroyed does not. In the creation of the gold statue, for example, the gold existed before the statue. So they must be distinct things. Wiggins points out that the correct version of the principle in question is that formulated by Locke: that no two things *of the same kind* can be in the same place at the same time. The gold and the statue are of different kinds in this sense because, as Wiggins explains, they satisfy different identity conditions. Despite this clarification, however, many philosophers (besides Burke) have been dissatisfied with Wiggins's solution and they have attempted to carve a variety of different positions which avoid the conclusion that distinct things can spatially coincide even when of different kinds.

Another way of preserving just one thing thing in a place is to deny the reality of substantial change altogether. This is an idea of ancient appeal, represented famously by atomists such as Democritus. Suppose, for example, that there really are nothing but atoms and the void. Then we are mistaken when we think that things come into and pass out of existence. All that really happens is that eternally existing atoms rearrange themselves. To rebut this view would require showing that we are justified in acknowledging the existence of things which are genuinely created and destroyed. Since the next chapter will be devoted to such questions of justification, we will postpone the discussion of this form of reductionism. In the present chapter we are assuming that there are substantial changes and wondering how we should think of them.

---

148. Wiggins 1968.

Some philosophers are not much bothered by the idea that the gold and the statue are not the same and end up in the same place at the same time because, they think, the gold is not really one thing but a plurality of gold atoms. What bothers them is the idea that exactly two things could be in the same place at the same time, and not that one thing could spatially coincide with the plurality of its parts by having its parts spread out within it. Simons complains that since pluralities are just as real as single things even this should be considered a case of spatial coincidence between distinct things.[149] Be that as it may, it is certainly not clear that all cases of substantial change involve many things undergoing the change. In Aristotle's case of Socrates's sitting, the "matter" is the individual, Socrates; less fancifully, it is certainly arguable that a person comes into existence when the fetus obtains a certain internal (especially neural) structure. So, it does not seem that we can dismiss the importance of allowing the spatial coincidence of distinct things by saying that in all these cases it is really a relation of one thing to its many parts. It is at least far from obvious that this is so, and would require considerable argument, showing why the apparent exceptions are not really substantial changes. This is the sort of issue that is the subject of the next chapter. And since I will argue eventually that we are distinct from our bodies, I will say in this case, at least, that we do not have one thing and its many parts.

As we saw, Wiggins argued that in substantial change there are two things which, at some time, occupy the same place at the same time, and they are distinct because they are of different kinds, satisfying different identity conditions. It seemed to him that one thing could not be of different kinds, since this idea appears to land in contradiction. If the gold is the statue, then, when smashed, it would seem to perish according to the conditions of statues and not perish according to the conditions of gold. What a number of philosophers have done is to do deny the assumption that one thing cannot be of different kinds by somehow "relativizing" the notion of identity. Peter Geach suggested that identity was relative to its kind, and the idea was

---

149. Simons 1987, p. 212.

worked out by Nicholas Griffin.[150] The idea would be that the gold statue would perish relative to the kind, *statue*, but persist relative to the kind, *quantity of gold*. This is really quite similar to the idea held earlier, for example, by Quine, that the essence-accident distinction is not absolute.[151] Quine held that what a thing is essentially is not an absolute matter but depends on how we choose to think about it. If we fasten our attention onto the material composition of the gold statue, we can think of it as some gold; if we redirect our attention to its shape, we can think of it as a statue. The identity conditions of the thing would not be absolute, but relative to the way we think of the object. If we can "make" the essence of the thing some gold just by thinking of its material composition, then its identity through time would depend upon how we think of it. This would be the ultimate form of that conventionalism, which, as we saw in the last chapter, Wiggins wanted to deny in the case of persons. Geach and Griffin are plainly committed to this. For if the gold statue really does have different identity conditions for each of its different kinds, there can certainly be nothing wrong with choosing the kind by which we wish to think of the thing.

Wiggins would have done well to stress the revisionist nature of relative identity. For he was assuming our ordinary way of thinking of things (provided this was coherent), and it is surely part of this that existence is absolute. We commonly say that something ceased to exist or came into existence. People die: they do not die "as persons" and continue "as corpses." Since we are taking revisionist alternatives seriously, however, we cannot dismiss the present idea simply because it departs from ordinary thought and talk.

A similar way to avoid Wiggins's conclusion that two things can spatially coincide was suggested by Grice and worked out by George Myro.[152] Grice's idea was that identity could be relativized to a time, so that even though *a* and *b* were distinct at other times, they could still be identical at the times of coincidence. All such attempts to relativize identity seem subject to Wiggins's charge that they violate

---

150. Griffin 1977. See Griffin 1977 for references to the literature, including Geach's, which are sympathetic to "relative identity."

151. Quine 1960, p. 199.

152. See Myro 1986.

Leibniz's Law. How could the gold be the statue if, for example, the gold persists after smashing but the statue does not? Why not say that this one difference is enough to show that there are really two things? It is noteworthy that both Griffin and Myro took the same kind of tack: they *restricted* Leibniz's Law, weakening it, so that it guaranteed only that certain kinds of properties, and not all properties, would be shared by identical things. In light of this countermove, Wiggins allowed that "the final test of a theory of relative identity is not its internal coherence, but how it subserves a total theory of the individuation and existence of particulars."[153] I have objected that this concedes far too much; let me repeat my original objection to "relative identity."[154] For *any* form of similarity we can write a law that looks like Leibniz's Law except that it will be restricted or weakened to ensure that only the similarity in question is shared. Would this allow us to "identify" things "relative" to this form of similarity? If so, then for any similarity there is a corresponding form of "relative identity" and the distinction between identity and similarity collapses. Between a thing and its surface there are certain similarities: they are, for example, of the same texture, shape and color. Can we restrict Leibniz's Law to only such surface properties and identify a thing with its surface "relative" to the "kind" of thing to which both belong by sharing these properties? Since any form of similarity can be dignified by calling it a form of "relative identity" the term is, or ought to be, considered a misnomer for similarity. Identity at a time is nothing but temporal indiscernability; kind-relative identity is nothing but similarity in respect of the properties of that "kind." This does not make them identical because identity is different from all other forms of similarity precisely by ensuring that there are no restrictions on which properties are shared by a thing with itself.

There is, however, a way of understanding Wiggins's remark in light of my objection. We can question whether this relation of similarity could replace altogether the relation of true identity. I say "altogether" because it will be no challenge at all merely to have this relation along with identity. Myro wanted the absolute sense of identity along with his temporally relativized one, since he thought of his

---

153. Wiggins 1980, p. 23.
154. This was presented in Doepke 1982.

objects as continuants that can be (absolutely) identified at different times. But it might be thought that since kind-relative "identity" can apply over time it can entirely substitute for true identity. The question is whether we must allow that this proposal should be tested by "a total theory of the individuation and existence of particulars" or whether we can scotch the idea from the start. It is easy to see, however, in light of our present discussion, that the problem is much deeper. Since between any two objects we wish to distinguish from one another there will be *some* similarity, however strange, and since relative identity is really just similarity, we will always be able to identify the things relative to this similarity and will thus not really be able to distinguish them as distinct things. Suppose a pen is on the table. We ordinarily think these are two things. But they share the same property of being in the same general vicinity. If we are free to decide what property is essential to things we might as well fasten on this vicinity and say that it indicates a kind of thing to which the pen and table belong, in which case we have no grounds for thinking there are two things. To make the point more vividly, suppose we call a "pentable" something which has a pen and a table as its parts. Then when we point to either the pen or the table we are pointing to one pentable, just as when we point to a person's head and torso we are also pointing to one person. Now, the pen and table, *as* a pen and a table, are distinct things, in distinct places. But according to relative identity theory, we must shake ourselves of the temptation to think of these descriptions as absolutely essential. It is just as indicative of their identity to think that the pen and the table are in the general vicinity of the pentable. But when we think of the pen this way we are not distinguishing it from the table. When we "make" this property essential, in pointing to the pen and the table we are pointing to one pentable. What must be emphasized is that there would be nothing wrong with this choice. We would have no more reason for thinking of a pen distinct from a table than for thinking of one pentable. The point is not that relative identity or relative essence is logically impossible. I am sure that the notions lead to no contradiction. It is rather that without absolute identity individuation is impossible. Any attempt to individuate will strike us on reflection as *arbitrary*. For we will always be able to ignore the differences on which we are relying to distinguish the two things by making the appropriate "restriction" of Leibniz's Law. And since there will be nothing wrong with this, our original basis for distinguishing objects will appear ungrounded. But then we will be forced to retract our original judgment that we knew which thing we meant.[155]

A similar case can be made against Lewis's idea that we can count with the relation of identity-at-a-time.[156] Lewis admits that if we count by "identity simplicitur" in a case of personal fission, then there are two people about to separate, and it was on the basis of this that I said in the second chapter that he allows distinct persons to spatially coincide. He maintains, however, that there is only one person if we count with identity-at-a-time. But what is "counting" by this relation except merely uttering the word, "one," while *thinking* that there are *two* things that are temporally indiscernible? And if we do *not* think that there are two things there, why is not our thought about something *else*? We might as well suppose that we can count by the relation identity-in-species so that all lions are "one." But would we, in referring to this "one thing," be referring to the species itself or describing a similarity between individual lions? If we cannot make this distinction, then we cannot individuate, for as we saw, anything is "relatively identical" with anything else in some respect. But to make this distinction, we must distinguish counting by identity from "counting by" various forms of similarity. "Counting by identity-at-a-time" is a misnomer for describing things as temporally indiscernible.

Relative identity would have enabled us to admit substantial change without admitting that it involves, at some time, distinct things in the same place at the same time. Having defended Wiggins's position (which accords with ordinary thought and talk), that identity and essence are absolute, we cannot avoid the spatial coincidence of distinct continuants without denying substantial change (a subject of the next chapter). For we have rejected the alternative that the matter and the thing exist only in temporal succession, like beads on a string. Since the matter exists throughout the whole change, it exists with the

---

155. This argument owes much to Manley Thompson's reconstruction of Aristotle's reply to Protagoras in Thompson 1983. For more on Aristotle's argument see Irwin's reconstruction of Aristotle's defense of the principle of non-contradiction and its application to Protagorean relativism in Irwin 1988, pp. 181–92.

156. Lewis 1969, pp. 200–01; Harold Noonan concurs in Noonan 1989, p. 167.

created or destroyed thing. Since these are of different kinds, satisfying different identity conditions, and since identity is absolute, they are distinct things in the same place at the same time.

Burke has raised another objection to the idea that distinct things can be in the same place at the same time which I think demands an answer.[157] I have said, following Wiggins, that the things in question are distinct because they satisfy different identity conditions. The gold can be re-identified after smashing the gold statue, but the statue presumably cannot be. What Burke finds unacceptable is the idea that the fact that they satisfy different identity conditions is just a brute fact about them. Surely, he claims, there must be some fact about each which explains why its identity is different from the other. If the gold survives the gold statue when the statue is smashed, what is it about the gold that explains this? My account offers an answer to this question. Let us suppose, for the sake of illustration, that what determines the identities of the gold and the statue respectively are two tendencies, one to preserve a certain amount of gold and one to preserve the shape of the statue. Then, if the statue is smashed, the tendency to preserve the shape is lost, and that fact explains why the statue (but not the gold) ceases to exist. Since each tendency, we are supposing, determines the identity of the thing in question, the possession of that tendency is fundamental to its being of the kind of thing it is, and so there is no more explanation possible for why the thing has that tendency, though there are of course legitimate questions about why that thing exists or what reason we have for thinking that it does.

Burke may object that this appeal to tendencies is subject to the same problem. If the statue has a tendency to preserve its shape, it is surely tempting to say that this cannot be just a brute fact about it. In the case at hand, surely there is some reason why the statue has this tendency, and when we spell it out, will we not be describing the gold? Does not the statue stay together because the gold atoms attract one another? But is it not, then, the gold which has the tendency which was supposed to distinguish the statue from it? Since I will discuss these cases at more length in the next chapter, I give now only an analogy which shows how this conclusion can be blocked. Suppose a

---

157. Burke 1980.

committee is formed to make rulings which no individual can make. And suppose that deliberations of this committee take place over a period of time in which several members are replaced, and the new members participate vigorously in the discussions, as did the former. We might describe various tendencies discernible in the behavior of the committee over this time, say, of avoiding certain issues, or of settling disagreements, which could not be attributed to a particular set of members, since different sets would be involved, owing to the replacement of certain members. And yet it would be plain that these tendencies of the committee would not be merely brute facts, but would be explainable in terms of how members, at various times, behaved. So the tendencies, though explainable by reference to how the "matter" is (the people composing the committee), can still belong to something distinct from the "matter." I also want to allow, however, that some tendencies may be brute. Suppose that there are, in fact, fundamental constituents of matter, small entities not constituted by things of other kinds, as Democritus supposed his atoms to be. Since the laws which describe most fundamentally what they do would presumably be brute, we might accordingly describe some tendencies which they have, the presence of which in nature would have no explanation. It is possible, for example, that photons are basic entities, not composed of anything simpler, and that their tendency to travel in straight paths at a certain high speed is essential them and not explainable, therefore, in terms of how they are composed. Since I do not see how to rule out such possibilities, I for one am willing to allow the possibility of brute tendencies in nature.

I have avoided expressing the position I am defending in terms of how many "substances" can share the same place at a time and have used instead more neutral terms such as "thing" and "plurality." My terms are meant to be neutral in not being associated with certain traditional doctrines in metaphysics. It is not that I think such doctrines are not worth considering, but that I think that the notion of substance is somewhat heterogeneous, so that these doctrines, and the notion of substance itself should be explained in more neutral terms. Michael Ayers concedes in effect that the notion of substance is a bit heterogeneous, since he allows that in addition to such "paradigm" substances as a gold ring or a horse, there are "homeomerous substances" such

as the gold of the ring or the flesh of the horse.[158] Paradigm substances
are to be distinguished from such "modes" as attributes, events,
actions and processes, according to Ayers. Above all, Ayers wants to
defend the traditional notion of substance against that form of "conceptualism" which conflates this distinction by treating substances as
just another kind of mode. Modes are creatures of the mind, according to Ayers: the (particular) brown of this curtain, for example, owes
its identity to our concept of brown. For creatures with different ways
of perceiving the curtain, this brown might be quite inaccessible. What
the "conceptualist" (such as the ontological relativist) wants is to see
even paradigm substances in this way, so that it is a peculiarity of
ours that we encounter the horse as a continuant horse, and not, say,
as a sum of horse stages or a sum of undetached horse parts. In
defending the non-conceptual status of substances, Ayers upholds (and
inter-relates) a number of metaphysical doctrines, one of which is "The
traditional view that substances are distinguished at any one time by
their matter," which he glosses as "the principle that two individual
substances cannot be composed of the same matter at the same time."[159]
He adds that "Modern philosophers often deny" this principle—"So
much the worse... for modern philosophy."[160]

It is clear that the metaphysics we are developing in this whole
work is in complete harmony with Ayers's attack on "conceptualism."
Not only have we defended the epistemic priority of continuants (in
Chapter 4), the doctrine of relative identity which we recently rejected
is evidently related closely to this form of conceptualism. (Recall that
Quine embraced this doctrine by holding that the identity of a thing
depends on how we think of it.) Should we then deny the principle
that two substances can share the same matter at the same time? I
have argued that two "things" can, for instance, the gold ring and the
gold of the ring or a person and his or her body. There is no reason to
insist that these are pairs of "substances," however, and by one of
Ayers's own criteria there may be good reason to deny it. Paradigm
substances, as he repeatedly emphasizes, are "given" rather than "constructed." They are, in our terms, the epistemically primary subjects

---

158. Ayers 1991, p. 69.
159. Ibid., p. 84.
160. Ibid.

of predication. It seems quite plausible, and may be an important principle, that only one such substance could be in a place at a time. (As Ayers seems to suggest, this may be necessary for them to be truly *discovered* by us.) But there is no reason for us to classify such things as the gold of the ring or a person's body as a substance in this sense. And indeed it does seem that we identify such things, at least normally, only in relation to something else in the same place, such as the ring or a person. With this clarification we see that Ayers's principle is not opposed to the one that we have followed Wiggins (and Locke) in accepting. And I cannot think of a single philosopher in "modern philosophy" who would claim that when distinct things share the same matter at a time they are distinct "substances" in this special, technical sense. The correct claim made by the traditional principle that distinct substances cannot share the same matter at the same time is, I submit, that two things of the same kind (with the same sort of identity conditions) cannot share the same matter at one time. And there is a metaphysical reason for accepting this. The identity of a continuant is determined in its creation by the fact that a certain "matter," at that time, underwent a certain change, for example, the gold received the shape of a ring. If we allow that two rings could thereby come into existence it would be utterly mysterious how they would be distinct.

Having allowed that in substantial change there are two things which are very similar, indeed which appear just the same, the question arises as to why this is so. This problem was first impressed upon me by Myro.[161] He argued that by identifying them we *explain* why the things are alike in all these respects, for there is surely no mystery in a thing's being of the same weight, shape and so forth as itself. What we need now is an *alternative* explanation of the variety of logically independent similarities between spatially coinciding objects.

Identity explains the similarities in question because it explains the possession of *all* properties in common. But I claim that invoking identity for this explanatory job is excessive. All that we need to explain is the common possession of those properties which do not distinguish the objects at the times of coincidence. Now, there is a

---

161. George Myro impressed this upon me while a member of my doctoral dissertation committee; I am accordingly grateful to him for pointing out the need to develop this part of my account of constitution.

relation, weaker than identity, which explains all the properties we apparently need to explain. Objects which share the same *parts* at a certain time will evidently also share exactly the variety of properties which Myro rightly found to be logically independent when considered apart from this source.[162] The statue and the gold are now in the same place, of the same weight, shape, color and so forth. These similarities are perfectly well explained by the fact that they are made of the same parts, say, the gold atoms, and that these atoms are in this place, arranged in a certain way, of a certain amount, and so on. Such objects as the statue and the gold need not share all their properties, however, since they may differ in how they retain these parts over time. Again, the statue, but not the gold, can lose some of these parts, and the gold, but not the statue, can lose their internal arrangement. Once we see the matter "supplying" the parts of the created or destroyed thing, and see these parts arranged in the same place in the same way, the variety of similarities are fully explained. Indeed, now is when we might well appeal to Occam's Razor. Since the similarities in question are fully explained by the logically weaker relation of sharing the same parts, it is gratuitous to explain them with the excessively strong relation of identity.

Although the relation of sharing the same parts at time *t* suffices to explain the relevant properties, it may be desirable to have an even weaker relation to accommodate all the possible cases. Since we are concerned mainly with a metaphysical account of such issues only insofar as it eventually bears upon our own identity, I will now give only an indication of what this weaker relation might be.[163] Suppose that a large plurality of wood cells are separated into various portions, and each portion is then compressed into a wooden piece. And now suppose that these pieces are put together to make a ship. The ship would coincide with not only the plurality of wooden pieces but also with the plurality of wood cells. Yet is not obvious that these three things share all the same parts, since it might be held that the wooden

---

162. I presented this in Doepke 1982 and learned in correspondence with Peter Simons that he had arrived at this same solution independently. Ayers also rejects a similar principle stated in terms of "substances" (Ayers 1991, p. 84); for reasons given above we have no reason to dispute this in his special terms.

163. For a fuller account see Doepke 1982 and Peter Simons's careful and expert discussion of my account and related matters in Simons 1987, Ch. 6.

pieces, though parts of the ship, are not parts of the original batch of wood cells. Simons has effectively criticized and modified previous attempts of mine to capture the relevant relation.[164] Without going into all the subtleties, I think it is clear how we would go about attempting to capture them. For surely, even if the wooden pieces are not parts of the original batch of wood cells, it is these wood cells themselves which have been merely rearranged to form these pieces. This being so, it is the fact that the wood cells are arranged as they are that determines the places, shapes, and so forth, of the wooden pieces, and thereby the place, overall shape, and so on, of the ship itself. So we might say simply that the logically weaker relation that also captures the relevant similarities is that of being "built of" a common batch of parts.

By requiring that objects in the same place at the same time share the same parts, or at least that they be built of a common batch of parts, we have an adequate explanation of why they are in the same place and of the same shape, weight, color and so forth. Such objects are, however, also strikingly related in a different way, which surely calls for explanation. To say only that they "coincide" misses the fact that they seem to be arranged in some kind of *hierarchy*. Having denied the identity of a thing with its matter, Wiggins said perceptively that the thing was "constituted" by its matter. Now, mere coincidence, like identity, is an equivalence relation, symmetrical and transitive. If a coincides with b, then b coincides with a, and if b also coincides with c then a coincides with c. This is really explained by the equivalence of identity, since coinciding is just being in the "same" place. But Wiggins's constitution relation, though evidently transitive, strikes us as *asymmetrical*: if a constitutes b (at time t) then b does *not* constitute a (at time t).[165] Relations which are both asymmetrical and transitive are just those which allow us to arrange objects in a *series*. It was evidently such a series that Aristotle had in mind when he spoke of the wood of the basket and the earth of the wood, wondering if continuing in this way would lead to a primary kind of matter.[166] Indeed, the very notion that the matter of a thing is unique, implied

164. Simons 1987, Ch. 6.
165. This was first pointed out to me by Charles Jarrett.
166. Aristotle 1941a, Bk. 9, Ch. 7, 1049a20–1049b.

by such phrases as "the matter" or "the proximate matter," indicates that a relation of order exists between the objects in question.[167] And assuming that there cannot be "loops" with this relation, that we have series which do not come back to the same things, there must be such a relation which is also transitive, so that the asymmetry is, so to speak, passed along the series. Constitution (at time t) seems to be an asymmetrical, transitive relation in virtue of which spatially coinciding objects form series. Let us see now how to understand this relation so that we can see why it has these formal properties.

It may seem that the asymmetry of constitution (at time t) is easy to explain. After all, is not the one which constitutes the other the one which underwent the substantial change, whereas the constituted object is the one created or destroyed? This is no doubt close to the right answer. But a certain amount of refinement is needed. A feature of many cases is that the matter of a thing's creation is replaced somehow by something which comes to be the thing's matter at a later time, so that there can be a succession of distinct objects taking turn as the matter of the thing. This happens vividly in organisms in which there is quite a bit of material replacement. The cells which constitute an organism at one time can be an entirely different batch from those which constitute it at a different time. And since a "batch" is just a plurality which, like a set, is defined by its members, all it takes to have a different batch is the addition or loss of one cell. And we cannot assume that this is always a gradual affair. Many, if not most people, would say that if the brain of a person were put in a different body, the person with the new body would be the original person even though the change of parts was sudden and great. There seems to be something in common, however, between the objects in a series which take turn constituting a persisting thing, and that is that each thing

---

167. With considerable textual evidence, Irwin claims that the proximate matter of the thing, for Aristotle, is identical with that thing (see Irwin 1988, pp. 241--42). If so, then the notion of proximate matter provides just a specialized notion for describing a thing. Even if there is a use for such a notion we still need a notion to describe the subject which goes all the way through the creation or destruction of a thing and which must therefore be distinct from that thing. And if we want the notion of something which would undergo such changes with nothing more gained or lost than the essence of the thing created or destroyed, then it seems appropriate to call it the "proximate" matter. I suggest further that this notion is more basic, in that we understand the notion found by Irwin only by analogy with this notion.

could undergo a change which would be the destruction of the persisting thing. Even if the wooden parts of a ship are continually replaced, at any time we can point to the batch of parts which currently constitutes the ship and say that if they were to be dispersed, that would be the destruction of the ship. And the fact that this is not happening is a contingent fact which therefore explains the actual *persistence* of the ship. So the point is that describing what, as a matter of contingent fact, is going on in the constituting object enables us to explain whether and how the constituted object persists or perishes.

The question now is how this fact provides an explanation of the formal properties of the constitution relation. Let us consider the asymmetry first. Why is it that if *a* constitutes *b* (at time *t*) *b* does not constitute *a* (at that time)? If (at time *t*) *a* could undergo a change which would be the destruction of *b*, does it follow that *b* could not undergo a change which would be the destruction of *a*? Simons has presented an apparent counterexample.[168] Imagine a wall made of stones which in turn are made of some stone-stuff. Since the plurality of stones which constitute the wall are just "these" stones, with the loss of even one this very plurality ceases to exist. But suppose this happens by the disintegration of a stone while the wall, in suffering only this one loss, continues to exist. Would not the wall thereby undergo a change which would be the destruction of the plurality of stones (even though it is this plurality which constitutes the wall)? Simons suggests that we modify the original idea by saying that the object which constitutes the other can undergo a change which would be the *complete* destruction of the other. The idea is that if all the stones of the wall are scattered, the wall is "completely" destroyed, but the wall cannot undergo a similar change in which the plurality of stones is "completely" destroyed. It is not clear to me that this is correct. Suppose that over time the elements cause the gradual collapse of all the stones, leaving the same stone-stuff in the shape of the wall. It is plausible, at least, that the same wall would persist throughout the "complete" destruction of the plurality of stones which originally constituted it. To avoid such apparent counterexamples I suggest we attend to a feature of constitution in my original account. What needs to be emphasized, I

---

168. Simons 1987, p. 239.

suggest, is something evidently implied in Aristotle's notion of the material "cause": that in the substantial change of the constituted object the fact that the constituting object undergoes that change *explains* the creation or destruction of the constituted object. What explains the destruction of the plurality of stones when the elements cause them all gradually to collapse is not the fact that the wall undergoes some change. Whether the wall continues to exist throughout the destruction of the plurality of stones is sheerly a coincidence, due to the fact that the stone-stuff happens to retain the shape of the wall. But this fact about the stone-stuff is incidental to whether the plurality of stones persists or perishes. It is accordingly pointless to refer to the wall in explaining the destruction of the plurality of stones, and because of this, such references do not really belong in the correct explanation. This is what, I submit, accounts for the asymmetry of the constitution relation. When *a* constitutes *b* at time *t*, there is some property that *a* happens to have at *t*, possession of which explains why *b* exists at *t*; and whether *b* continues to exist is explainable by whether *a* retains or loses this property. But since it is not essential to *a*'s persistence that it happen to retain this property, if it does, the persistence of *b* throughout this time (by the retention by *a* of this property) is incidental to *a*'s persistence. Any reference to *b* throughout this time will, therefore, be gratuitous in explaining *a*'s persistence.

Why, then, is constitution (at time *t*) a transitive relation? If the "matter" can undergo a change in virtue of which the thing in question would be destroyed, then in that change the "matter" would change with respect to a property which would be an accident of it. A similar point pertains to creation. If the thing in question is created by the "matter" undergoing a change, when the "matter" started the change it did not have the property with which it ends up. When one object constitutes a certain thing, the existence of this thing (at that time) is explained by the fact that the "matter" possesses a certain accident. Returning to our example of the wooden ship, we can say that the planks of the ship exist because the cells of the planks happen to be arranged in a certain way, the way which results when we separate them into heaps and compress these into planks. Now notice that when the ship is created by arranging the planks, this involves a *further* arrangement in the wood cells. To describe this arrangement as one that is "further" is to suggest that a relation of one-way entailment obtains. To describe the arrangement of the wood cells in virtue of which the ship exists (at that time) we *add* to the description which explains the existence of the planks (at that time). There is, therefore, a one-way entailment relation between the two descriptions. Now, this logical relation is not only asymmetrical but transitive. And it is, I submit, what explains the transitivity of constitution. The first constituting object in a series of constituting objects possesses a series of (accidental) properties, each successor of which is a restriction (in some general way) of its predecessor. And since the possession of each property in this property-series explains the existence of a corresponding object, the first property is the series (which thereby entails all the rest) can be lost (by the first constituting object) in such a thorough way that all of these (constituted) objects would thereby perish together. This would happen, for example, if the atoms of the ship were to be so dispersed that the pluralities of molecules, wood cells and planks would all cease to exist with the ship.

Constitution (at time *t*) is both asymmetrical and transitive, and it is just such relations which create "total order." The relation of being greater than is such a relation, and it is only because of this that it suffices to determine the exact order of a set of numbers. This does not mean, however, that given any set of objects in the same place at the same time, they can be totally ordered by the constitution relation, even if every one of them is related directly or indirectly to every other one by this relation. A set of numbers is this way because they owe their whole identity to the fact that they stand in this relation to one another. But objects are ordered by the constitution relation in virtue of the fact that they are correlated with a certain kind of generic property (such as the arrangement of wood cells). There is nothing that we have seen so far that would rule out "tree-like" formations, owing to the fact that an object is constitutionally related to different objects in virtue of quite different generic properties, so that neither of these objects constitutes the other.[169]

---

169. I first suggested this in Doepke 1986. I believe the present account offers a more accurate explanation of the transitivity of the constitution relation.

There is a kind of restaurant in which the rooms are railroad cars. We might imagine that the restaurant is distinct from the plurality of cars because we can replace cars and still have the same restaurant. The plurality of cars at any time forms the restaurant because the cars are arranged in a way that is favorable to serving food. Let us suppose that a given plurality also just happens to be arranged in the way that is usual for trains, and that the train is also distinct from the plurality because it can suffer replacement of cars. It appears to be a sheer accident that a given plurality of cars constitutes both a restaurant and a train, so that we have a certain "tree" formation.

I have allowed at least the possibility of what we might call "upright" trees, in which an object constitutes two objects neither of which constitutes the other. But can there be "inverted" trees? I submit that these are impossible. Suppose an object is constituted by two objects neither of which constitutes the other. Each of these objects will have a certain accidental property which it could lose to explain the destruction of the constituted object. But since neither of the objects constitutes the other, it appears that either could lose this property, thus explaining the destruction of the object, while the other continues to retain its property, thus explaining the continued existence of the same object. So it seems that while upright trees are at least possible, inverted trees are quite impossible.

Showing that inverted trees are impossible vindicates Aristotle's idea that for an object we can pick out only one thing as its "proximate" matter, the unique thing that is immediately "below" it in a constitution series.[170] But we have seen that we cannot assume that we are always entitled to talk of "the" thing which something immediately constitutes. That there are such structures among coinciding objects is of interest for metaphysics. Our main reason for going into these matters, however, is to defend the constitution relation, which we have seen should be accepted with the acceptance of substantial change. I have tried to take the mystery out of this relation by explaining its formal properties. There is, however, some importance in the actual results we have reached. When we are dealing critically with questions of identity, we have to consider subtle differences between

---

170. See note 167 above for different interpretations of this term.

objects in the same place at the same time. For when we are trying to determine whether to interpret experience by treating a certain property like rationality as essential, the alternative is turn to another object in the same place, like our body, perhaps, which does not have this property essentially. Understanding the possible patterns in constitutionally related objects helps us to see what are our choices. For example, since we now know that inverted trees are impossible, when we consider "reducing" an object, we are assured that there is one best candidate, "the" object immediately below.

There is a certain virtue of our account of the constitution relation to which I would like to call attention. Nothing in our account either requires or prohibits that there be an infinite series of objects, each successor the "matter" of the one before. We saw that Aristotle wondered whether a series consisting of the basket, the wood of basket and the earth of the wood, would eventually lead to a "primary" kind of matter. There is, however, good reason to think that the answer to this question is unknowable. The disagreement between thinking that there are "simples" which are the fundamental building blocks of all larger material objects or that there are not, since there is an infinite series of ever smaller parts to these things, created the "Second Antinomy" discussed by Kant. As I understand his position, neither of these is knowable by us, since the issue would take an infinite amount of empirical data to decide. Of course, at any given time, physicists will offer a theory in which some entities are depicted as basic, but what rules out an infinite series of modifications to such a theory in which an infinite series of ever more basic entities are revealed? Again, Kant's point, as I take it, is the evidently correct response that nothing rules this out except an infinite amount of data, which we can never collect. Some philosophers discuss constitution and substantial change by assuming that there are simples. Van Inwagen, for example, in taking a hard-headed stand on admitting constituted objects, ends up with an ontology of simples and organisms (so that living things are the only things that are constituted by anything).[171] The simples he has in mind are the basic entities of current physics. But there is no reason to think that this theory would survive infinite testing. And if

---

171. In Van Inwagen 1990.

there is an infinite series of "matters," as envisaged by Kant in the "Second Antinomy," then in fact there are no simples: every material object will be constituted by something else, and Van Inwagen's ontology will be false. I admit this is a hard possibility to envisage, but is it any easier to accept the idea of an infinite past (to allude to the "First Antinomy")? A virtue of our account is that it remains properly agnostic with respect to this issue.

We have assumed in this chapter that there really are generable and perishable objects and have asked, on this assumption, how substantial change should be understood. We rejected the idea that substantial change involves a mere temporal succession of objects on the ground that this would require a revisionist ontology with rules of identity which were less well-supported, owing to their lesser generality. Since the matter of substantial change is a single continuant (or plurality of them) persisting throughout the whole change, it begins or ends in spatial coincidence with the thing created or destroyed. This thing and its matter belong to different kinds, and so are identical only if identity can be somehow relativized, perhaps to a kind or to a time. To avoid contradiction, identity has been relativized only by restricting Leibniz's Law. But this shows that any form of relative identity is really just a form of similarity. The attempt to replace true or absolute identity with relative identity failed, not because relative identity is logically impossible, but because it is self-refuting: attempts to individuate are undermined by arbitrariness in our choice of identity conditions. This forced us to admit that substantial change would involve distinct objects sharing the same place at the same time. I argued that the counterintuitive status of this claim should not be given evidential weight since it might well be due only to the ease of being able to ignore differences between distinct things which appear the same. And there is no violation of Occam's Razor, properly understood, since this pertains not to simple numbers of objects at a single time but to whether a theory makes gratuitous assumptions. The fact that distinct objects in the same place appear indistinguishable did, however, call for explanation. This problem was solved by appealing to the fact that spatially coinciding objects would share the same parts, or at least be "built of" a common batch of parts. This alternative was actually favored by Occam's Razor, properly understood. A further problem arose, however, since it seems possible to order spatially coinciding objects, as reflected in Wiggins's idea that one "constitutes" another. An analysis of the relation was provided, explaining its formal properties and its role in explanations of existence, persistence and perishing. Although of intrinsic metaphysical interest, the chief reason for providing this analysis was to make the constitution relation more acceptable. For we have seen that if there is substantial change, there are objects standing in this relation. Any resistance to accepting the constitution relation, perhaps because it is not understood, is bound to undermine confidence in substantial change and thereby encourage reductionism such as envisaged by Democritus. The question of whether there is substantial change at all, and if so, when it is going on, is the subject of the next chapter. We have seen that this is intimately related to our question of how to know if a property is determinative of identity. And it is just this sort of question that we must be able to answer to make a principled decision between a "short" and "long" view of personal identity.

8

Establishing an Essence

In the last chapter we assumed that there are "substantial" changes, in which things come into or pass out of existence, and wondered how, on this assumption, we should think of these changes. I argued that in substantial change there ends up (in creation) or begins (in destruction) two things in the same place at the same time: the thing created or destroyed and the "matter" which undergoes the whole change. Following Wiggins, I said that the matter would at the time of spatial coincidence "constitute" the new or old thing and I spent most of the chapter trying to win acceptance of the relation by explaining it. We need to understand constitution because we need to understand substantial change. And we need to understand the latter because the question of when there is substantial change is virtually the same as the question of whether a property is determinative of identity. For a property is this way just in case its gain or loss would be a case of creation or destruction. If it is not sufficient for the existence of the thing in question then its gain would not be the creation of that thing; if it is not necessary, with its loss the thing would not perish. In the present chapter we go deeper, by questioning whether there even are substantial changes. Our hope is that by seeing why we are entitled to think that there are any of these changes at all, we will be able to tell whether a particular case before us is truly such a change or merely an alteration in a single thing.

This in turn will involve knowing a good deal more than we do now about how to apply the concept of identity in the interpretation of experience. We saw in the fourth chapter that we are entitled to apply the concept in the first instance to "continuants" which genuinely undergo change, bearing in succession manifest properties of experience. In the fifth chapter we found that what entitles us to individuate in the first place is that it enables us to exercise reason in that "conscious" way that is necessary to confirm our empirical judgments. In the sixth chapter we saw that this "Kantian" way of justifying individuation leads to an "Aristotelian" conception of identity, idealized by Leibniz. Although this conception is not vacuous, it was still not clear how to tell whether a tendency of an object to produce its own future states is truly determinative of identity or merely accidental. Now that we have a conceptual structure for thinking of substantial change, we are ready to apply the results of these earlier chapters to deal with this question. It is in learning how to answer it that we will learn more about how to apply the concept of identity over time. In the next and final chapter we will apply this enriched metaphysical account to ourselves to see whether to favor the "short" view of personal identity which Rawls associated with Hume and Parfit or the "long" view which he associated with Kant.

In our ordinary ways of thinking and speaking we admit a wide variety of generable and perishable objects. People unfortunately die: they do not simply "become" corpses. Works of art are created, molecules are destroyed and stars are born. If we were content in this work to describe our common metaphysics it would, I am sure, be sufficient to establish a property as what determines the identity of its bearer by employing the "method of cases" discussed at length in the first chapter. Within this framework it is sufficient to establish, for example, the identity of this water. By reflecting on how we think and speak of it, we see that (according to our common ontology) its identity is determined by the fact that it neither gains nor loses water . We do not say that it ceases to exist when portions of it are separated and we do not allow that it can grow or diminish in the amount of water it contains; on the other hand, we do not allow that this water continues to exist when its hydrogen and oxygen become separate gases. It is tempting to say that this shows that being of a certain amount of water is a property which determines identity. This is fine if we are entitled to assume the metaphysics of ordinary thought and talk. But as I have often reminded us, we are taking revisionist alternatives seriously. This is not only of interest for metaphysics, but it is absolutely necessary for providing an adequate response to a view of the self, such as Parfit's or Hume's, which admittedly has revisionist roots. Now, among the revisionist alternatives which have been put forth with conviction is that which denies substantial change altogether by "reducing" all continuants to their fundamental constituents. Although this view is traditionally associated with atomists such as Democritus, is was also espoused by Kant himself. Since we share starting points with Kant, we would do well to see if we really are forced to this conclusion.

Kant claimed that "the unity of experience would never be possible if we were willing to allow that new things, that is, new *substances*, could come into existence."[172] As we saw in the fifth chapter, the unity of experience is effected by the possibility of attributing different states to oneself, which in turn is a condition of conscious rationality (the capacity to be aware of reasons as such). If the admission of substantial change really did make the unity of experience impossible, we would have to deny such changes, and with them, that things really stood in the constitution relation, since this would undermine our own starting point of conscious rationality. Guyer has given a clear explanation of Kant's point (and even accepts it himself).[173] If a porcelain pig were to disappear apparently without a trace, we would never be justified in thinking that it vanished into nothing, because for all we could ever know, it would have transformed into something very different or suddenly changed location.

Guyer's argument against substantial change clearly involves a certain *conception* of it, in which something passes into (or comes from) *nothing*. This is of course not the conception which we developed in the last chapter. I argued there that in substantial change the new thing

---

172. Kant 1968, B229/A182.
173. Guyer 1987, p. 232.

does not come from nothing nor does the old thing pass into nothing. There is one thing persisting throughout, the "matter," which is a distinct continuant (or plurality of them) which "supplies" the parts of the thing created or destroyed at the time of coincidence and whose change explains the creation or destruction by gaining or losing a certain accident. According to our conception of substantial change, every case of creation or destruction is *also* an alteration in a persisting thing, so that things come from and pass into, not nothing, but this "matter." Since Guyer's argument against substantial change clearly depends upon the alternative conception, we have no reason to think that the "unity of experience" is incompatible with substantial change.

It might be thought that in denying "substantial change" Kant meant only to exclude that conception of it in which something comes from or passes into nothing, so that he did not mean to embrace a reductionist metaphysics. But Kant repeatedly claims that the *only* real bearers of properties are things which exist "throughout all time."[174] Guyer supports Kant on this very point by claiming that it is only such things which have been justified as necessary for the unity of experience.[175] His general attitude toward questions of existence is one which we have firmly adopted in this work. The existence of things of a certain kind must be justified: it is not enough that we ordinarily think of them or that thinking of them leads to no contradiction. So we must meet Kant and Guyer on their own ground. By showing that the unity of experience is compatible with substantial change I have shown only that substantial change is *possible*, in that it does not contradict our starting points. Clearly, more must be done to show that it is *actual*.

In the last chapter I pointed out that our account of constitution had the virtue of not committing ourselves to something Kant held is unknowable by us, namely, that there are "simples" which constitute all complex material objects and are not themselves constituted by anything. Does Kant himself (and Guyer with him) now violate his own restriction of knowledge by denying substantial change? I think

---

174. Kant 1968, B228/A185.
175. Guyer 1987, p. 235.

not. I will say what I take to be Kant's position without, however, doing much to defend my interpretation. I want only to show that it is plausible that there is not an obvious contradiction in positions. The idea that the existence of entities which exist "throughout all time" is a condition of the "unity of experience," or empirical knowledge, seems to require that *within* any physical theory, empirically justified at a time, there should be posited such basic entities (to "unify" the experience on which the theory is based). This means that at any time we are empirically justified in thinking that there are basic entities of a certain kind, but for all we know, there will be an endless series of modifications in this theory forcing the admission of an endless series of ever more basic entities. Even if there may be such series in the future, it could still be that at any time we were entitled to think only of the basic entities of current physical theory and not additional entities which they constitute. These would be the entities which, according to that theory, exist "throughout all time."

It might seem that results of previous chapters already show that there is substantial change. In the second chapter we saw that we must individuate ourselves to individuate anything at all and in the fourth chapter we saw that this would involve seeing ourselves as manifest continuants among others. We know empirically, however, that each of these are composed of many small entities, so that it might seem that to deny substantial change we would have to think of each of these macroscopic objects as a plurality of small entities. But this has already been ruled out, if only for the reason, given in the second chapter, that we cannot think of ourselves as pluralities of anything. To avoid this objection let us grant (what we have not justified) that for any plurality there is a "sum" which, like the plurality, is identified by its members, but unlike the plurality, is a single thing. Now we may consider whether we and other manifest continuants are really just sums of smaller entities. This will allow us to see each of these as a single thing while still preserving the reductionist idea that there is no substantial change. Since a sum of basic entities persists just so long as they do, it does not really come into or pass out of existence when their members mix with other entities in the world. For entities like us which appear to undergo material replacement, this will have the extraordinary result that with each such replacement a new sum of smaller entities appears in our place. After breathing in or out my I-thoughts will belong to a new sum of these particles. We saw in the first chapter that this sort of thing could not be ruled out a priori, for this would be like Kant's example of consciousness being "passed along" a series of subjects as motion is transferred from one billiard ball to another.[176] We cannot avoid these extraordinary results by claiming that we are "sums" which can undergo material replacement, since this will be to extend the notion of "sum" to any material object. As physical objects we are of course *composed* of smaller particles. But manifest objects such as ourselves, as we ordinarily think of them, cease to exist with the dispersal of these particles just because they are not (we think) merely sums of them.

I have suggested that we see what reason we have for thinking there are substantial changes by considering the alternative of reducing manifest continuants, including ourselves, to sums of "particles." And we will think of these smaller entities as continuants which compose the larger objects. This might seem to fly in the face of the idea that the most fundamental constituents of physics are not even continuants, but are more like events. What we need to realize about this objection is that in light of the arguments of the fourth and fifth chapters, it would show that we cannot be reduced to such entities. For since we found that a condition of making true empirical judgments is that we think of ourselves as continuants among others, we and they cannot be identical with sums of things which are not continuants. Sums of events could only constitute us as distinct things which would be created and destroyed by certain (trans-temporal) relations between these events. To give our reductionist a chance, we will consider reducing manifest continuants to sums of entities which are themselves continuants.

When considering (in Chapter 6) the view of identity we had justified, it appeared to us (as it did to Aristotle) that organisms would be our best examples. Although they genuinely interact with other things, they approach relatively well that Leibnizian ideal of being independent of their surroundings, since they are evidently responsible for many of their own future states. While attending to their behavior,

---

176. Kant 1968, A362–366, footnote.

the view of the reductionist is bound to seem most strange. When an animal eats and assimilates its food, the reductionist must see only two sums of particles coming together. The idea that one thing is literally taking in something else and making it a part of itself cannot be admitted. When the animal breaths out, all the reductionist sees is the fact that one sum separates, so that a larger and a smaller portion of particles go in different directions. The problem is not of course that what the reductionist sees is not there: it is that the picture seems incomplete. Even if what is before us can be explained and predicted by referring to only the shifting particles, it seems that we are entitled also to explain things by attributing properties, such as eating and breathing, which we see, on reflection, cannot be attributed to the particles themselves. But as I pointed out in the last chapter, the mere fact that we can explain more is not enough for us to admit the new things in question. In this we followed Harrison, who defended laws of greater generality not because they explained more but because the judgment that they apply is supported by the more instances which they cover. In admitting the existence of generable and perishable things we make new judgments, applying the concept of identity in new ways. Even if this allows us to explain things or to explain them in a different way, we still want to know why we are justified in accepting these new explanations as true.

Plato argued that within the soul reason and appetite are distinct parts.[177] His point was not merely that these are distinguishable aspects, like the color and shape of an object, but that these are really distinct things; and his reason was that we sometimes see them in *opposition*. This is evident whenever we exercise reason to control appetite. Without reason we would in these cases act *differently*: reason constitutes a kind of external force for appetite. I want to use this general principle of Plato's for acknowledging distinct things to show how to justify thinking that one thing genuinely constitutes another.

For the principle to be really effective it must not allow us to see every change as substantial. When Aristotle wondered whether Socrates and Socrates-seated were the same, he no doubt thought of Socrates's sitting as an arbitrary example of what appears to us to be a

---

177. Plato 1969.

mere alteration. If our Platonic principle could not show that this sort of example is not substantial, it is utterly vacuous. Since we will discuss personal identity in the next chapter, let us look at another arbitrary example of a mere alteration. When water freezes it "becomes" ice, but we do not think of this as the literal creation of some new thing. Nevertheless, the water certainly "behaves differently" in the frozen state. Now that it is rigid it resists distortion, yet before it was fluid. Does this force us to say that the liquid water and the ice are "in opposition," since the presence of the frozen state constitutes an "external force" altering the way the water behaves, as the presence of reason opposes the natural behavior of appetite? The problem is clear: since the addition of any accident will alter the way the thing behaves, it is not clear why we cannot see in any alteration two things "in opposition."

I think the solution to this is that the fact that the water is ice merely *follows* from the fact that the water is in the circumstances in question, so that when we omit reference to the fact that ice is present, it does not alter how we describe what happens to the water. Suppose that the water freezes because it is on a very cold sheet of metal. Then the relevant "circumstances" include just its presence on this cold metal; the water becomes frozen because it is in these circumstances, and it follows logically that ice is present. Because the presence of the ice merely follows logically from the facts about the water, the ice does not appear as an external force. Now contrast this with a true case of an external force. When one billiard ball is deflected in its path by another the presence of the other cannot be simply inferred after we have an adequate explanation of the direction of the first ball. If we do not mention the presence of the second ball in the explanation itself, the change in direction of the first ball will be utterly mysterious.

We have seen how our Platonic principle counts some changes as mere alterations, and thus, some properties as mere accidents. This should become clearer when we contrast it with a case involving a genuinely constituted thing. I said before that our best examples would be organisms. So let us consider a typical example, and see how our Platonic principle (if defensible) would let us rebut the reduction of the organism to something which constitutes it. But first, I will say generally how I will apply the principle. In the example of the billiard

214

ball the behavior of the deflected ball could be explained only by mentioning something else (the ball which hit it), which therefore appeared as a distinct object, exerting an external force on it. I want to consider a different kind of case, in which the alternative is not to avoid mentioning something else of the same kind, but to ignore all things of a certain kind, the things that we think are constituted by more basic things, such as atoms. What I want to show is that without being able to mention the constituted thing in question, there will be some facts which, even when reported by mentioning only the more basic things, will still be unexplained. But it will not be, as with the deflected billiard ball, that we cannot explain the behavior of a certain sum of particles by mentioning what *it* does in the relevant circumstances. The facts in question will pertain to how *different* sums of particles are related to one another, so that reference to the constituted thing will help us to explain these interrelations. It is in this perhaps attenuated sense that the constituted thing will appear as an "external force." (After explaining how the principle applies, I will show why we are justified in applying it.) Now to the example in question.

Suppose that a dog decides to bolt and takes off running. Since it will exchange particles in its run, there will be no single sum of particles tracing the same path. In fact, if we begin with the initial sum of particles and consider what will happen to it in these circumstances, we see that it will separate with the first exhaling. When the dog finishes his run this original sum will be in a different place from that of the dog. Of course, much of it will be where the dog is, but some of it will be spread out along the path. If we followed the dog to old age we might find none of the original particles with him. But this possibility (of complete material replacement) offers only an extreme example of the relevant point. With the first breath the dog and these original particles are in different places. And from the fact that these original particles are in the first place, all that follows about these particles is that they will be in a series of spread out places. This is what makes this case notably different from that of water turning into ice. Describe what happens to the water and it simply follows that the ice is present. But describe what happens to the original particles and the presence of the dog along the path cannot be simply inferred. This is why the dog seems to "take on a life of its own." The dog has a tendency to act in these circumstances which cannot be attributed to the first sum, since this sum (in separating with the first exhaling) does not behave like the dog. Nor, of course, does any other sum in the sequence of sums which constitute the dog throughout the run exhibit the dog's tendency to act as it does. Now consider this sequence and ask why each member appeared when it did along the path. The obvious explanation refers to the dog: it is because these are the particles of a dog who is running along the path breathing in and out. The members of this sequence are interrelated in such a way that is explained only by referring to the dog, and it is in this (perhaps attenuated) sense that the dog exerts an "external force" on the members of this sequence.

It will no doubt be said that we could have explained the appearance of each sum on the path without referring to the dog. Consider the entire plurality of particles the members of which appear at some time on the "run." Surely these behave according to laws of their own which are sufficient to explain why various portions of them appear in succession along the path. There is not, the objection goes, a distinctive "tendency" to act which can only be attributed to the dog. The appearance of this tendency is only an appearance, due to focusing on one small portion after another of this entire plurality. If we could keep track of all the particles of this larger plurality we would see them in interaction, and everything that led us to think of the dog would be adequately explained, without, of course, referring to the dog as such. Naturally, in normal life it is convenient, even practically necessary, to ignore all the relevant facts and suppose there is a "dog" there. But in "serious metaphysics" we abstract from these parochial constraints.

There is no reason for me to deny the facts on which this objection is based. Let it be granted that the members of the entire plurality of particles involved throughout the dog's run comply with their own laws that enable us to explain why various smaller portions of them appear in succession along the path. The fact remains that at each time in the run the state of the plurality which constitutes the dog *depends* on the state of the plurality which preceded it in the sequence, so that there is a chain of such dependencies which makes the members of this sequence specially related to one other, and the question is why this is so. There is, in traditional language, a continuity or preservation of "form" (the form in virtue of which each constitutes the dog) throughout this sequence. Because of this there is a lawlike connection between the members of this sequence. But no member of this sequence complies with the law that would describe this (since each is coming or going out of the process the law would describe). We can acknowledge that this lawlike process takes place, therefore, only by referring to that one thing that does undergo the whole process: the dog. This process is not merely an appearance that disappears in the divine image of the entire plurality involved. To say this is to fail to distinguish this process from any other arbitrarily chosen sequence of smaller portions within the entire plurality. This sequence is not arbitrarily chosen because the chain of dependencies between the members of the sequence enables us to explain how each gives rise to the other in the sequence *without* referring to the surrounding particles which have been or will be involved in the run but are not currently involved. We have allowed that the entire plurality in question will have its own laws which will explain where the members end up from moment to moment. If we trace this entire plurality from the beginning of the run to its end, it will of course follow that the members of sequence which constitute the dog in succession will end up on the path. But the crucial point is that this will be a *different* lawlike process. The entire plurality, after all, is not where the first plurality is at the beginning, and it is not where the last plurality is at the end. There is no reason for us to deny that this complex process *also* occurs, beginning and ending over a relatively spread out area. What I want to insist upon is that this is compatible with a very different lawlike process occurring within this area, the explanation of which requires reference to something constituted by these particles.

Let us see, then, what *entitles* us to infer from these facts that the particles in question do indeed constitute a "new" entity, the dog, which is identical with no sum of them. What I want to do is to show how our general account of what kinds of continuants we are justified in thinking there are can be applied to the present case. Let us recall that the basic rationale for admitting kinds of continuants was that references to them enable us to apply Harrison's rules of confirmation. The fact that a certain rule applied was itself something judged to be true and in need of its own justification. With this justification, we apply the rule to things of an associated kind, and it is only because the rule is justified that references to these things are justified. Rules are justified only by judgments that instances of them have occurred. Of course, a rule can be trumped by a more general one, and we have seen several examples of this. But when this is not so, to fail to acknowledge the rule is to fail to make connections between the judgments to which the rule applies and thus to have fewer reasons in support of one's judgments. Now, the point that I have been making about the dog and the entire plurality of particles involved in its run can be understood in these terms. The crucial point is that there *is* such a rule which can be applied only to the dog and not to any sum of its particles. What I have in mind is a complex rule that would describe all the relevant facts that we would normally invoke to explain how the dog runs down the path, breathing and so forth. Since the rule describes a process which "involves" eventually the entire plurality in question, the only plurality to which it could apply is this whole plurality. But it does *not* apply to this plurality. This larger plurality starts off and ends up in different (larger) places than anything to which the rule could apply. The rule applies only to something at the beginning and end of the path and no single sum of particles fits this description. There is accordingly a judgment that we can make about the state of affairs at the beginning of the path (which we would normally state by describing the dog) which is *confirmed* by judgments that we would make about the states of affairs along the path. Suppose we judge that the dog has decided to bolt, say because it has opened its eyes and turned up the path. This judgment would be confirmed by seeing its legs propel it up the path. What *entitles* us to make such a judgment as the first one, in which we refer to the dog, is really very simple. It is that there *is* confirmation for it, which is to say, that *there are reasons* for it, the reasons that we report with the future judgments in question. The difficulty of seeing this as justificatory is that we need to see that the rule in question which links the relevant states of affairs is not one that can be applied to any sum of particles. That is why I labored so much to show that. But once this is seen, the justification for admitting a constituted object is rather simple. Again, if the rule can apply only to a constituted object, and it enables us to make a link between two states of affairs that we could not make without it, we are justified in admitting the new object since this enables us to report the first state of affairs and *support* this judgment by reporting the second state of affairs. In this way we "have a reason" for admitting the new object.

It might be helpful to re-express the main point in the language of "interpreting experience." We begin by imagining that we have now certain empirical data which we ordinarily interpret by judging that there is a dog here. The reductionist claims that the data are better interpreted by judging only that there is a sum of particles here with a certain internal structure. I do not deny that the data do reveal the sum of particles in question but insist that they also reveal a dog genuinely constituted by these particles. The reason for this is not evident when we focus on only this current circumstance since, as we have seen, when one object constitutes another they appear the same at the times of coincidence, so that reference to either is sufficient to describe how it appears at these times. What justifies the additional interpretation of the current data with the concept of a dog, with its different application of the concept of identity, is the fact that there are reasons for it which are expressed by interpreting different sets of data, at later times, again with the concept of a dog. At such a later time, these data can also be interpreted as revealing a sum of particles (a different one), but when they are, the judgment made does not support the first judgment (about the first plurality). This later judgment (about a later plurality) does support other judgments, made in the interpretation of other data, collected in different places (pertaining to how this different sum was before). But by not availing ourselves of the concept of a dog we miss the opportunity of interpreting this later set of data in such a way as to provide a new reason, one which supports the earlier interpretation of the original data. Simply put, there are reasons for thinking there is a dog here, including the fact that a dog is down the path. This claim no longer seems banal when we see why the reductionist is not able to accommodate it within his scheme.

To defend this account, I want to consider one more objection. I have argued that in the case of the dog, recognizing a distinct thing (the dog) in addition to the sums of particles enables us to make a direct link between the states of the dog at the two times which we cannot make while restricted to the sums. So, why are we not entitled to make such a link whenever one thing affects another? Suppose that one billiard ball deflects the path of another. We cannot explain the new direction of the other ball by referring only to the first ball, since the other ball contributes to some extent to its own new path. But suppose that we claim that there is a new entity, a "bridge-ball," which is constituted first by the affecting ball and then by the affected ball. Unlike the "extraordinary" balls that we considered in the sixth chapter, bridge-balls are not supposed to replace ordinary balls but are supposed to exist in addition to them, as entities constituted by them. When one ordinary ball hits another it is as if one bridge-ball hops from one to another. Since the motion of the ball which is hit does depend upon the ball which did the hitting, there is a rule which links these two states of motion. The problem is to show that our account has the resources to avoid concluding the additional existence of a bizarre bridge-ball.

To avoid this unwelcome consequence, let me point out that the only way in which we would know that a bridge-ball exists would be by knowing first that two ordinary balls had made contact and then *inferring* the existence of the bridge-ball from this. We could not (I am supposing as obvious) predict where the bridge-ball will be merely by describing what will happen to it, given that it is in the initial circumstances of the affecting ball. (This would be like describing the effect on the ball which is struck without describing how this ball contributed to the result.) In this respect, the case is just like that of water turning into ice. Just as the existence of ice follows logically from the fact that water has frozen, the existence of a bridge-ball would follow logically from the fact that one ball has deflected the other. And the crucial point is that the only way that we could know about the existence of the bridge-ball is by making this inference. Because our knowledge of the bridge-ball would be obtained only by inferring it from what we already know, *without* making independent contact with the world, judgments about bridge-balls would add no new confirmations for our previous judgments. In this respect they are like Shoemaker's klables, which we discussed in the sixth chapter. A klable, we recall, shares the history of a kitchen table for half the day and then that of living room table for the other half. What we found was that the judgment that a klable was before us just after a "jump" did not really help in confirming our prior judgment about the klable, since to know that this was indeed a klable before us, we would already have to know where it was before. This showed a sharp difference between ordinary sortal concepts like that of being a table and phony ones like that of being a klable. We can know (corrigibly) that a table is before us without knowing its past, and it is only because of this that judgments about tables provide genuine confirmation of past judgments about tables. I am making a similar point about phony sortals like those of bridge-balls. Since the only way to know that a bridge-ball is before us is to know of its past (the contact of two ordinary balls), acknowledging a new bridge-ball provides no real confirmation for our empirical judgments. Reference to the bridge-ball is thus crucially different from reference to the dog. The fact that the dog is running down the path is not merely inferred from what we previously knew, but is confirmed by future perception. This independent contact with the world provides genuine confirmation of previous judgments about the dog. We are not, therefore, forced to see whenever one thing affects another a strange new thing constituted by the two, since our account distinguishes these from genuine cases of constitution.

I would like to compare my account to another, by Samuel Wheeler, which is in certain respects remarkably similar.[178] Like me, Wheeler thinks that the addition of new entities will be justified only by the justification of new laws which apply to them and not to the particles of which they are composed. But unlike me, he thinks that whether these new laws can be justified turns on the issue of whether there is *indeterminism* among the particles. His point is that if the particles behave deterministically, there will be nothing left for the new entities to explain. Suppose that Jones reads about a sale at the A&P and travels for thousands of meters to get there. Although we could predict with accuracy where Jones will be on the basis his beliefs and desires, "current laws about micro-particles"[179] might make it impossible to predict where the micro-particles which constitute him will be after

---

178. Wheeler 1986.
179. Ibid., p. 339.

such a large stretch in space and time. But since Jones will carry his micro-particles with him, according to Wheeler, the presence of Jones will enable us to make predictions about the micro-particles which are not yielded by laws which apply to them alone. This illustrates the "bare possibility"[180] that a complex object like a person can be justified as a new object; but the justification would require that indeterminism holds among the old objects.

Even if the actuality of this "bare possibility" would be sufficient to justify new objects, we may wonder if the whole case for new objects really *relies* on causal indeterminism. It would certainly be desirable to be able to justify the existence of the generable and perishable objects which we think we find about us without relying on a thesis which has emerged only in modern physics. I hope it is clear how our account does not depend on such an extraordinary basis. Even if the particles behave deterministically, the fact that Jones ends up with certain ones cannot be predicted from the fact that the first ones were in his original circumstances. As I have emphasized, Jones does not carry all of his particles from home to the store since he undergoes material replacement along the way. This means that the particles which end up at the A&P are not those with which he began. Even if we can turn to a larger plurality which includes these and deterministically predict where the last ones will be, this does not mean that there is nothing left to explain. What may be explained is the movement of Jones to the A&P, given his initial circumstances, which do not include the larger plurality. There is, we are supposing with Wheeler, rules or laws which make reference to Jones's beliefs and desires and which enable us to link judgments and corresponding states of affairs. But as I have argued, we simply cannot link these in the same ways when restricted to his particles. And since these judgments are made not merely by inference, but by perception, our reference to Jones's arrival at the A&P genuinely confirms our judgment that he read of its sales. New objects, constituted by their constituents, can be justified even if these constituents behave deterministically.

To make the case that there is substantial change and therefore

---

180. Ibid., p. 342.

that objects sometimes constitute others in their same place, I have focused on the case of organisms and particles of which they are composed. This was natural, since we expect organisms to approach relatively well the Leibnizian ideal of being independent of other things. Other cases are thus bound to appear less compelling. Nevertheless, to have a clearer view of what our account can admit, we should address these cases too. For example, is an artifact like a ship or watch constituted by its parts? Is a lump of gold or a rubber ball constituted by a quantity of gold or a quantity of rubber? These are surely less attractive examples to illustrate the constitution relation. But let us see what kind of case can be made for them. Perhaps in seeing why they are unattractive we will understand better why so much attention has been devoted to problems of their identity.

Let us begin with the case for artifacts. Hume held that artifacts differ from organisms in the way in which their parts are interrelated: in artifacts the parts only serve a common purpose, whereas in organisms a common purpose is served by the mutual influence of the parts.[181] This is reminiscent of Wiggins's idea that the identity of an artifact is determined only by the purpose it serves, indicated by a term such as "watch" or "pen," whereas the identity of an organism is determined by a natural kind term such as "horse" or "human" which indicates a characteristic kind of development.[182] Once again engaged only in psychology, Hume observes that the mutual influence of the parts of an organism makes us think that we have more reason to think that an organism is a genuine unity. In our terms, this is to say that it seems to provide more compelling reason for recognizing the organism as a thing genuinely constituted by its parts, and that conversely, there seems to be relatively less reason to resist reducing an artifact to its parts. Although Wiggins considers the reduction of artifacts to their parts, he does not concede this. But this is because he is working within our common metaphysics, and since he thinks our thought of artifacts is coherent, he allows that they are constituted by their parts. Since we are standing outside this metaphysics, we must

---

181. Hume 1968, Bk. 1, Part 4, Sec. 6. For a philosophically subtle and formally rigorous discussion of the notion of integrated wholes, see Simons's chapter on that topic in Simons 1987, pp. 324–60.

182. Wiggins 1980, Ch. 3.

find more justification for not succumbing to reductionism. And since our standards are more stringent, we should not be surprised if that justification is harder to find or less compelling. Nevertheless, let us see if our account can provide any resistance to the reduction of artifacts to their parts.

It may seem that Hume's account of the difference between artifacts and organisms is correct. It is certainly impressive how the parts of an organism influence each other to preserve life. But this is so, I suggest, because, like organisms themselves, the parts are energetic in serving their various functions. When we turn to something like a statue, it may seem that all that the bits of stuff have in common is that they serve to present a certain shape. But consider a really clear example of things which merely serve a common purpose. Suppose that to block the sun, we cover a window with many separate pieces of paper. These serve a common purpose, but it seems that there is no temptation at all to think of them as constituting a distinct thing. Now contrast this with something like a ship. It is true that when the ship loses a plank in a storm it does not create or search about for another. But I suggest that there is still some reason for thinking of the ship as distinct from its parts. It seems that the ship behaves in certain regular ways that permit gradual changes in its parts. When the sails are unfurled, it lurches forward; when the rudder is turned, it veers to one side. These lurches and veerings could take place even if a part were added or lost, in which case they would not really be undergone by a single plurality of parts. I suggest that such changes are possible because the ship really is like an organism, though to a modest degree. The parts of a ship are not merely in the same vicinity, serving a common purpose, like the pieces of paper. They are fitted together in such a way that they do mutually influence one another. To explain the behavior of each part, it is necessary to refer to surrounding parts, such as nails and the like. The parts of the ship thus have an internal arrangement which can survive gradual changes of parts, and it is the preservation of this structure even through a succession of distinct pluralities which accounts for the behavior of the ship. If this behavior allows us to see a persisting thing, this thing cannot be the parts themselves, but must be something constituted by them, since it is a kind of behavior that permits material replacement.

To see more clearly how our account resists the reduction of (some) artifacts, contrast Hume's account of them with Locke's: ". . . what is a Watch? 'Tis plain 'tis nothing but a fit Organization, or Construction of Parts, to a certain end, which, when a sufficient force is added to it, it is capable to attain."[183] Wiggins thought without question that the sortals of artifacts would be such terms as "watch" or "ship" which indicate only their function, and it was because of this that he thought that their identities were to a large extent up to us to decide. But suppose that we follow, not Hume but Locke, by thinking that their identities are determined by a "fit organization or structure." Since this is the sort of thing that is depicted in a blueprint, the proper sortal for each artifact would not be something so general that it indicated only its function, but would rather be something specific, like a certain model of watch or car. To say what, for example, my watch *is*, I would say not merely that it is a watch, but that it is a Swiss Army Watch. Watches of this kind have a distinctive internal structure. To say how they operate, we say how their parts interact or "mutually influence" one another in order to tell time. The state of the parts at one moment predicts their state at the next, so that judgments about the first state are confirmed by judgments about the next. Now, if parts of the watch could not be replaced, there would seem to be no reason not to attribute these machinations simply to the parts themselves. But if this behavior can sustain even small replacements, then it would seem to be the watch and not the parts in which the machinations properly take place. An important point to realize is that if the parts themselves do not really perform these machinations, then these do not really "tell time"; of course, we can tell the time by looking at how the parts are arranged at one moment, but only the watch, and not the parts, will be "telling time" in the sense of operating in that regular way which permits us to read it over long periods. This will be the distinctive form of activity that distinguishes the watch from its parts. The watch, to exist, will not have to be actually performing this activity. Since it is what is "responsible" for this activity it can be re-identified after a period of inactivity on the ground that Locke's internal structure, which explains how it is so responsible, is preserved. Locke

---

183. Locke 1975, 331.

distinguished artifacts from organisms on the ground that only in artifacts did a "sufficient force" have to be "added." We have to wind the watch or replace the parts ourselves. Although this is certainly an impressive difference, it does not seem to me enough to show that artifacts are identical with their parts.

It is not necessary for me to be completely convincing about artifacts, but only to show how the case should be argued from our general metaphysics. According to this account, the identity of each (epistemically primary) continuant is determined by a certain tendency to produce its own future states. For each kind of thing there is accordingly a distinctive essential tendency which all members of that kind share. When one object genuinely constitutes another, there must be different tendencies which cannot be attributed to the same thing. If an artifact is distinct from its parts, it must have a tendency to contribute to its own future which is not due simply to its composition. What would this be? I have suggested, following Locke, that it would be a tendency to preserve a certain internal structure. It is certainly tempting to think that this structure is preserved by the parts; we explain how the structure is preserved by saying how the parts hold together. But the temptation to reduce diminishes, I think, when we realize that the way in which the structure is preserved permits replacements in the parts. It then seems that it is not a certain plurality of parts, individually nameable, which undergoes the changes in question, but that it is because these parts are serving functional roles with respect to one another that the structure is preserved. It is then that the artifact seems to "take on a life of its own."

Van Inwagen denies that artifacts are constituted by their parts and imagines cases in which the idea is unattractive.[184] If a snake were wound up to make a hammock, would the hammock be distinct from the snake? Many examples are like this. If I use my pen as a paperweight do I bring into existence a new thing when I lay my pen on paper? Nothing in our account forces us to admit such things. I have denied Wiggins's idea that terms like "hammock" and "paperweight" (which indicate only a purpose and not a structure) are sortals for artifacts. There is no reason in our account why, for example, a term

---

184. Van Inwagen 1990, pp. 124–27.

like "hammock" might not apply to things of a variety of kinds, with very different identity conditions. It might apply to a snake, with identity conditions associated with a form of life, so that being a hammock is simply a temporary state of the snake. The term "hammock" might apply also to something with a certain essential structure, genuinely created by intertwining many small pieces of rope. I argued that *some* artifacts have parts that mutually influence one another to a common purpose and serve their purpose by playing roles that allow them to be substituted; *when* this is so, the activity in question cannot really be one created by a particular plurality of parts. There is no reason to think that all artifacts meet this condition, and for those which do not, there is no evident reason to think that when the artifact is "created" something new comes into existence.

I have made a case for thinking of (some) artifacts as constituted by their parts. Brennan would no doubt reject my conclusion since he claims that "there is no counterpart in artifacts to the law-governed development, and retention, of structure that we find in natural kinds."[185] I think that there is a modest counterpart, but let us suppose that Brennan is right. Then I would say that we ought to reduce artifacts to their parts. I believe that the plausibility of artifact reduction has a good deal to do with the fact that there are such problems surrounding their identity. Let us recall the case in which parts such as construction toys are repeatedly taken apart and put back together to make the same structure. I admit that there is a temptation to say that it is the same toy existing intermittently even though I argued against this in the sixth chapter. But a large part of the temptation, I believe, is due simply to the fact that it is tempting to see the toy as only the parts themselves. The fact that there is relatively little reason to distinguish an artifact from its parts (even if there is enough) must affect our intuitions, so that when presented with the same parts in the same shape it must seem to some appreciable extent that the same thing is present. I submit that it is precisely this ambivalence that creates the problem of the ship of Theseus. To the extent to which we have good reason for thinking of the ship as being like an organism, we have reason for thinking that the ship has simply undergone

---

185. Brennan 1988, p. 201.

replacement of its parts. But the case for this is relatively weak, so that we are also tempted to reduce the ship to its parts and think of a ship as simply being the parts, which are called a "ship" whenever properly arranged. This gives rise to the conflicting intuition that when the old parts are put back together the original ship is there.

It is, I believe, a virtue of our account that it explains these conflicting intuitions. As I have argued, our account provides sufficient (though slight) reason for thinking that an artifact like a ship is constituted by its parts, thus supporting and thereby explaining the intuition that the ship with the new parts is the original ship of Theseus. A satisfactory philosophical account of the matter will, however, not merely come down on one side of the issue but will explain, or "explain away," the contrary intuition. I have done this by showing how the case for resisting reduction is relatively weak. Since, as Locke realized, it is up to external agents like ourselves to animate them and repair them, their tendency to create their own future seems less distinctive. This explains the conflicting intuition that the original ship reappears when the old parts are reassembled, since it explains the intuition that the ship is really just the collection of parts. Together, this is my solution to the problem.

I have been emphasizing the fact that the parts of an artifact or organism mutually influence one another while neglecting the point, mentioned by both Hume and Locke, that a certain end is served. Without this qualification, it would seem that if we took any arbitrary portion of an integrated object we could say that the parts involved constituted their own object. The left half of the torso of an animal certainly contains many parts in vigorous interaction, but it hardly seems that these constitute a distinct entity. It seems that to point to this half is to point to only these various parts and that we see a genuinely constituted entity only when we see them in interaction with more things, the other parts of the animal. The difference seems to be that the left half does not serve a distinctive purpose. The question is whether our account will enable us to reduce this half to its parts.

Our account is "Aristotelian" by identifying the "formal cause" with the "final cause:" we say what a thing is by saying what it has a tendency to become. Understanding the nature of a thing thus becomes in large part understanding the "end" toward which its is "striving," for instance, the oak tree which the acorn is striving to become. Since the parts of an arbitrary portion of an integrated object are not cooperating to some common end of their own we have no reason to think that they constitute a distinct object. What distinctive tendency can we attribute to the left half of an animal's torso? Because there is none, our account creates no pressure to recognize a distinct entity. There are of course judgments about the left half of the torso which are confirmed by later judgments about this half. But it seems plain that these are easily regarded as judgments about the various parts, so that there is no reason to think of them as constituting their own new entity.

My stance on this last issue allows me to deal straightforwardly with a problem which has lately drawn a good deal of attention.[186] Consider a certain cat, named Tibbles, and let us call that portion of her which excludes her tail, Tib. There is no temptation to identify Tibbles with Tib while she has her tail since Tibbles but not Tib has a tail. But now suppose that Tibbles loses her tail. The problem is that we are now tempted to say that Tibbles just is Tib, since there is no evident difference between them. But unless we resort to some controversial measure,[187] we appear to contradict our previous judgment that Tibbles is not Tib. The mistake of all this, I think, is to suppose that just because we pick out some arbitrary portion of an object we have picked out a single thing. I claim that Tib is just like the left half of a torso, not a single thing, but a plurality of cat parts. It is for this simple reason that Tib never is identical with the single entity, Tibbles. I submit that the whole problem arises from that attitude of ontological liberty which I criticized in the first chapter, of supposing that we can name something real just by making up a word for it, with associated identity criteria, provided only that there are empirical data satisfying these criteria.

It is hard to imagine a more humble example of constitution than the constitution of a lump of stuff by the quantity of stuff with which it coincides. Are these really two things, or is a lump merely a quantity, so called when the quantity happens to be lumped together? Surely,

---

186. The example of Tibbles comes from William of Sherwood; Geach has brought it to our attention.

187. Simons canvasses these proposals thoroughly. See Simons 1987, pp. 118–21.

it is very tempting to say the latter. But let us consider a well-defined lump, such as a ball of gold. And let us suppose that the lump is rolled across a flat but rough floor, so that the path it takes is due largely to its shape, but during its journey some of the gold rubs off. Because a quantity of gold can neither gain nor lose gold, the quantity which ends the journey is only a proper part of that which began it, and so is numerically distinct. As in other examples of ours, there is really a succession of distinct quantities along the path. But there is surely a temptation to say that there is one lump or ball of gold rolling across the floor, and once we realize that this cannot be identical with any quantity of gold, we are struck with the possibility that the lump is genuinely constituted by each quantity in succession.

In light of our previous discussions, it is clear how to defend the constitution of the lump by the quantity. As I said, the path of the ball is determined largely by its shape, which it retains despite the loss of gold. The successive positions of the ball can be predicted by the fact that something made of roughly this amount of gold but having a tendency to preserve a spherical shape has been propelled in a certain direction in these circumstances. Since judgments to this effect are confirmed by perceptions of the ball at later moments, it seems that recognizing the ball itself does provide genuine confirmations that would be unavailable if we were restricted to the quantities of gold.

Although there seems to be sufficient reason to distinguish the lump of gold from the quantity of gold, the case is surely less compelling than that of organisms. To see why, suppose that the lump is smashed. Is it the same lump or a different one? The reason why there is no evident reason to think it is the same lump is that the change in shape is caused by an external agent, such as a person wielding a hammer. But this change is one that the quantity itself undergoes, so that there is no tendency to retain a shape that is distinctive of the lump and not the quantity that would enable us to re-identify the lump after the change in shape. And this seems to mean that with *every* change in shape, at least those brought about be external agents, the quantity

---

188. Van Inwagen finds this sort of possibility "incredible" (Van Inwagen 1990, p. 126) and concludes from this that artifacts should be reduced to their parts. I do not see the problem, especially when we admit that the grounds for distinguishing the lump from quantity, though sufficient, are only minimally so.

constitutes a different lump.[188] Since it is relatively easy to bring about such changes, and since the lump itself offers little resistance to them, the distinctive activity of the lump, that of preserving that shape, is not witnessed to an impressive degree. In an extreme case, such as a lump of dry dirt, there is no such tendency which permits us to see it behaving in a lawlike manner through changes in amount of stuff. Try to roll a lump of dry dirt and it simply falls apart. Since it behaves just like the quantity of dirt, there is no reason to see it as something distinct from the quantity. But other lumps of stuff are not much different.

Notice how we have a stronger case for constitution with something like a rubber ball which not only preserves its shape but which has a tendency to return to its shape after deformation. This latter tendency explains, of course, why it bounces, whereas the ball of gold would not strive to regain the spherical shape if deformed. Well, perhaps it would if deformed slightly, but there is still a great difference in degree. And because of this there is more reason to think that the same ball is undergoing rather great changes in shape as it bounces, since it is the ball itself which is responsible for repeatedly returning to the spherical shape. I say that it is the ball itself which is responsible for this and not a quantity of rubber of which it is composed because, as with the ball of gold, small amounts of rubber can be lost through the bounces. But because something persisting throughout these seems to be causing the repeated returns to the spherical shape, and since because of the losses of rubber, this can be no quantity of rubber, there is even more reason to think that a rubber ball is genuinely constituted by its rubber. The rubber ball seems a bit more like an organism which takes active steps to preserve a certain internal state.

We have been deliberately considering difficult cases in which to apply our account of how to justify thinking that there is a distinct constituted object to get a better view of how this account works. My last example of this chapter will have a more direct bearing on the account of personal identity of the next and last chapter. Aristotle held that our bodies are our matter, or as Wiggins would later say, that we

---

189. There is some reason to think, however, that Aristotle meant to identify the body with the person (see Irwin 1988, pp. 241–42 and footnote 167 above).

are constituted by our bodies.[189] I will defend this in the next chapter, though on grounds which are unusual. What I want now to consider is whether the same should be said for other organisms. Is an animal such as a dog really constituted by its body or merely identical with its body? Are there two things, the plant and its body, or only one? I want to defend Descartes's idea that other creatures, which lack our power of thought, are merely bodies. I will not of course say that we are different by the possession of a Cartesian soul, but I do want to capture eventually what I think is right in his position.

When I speak of other animals, what I have in mind are those which are not consciously rational, which lack our capacity for being aware of reasons as such. So, I will be arguing in the next chapter that it is because of this capacity that we are not identical with but are genuinely constituted by our bodies. Now, what do I mean by "bodies"? The term is used in a variety of senses. As with Hume, it can mean merely material continuants. Or it can perhaps be used to refer to ourselves insofar as we are such objects. But when a person dies we also say that the corpse is identical with the body of the person. I want to use the term in still a different sense. For the present purpose, a body is something which is essentially striving to preserve a certain organic structure. Activities of the body, in this sense, would clearly include such things as circulating blood, digesting and assimilating food and maintaining temperature. These sorts of activities contribute to preserving the organic structure which is distinctive of the kind of creature in question. A body in this sense is not of course just any material continuant; but nor will it literally become a corpse, since the corpse has no tendency to preserve the organic structure in question. I regard the corpse of any organism as merely a lump of stuff. But bodies in our sense are essentially alive. In the next chapter I will argue that in spite of this, we are still distinct from our bodies, thus paying homage to Descartes's position. Now I want to argue that plants and other animals are merely identical with their bodies, in this sense of the term.

My strategy will be to take what seems to be most distinctive in the activity of a plant and an animal and then to argue in each case that there is no reason to think of the organism as distinct from its body, since this activity does not put it in that kind of "opposition" with the body that we saw, when discussing Plato, is what distinguishes a thing from its matter. Consider, first, a typical plant, which puts down roots and turns its leaves to the sun. There are many other things it does, including reflecting light and resisting pressure. But since these latter sorts of things are done by continuants of many other kinds they do not promise to distinguish the plant from its body. I am assuming that if anything would distinguish a plant from its body it would be those sorts of activities which are distinctive of plants, such a extending roots and turning leaves. What I claim is that these activities can be easily attributed to the body in our sense, so that there is no reason to think that their presence reveals a distinct thing. I take this to be rather obvious. The plant puts down roots and turns its leaves to the sun in order to preserve its organic structure. We understand why it does these things by seeing them as normally serving to preserve this structure. I say that they "normally" serve this purpose to cover unfortunate mishaps. If a plant puts its roots into poison, this may kill it. But we would still understand this as the sort of thing which is supposed to preserve the organic structure in question. Malfunctioning is not the same as functioning for a different purpose. The case of the plant is much like the case of the water which turned into ice. The point there was that the ice is not distinct from the water since its presence merely followed logically from the fact that the water froze. Let us understand similarly "the plant" to designate whatever does such things as putting down roots and turning leaves to the sun. Now it is easy to see the body, in our sense, as doing just such things, so that we do not have to mention the plant as such to explain what happens to the body. Since the presence of the plant simply follows from our description of what the body does, there is no reason to think of the plant as a thing distinct from the body.

Perhaps we should add one qualification. In reproductive activities such as producing pollen, a plant is surely acting distinctively as a plant (and not, for instance, as merely a material continuant); and yet it is not acting to preserve a certain organic structure throughout a series of constituting bits of matter. These acts of the plant serve instead to copy its genes so that similar plants result. I think we can accommodate these sorts of activities, however, by a refinement of what we mean by a body. Let it be understood that a body is essentially striving to preserve "a certain organic structure" in the sense that includes not only the preservation of this structure in a series of constituting objects but also in offspring as well. My claim is that the activities of plants as such are easily attributable to bodies in this slightly extended sense.

I will assume analogously that if anything distinguishes another animal from its body it will be its sentience.[190] I assume that if an animal is constituted by its body this is because what is most distinctive of it, its capacity to perceive and feel and act on desire, cannot be attributed to the body. Its sentience would put it in "opposition" with its body; its body itself could not be sentient, so that given the presence of sentience, a distinct entity would have to be admitted. There are of course desires and feelings and perceptions that belong only to a consciously rational being. I will argue later that wanting justice or feeling indignation or seeing that there is a ball before me is a state which cannot belong to the body. But these are clearly not merely states of sentience. What we should have in mind are states such as desiring water or feeling nauseated or seeing how it looks (where this is described only in feature-placing terms). I have pointed out before (in Chapter 5) that sentience is enough for a creature to be "primitively" rational. When I assumed that my dog, Argus, was capable of only feature-placing and not individuation, I still allowed that would he *have* reasons, since he would have cognitions, assessable as true or false, but he would not know this. In perception he would have representations, true or false, which we could report on his behalf with feature-placing sentences, such as "Blue-here." But, lacking conscious rationality, he would not be able to "unify" them through self-awareness. What I want to argue is that even though he is primitively rational, if he is not also consciously rational, he is merely identical with his body. I think that once we have the right sorts of states in mind it will seem obvious that there is no reason not to attribute these to the body, in our sense. Argus, for example, has a desire for bacon which arose from his need for nutrition and his past pleasant experiences with its taste. Acting on this desire is one thing that is "supposed" to contribute to the preservation of his internal organic structure; we understand why he has the desire by seeing that this sort of

---

190. I am not implying that all animals are sentient. Those such as insects which appear to be "pre-programed" I take to be like plants.

thing normally serves to keep his body intact. As with the plant putting down roots in poison, this particular desire could lead to his demise. But once again, this would seem to be a case of malfunctioning rather than functioning with a different purpose. It is of course true that when Argus lunges for the bacon his only purpose is to get the bacon. But still, it seems plain that the reason why he has such purposes is that he has needs which when satisfied collectively preserve the organic structure of his body. As with plants, we want this notion of preserving a certain organic structure to cover reproduction as well. The desires which arise from Argus' sexual needs serve to copy his genes and thus to reproduce the sort of organic structure he has in his offspring. Again, my claim is that the desires of merely sentient creatures, such as we are supposing Argus to be, are easily attributed to such bodies. Similar remarks pertain to their feelings and perceptions. Argus's feeling of nausea after eating too much bacon may help to preserve his body by dampening his enthusiasm. At least, it is "supposed" to. If his desires all normally contribute to preserving an organic structure, then his perceptual experiences, which put him in touch with his surroundings, would seem to serve the same end. After all, we will know which cognitions he has only by seeing these as combining with his desires in the explanation of his behavior. There is certainly no mystery in the fact that a body, in our sense, would acquire sentience as a way of better promoting its natural end; my claim is that it exists merely in order to serve this end. We have, accordingly, no reason to think that even a sentient, primitively rational being, is other than its body.

In the last chapter I defended a certain conceptual structure with which to think of substantial change. The "matter" which undergoes the change exists at the end or beginning in spatial coincidence with the thing created or destroyed. What explains their similarities is the fact that they share the same parts or at least that they are "built of" a common plurality of parts. The matter also constitutes the thing, and since this relation is present outside of actual substantial changes, we need to understand how this is possible. My answer was that whenever one thing constitutes another it has a certain accident in virtue of which the other exists. This explains how a reference to the constituting object itself explains how the other thing might be destroyed.

The matter can undergo a change in which its loses this accidental property, thus destroying the thing constituted. In this chapter I have showed how, in many cases, we can defend the claim that the possession of a certain accident reveals the existence of a distinct constituted entity. When water freezes the ice is just the water in a new state. But the internal structure of the particles of the dog reveal the dog's distinct existence. We saw this was so when we saw that there was good reason to think that the structure was preserved even through replacements of particles. Our reason came, not of course from the ordinary observation that that is how we think of dogs, but from the fact that in so thinking we have more support for our judgments. The point is not that we should think of dogs instead of their particles. I have allowed that we can make all the same judgments about the particles that the reductionist wishes. It is rather that we find genuine confirmation for admitting that there is also a dog. Simply put, there really is adequate reason for thinking that there is also a dog since this is supported by empirical observations. The fact that the dog is off running supports the claim that the dog decided to bolt in the earlier circumstances. There is a direct link between the dog in the two places which cannot be seen as obtaining between one or more sums of particles. Since the whole reason for individuating objects in the first place was to make just such links, we have good reason for admitting the dog in addition to what constitutes it. Similar arguments were made, less compellingly, for artifacts and lumps of stuff.

This, then, constitutes my answer to Guyer and Kant. What Guyer argued on behalf of Kant was that fundamental constituents are necessary for the unity of experience; they were thus justified, and since nothing else had been apparently justified, we ought not to admit the new things of substantial change, for it would be arbitrary to do so. By going back and showing why—or at least offering one good theory for why—we are justified in thinking of objects in the first place, I have argued in effect that it would be arbitrary *not* to admit certain new objects. By admitting the fundamental constituents as well, there is no loss of justification. But in certain special cases, involving especially organisms, the recognition of their distinct existence allows us to make confirmations that would be otherwise unavailable. We simply do have reasons for admitting them. These reasons come from the fact that experience reveals natural regularities which themselves reveal persisting continuants with identity conditions which sums of the constituents cannot satisfy. In the fifth chapter I offered a picture of what justifies individuation in general: the natural regularities of experience which create unconscious expectations in the feature-placing brute emerge into the consciousness of the consciously rational individuator. What I have argued in this chapter is that our experience happens to be such that some of the regularities of which we are conscious involve generable and perishable objects, genuinely constituted by distinct things in the same place at the same time. I submit that Kant could have allowed "new things, that is, new substances" with no serious threat to the rest of his system. Indeed, the Kantian method of justification eventually leads to this anti-reductionist conclusion.

It might prove interesting to compare our metaphysics with those of both Leibniz and Spinoza. Both adopted an extremely strict view of substance in which a substance must be entirely "self-sufficient," responsible for all of its own states. Since Leibniz thought that part of God's goodness was that He would create many such things, he allowed that his monads, though depending for their existence on Him, would still be responsible for all their own properties, and would thus not really be in interaction with each other. Since Spinoza thought that ordinary objects were in interaction, he concluded that they were not substances, but only modes of the one true substance. Our metaphysics is like those of Kant and Aristotle in that we have a relaxed notion of substance which allows them to be in interaction and thus be only partly responsible for their own states. But in a certain respect our metaphysics is more like Leibniz's than Spinoza's. Like Leibniz, we allow that a substance can be created by another and still be responsible for (some of) its own future states. Assuming, for illustration, that my modest defense of artifacts is correct, we saw that although my watch is created, and thus its existence depends on something else, it is still what is solely responsible for its own activity: although we make the watch, only the watch tells time. This is like saying that although a martini glass was made at some time in the past, now that it exists, *it* holds the martini. It seems to me that reductionists like Spinoza and the Atomists make a certain, understandable mistake. From the fact that the constituted object depends for its existence on the constituting object and that wherever we see a constituted object we can turn our eyes instead to the constituting object, they infer that only the constituting object exists. By repeating this down the constitution tree they arrive at fundamental matter. But this ignores the fact that the fundamental constituents have different identity conditions than those which are needed for many manifest regularities. Once we realize this we become aware of things which, though they depend on their constituents, have "taken on a life of their own." I agree with Leibniz (and Aristotle) that substances can be created.

I do not claim that our metaphysics is sharp enough to decide clearly in any conceivable case whether a property determines identity. But I do hope to show that we now have enough to decide between the "short" view of our identity associated by Rawls with Hume and Parfit and the "longer" view associated with Kant.

9

What We Are

In the last few chapters we have developed an ontology of continuants which is deeply supported by transcendental arguments.
Although the issues with which we have dealt are of interest to metaphysicians, our purpose has been to have a well-defended general
conception of how to re-identify continuants which we can apply to
ourselves. I will try to show in this chapter that our account really has
been sufficiently developed to provide strong answers to a variety of
questions pertaining to our identity. But since our main interest has
been all along how to decide between the "short" view of our identity
associated with Hume and defended by Parfit and the "long" view of
Kant and common sense, we will begin with that project.

This is really a difference in what is essential to us. Consider Parfit's
own example of the Russian youth with Socialist ideals who fears that
he will abandon these when he later inherits wealth.[191] Parfit expresses
approvingly the youth's sentiment that he regards these ideals as
essential to him, and this is supposed to illustrate his Humean view
that even in normal human life it is as if a succession of different selves
exist. Parfit does not deny that the youth is identical with the older

---

191. Parfit 1984, p. 327.

wealthy man; his position is more subtle. He claims that it is relatively trivial to insist that they are the same, so that it is relatively trivial to press claims of responsibility and desert over long stretches of time. Hume held a similar, "short" view of our identity as a consequence of his general metaphysics: since "the relations [of similarity and causation between impressions], and the easiness of the transition may diminish by insensible degrees... All the disputes concerning the identity of connected objects are merely verbal."[192] I have argued in several ways against ideas that would lend support to Hume's general metaphysics and his particular view of our identity. In the first chapter I argued that the intuition that apparent similarity, even when uncaused, is evidence of identity should be given no evidential weight, since it may well be produced by the merely subjective fact of ignoring relevant differences. So also, the appearance of change may produce the intuition that the manifest difference is relevant, thus producing the intuition that distinct objects are appearing. But this temptation must, according to the argument of the fourth chapter, be resisted, for we can have a justified view of the world only if we ascribe the manifest changes to continuants, things genuinely undergoing the changes with no loss of reality. Hume's view of personal identity would also have been supported by the idea, argued against in the second chapter, that the self is identified only in relation to momentary states of consciousness of which alone we are acquainted. If this were correct, there would appear no clear way to determine persistence, so that claims of our persistence would seem as arbitrary and trivial as those for nations. By arguing against such ideas we have defended the "longer" view of our identity, but only indirectly and negatively, by removing support for the "short" view. We have yet to find reason for actually accepting the "longer" view associated with Kant and common sense.

Unlike Hume, Parfit argues for the "shorter" view, not by an explicit appeal to a general metaphysics of change, but by reflection on what he calls the "Combined Spectrum."[193] As we saw in the fourth chapter, this presents a series of persons, beginning with Parfit him-

---

192. Hume 1968, Bk. 1, Part 4, Sec. 6.
193. Parfit 1984, pp. 236–43.

self and ending with a replica of Greta Garbo; intermediary members of the series result by replacing, a few at a time, Parfit's cells with those of the Garbo replica. Parfit claims that we know enough about the brain to know that there would be no sudden change in personality, and he concludes from this that it would be trivial to pick one person in the series that is the last one which is he. This is, as I said that chapter, a perfect example of implicitly relying on the Humean metaphysics. Even if we allow that personality is what somehow determines personal identity, why should we accept that mere similarity in personality from one moment to the next itself provides grounds for re-identifying the person? Does it not matter what is *responsible* for the similarities? Our whole metaphysics demands that identity is determined, not by similarity, but by a natural tendency of the thing to be responsible, to some extent, for its own future. From the perspective of our "Aristotelian" metaphysics, what is striking about the Combined Spectrum is that the changes are so *unnatural*. The changes of cells do not occur naturally, as they do in normal organic life, but result (grotesquely) entirely by external intervention. From our point of view, there is accordingly no more reason to think that Parfit would persist longer than he would have if his cells were removed and not replaced. It is plausible, in fact, that this would result in a definite point in the series where Parfit would cease to exist. Since the tendency which determines Parfit's persistence is presumably realized physically, it is quite possible that this would be suddenly lost with the removal of a certain batch of cells. Parfit claims that the sudden loss of his identity in the series would be unknowable since there *"could never be any evidence"* for it (his emphasis).[194] But what counts as evidence depends upon how to interpret experience with the concept of identity, which has been our over-arching concern. There could be no evidence for it *if* we assume with Parfit that the evidence would have to come in the form of a sudden change in personality. But if the evidence could consist of empirical data which reveal that the underlying physical basis for the relevant tendency has been lost, it might well be, as I have suggested, that we could know empirically a definite point in the series where Parfit ceases to

---

194. Ibid., p. 239.

exist even if he is followed by a person very similar to him at his end.

Although Parfit ostensibly offers a different argument from Hume's for his "short" view of the self, we have seen that he silently falls back on the very metaphysics that underlies Hume's view of personal identity. Although we have found reason for rejecting this metaphysics, I admit that the "short" view of the self may still have serious appeal to many. But we must be critical about the source of this appeal. Let us put the "short" view in its most favorable light. Following Parfit, this seems most plausible when we consider the loss of deep affections or ideals. It seems that in changing with respect to what is of most importance to us, it is as if we die or become a different person. Although we may be tempted to say such things, there is surely the sense that this is just a dramatic way of expressing the matter. Parfit's whole position is in effect to deny that this is just a way of speaking and to defend to some extent its literal truth. It is only if we can somehow see it as literally correct that it will have the practical implication of shrinking our sense of responsibility. But how do we decide whether to take this way of speaking as literal or merely dramatic? Our approach has been to develop a metaphysics on independent grounds, which are as firm as we can find. In the absence of an established metaphysics, I suppose that there is nothing particularly implausible about the "short" view. But as I will now try to show, our metaphysics provides a way of thinking of identity over time that counts clearly in favor of the "longer" view.

According to our account, we are justified in re-identifying a continuant over time to apply rules which link states which are causally connected in such a way as to provide support for our direct empirical judgments. This does not mean that whenever a future state causally depends upon a previous one that we are justified in seeing one continuant throughout, for the case may involve one thing affecting another. As we saw in the sixth chapter, when one billiard ball deflects another, it is better to admit that the future state of the ball which is hit depends upon the state of a distinct ball than to admit that there is an "extraordinary" ball which persists throughout this transaction. The reason was that it is simpler to stick with the ordinary balls, since the rules which apply to them explain all the same events, whereas the rules that would be required for the "extraordinary" ball would be more complicated and of less generality. So also, when one person speaks to another, the first makes judgments that affect the other, but this is a case of one thing affecting another, for reasons analogous to that of the billiard balls. Acknowledging an "extraordinary" person who is identical with both the person speaking and the one listening would involve extraordinary rules of identity in addition to those rules which already adequately explain the personal transaction. Although Parfit, as we have seen, does not think that in a normal human life like that of the Russian's there is literally a succession of selves, it will be useful to discuss this more extreme view first.

The problem with this extreme view is that counting distinct persons would also require new rules, for no good reason, which would enable us to link the states of these persons. Suppose that the youth loses his Socialist ideals by rational persuasion, say, by becoming convinced that Socialism concentrates political power in a manner reminiscent of Fascism. Even if we disagree with his reasoning, we can see how it *seems* rational to him, even if this involves seeing him as ignorant or confused.[195] In seeing his change in ideals as something which is brought about by reasoning, we see how a future state of his, his disenchantment with Socialism, is dependent upon an earlier state, his previous deliberation. If we literally distinguish two persons, then we must see one person affecting the other, as one billiard ball moves another. We must see, not the Russian youth becoming persuaded of the evils of Socialism, but his ceasing to exist with the loss of his ideals and being replaced by an elder whom he affects in accordance with new rules, which link their various states. The reason why we ought not to think this is that it is unnecessarily complicated. Just as with the billiard balls, all that happens is sufficiently well covered by the old rules which apply, in this case, to normal persons. We should remember that the sort of change that explains the political conversion is witnessed in less dramatic but numerous other cases. The Russian youth will be involved in many other changes brought about by his own rational reflection. By seeing the loss of Socialism as an instance of this same general phenomenon, the situation is simplified.

---

195. I discuss this sort of thing more in Doepke 1990.

The alternative forced on us by the "succession of selves" view is to admit that in addition to the many smaller changes brought about through rational reflection there are others (such as the effect of the young Russian's deliberations upon the elder's political views) which are brought about by a quite new kind of effect, which must accordingly be governed by a new kind of rule. There is no reason to admit this alternative since this supposedly new kind of effect is already covered in the old ontology as due to the same kind of change as involved in the other instances.

The problem with taking the "succession of selves" view literally is not merely that there is no reason to do so; the fact that it unnecessarily complicates the rules that we must apply means that its rules will be not as well-supported. The general point was explained by Harrison and we saw how it applied in the case of the billiard balls. By admitting only ordinary billiard balls we were able to see all their events as covered by the same rule (for example, that such things would tend to retain their shape). This rule had greater generality, since all the various bouncings and rollings of the balls were covered by it. And as Harrison explained, such rules are better supported because they are confirmed by the greater number of instances that they cover. Our ordinary view of the self is simpler than the "succession of selves" view. By allowing that we persist even through changes in deep affections and ideals we can see these changes and many others as of a piece. This is possible by seeing ourselves, not as the Russian youth does, as essentially striving to promote a specific ideal, but more generally, as changing ourselves through rational reflection. Suppose for the moment that it is this more general tendency which determines our identity. It is easy to see, in light of our general metaphysics, why this view is superior to that of the "succession of selves." Since this more general tendency is witnessed in more cases, the claim that we conform to it is better supported: every observable act which would support the claim that the Russian youth is striving for Socialism would also support the claim that he tends to change himself through rational persuasion; but such events as his political conversion also conform to the more general tendency (to change himself through rational reflection) but not to the more specific one (to strive for Socialism).

As we have seen, Parfit himself does not really subscribe to the literal version of the "succession of selves" view; he holds that the Russian youth is identical with the elder Russian, but that this is relatively trivial, since it is based on overlapping psychological connections which have collectively eroded over time. What is useful about discussing the literal version of the "succession of selves" view is that it brings to light the fact that our general metaphysics always favors a "longer" view (other things being equal). This is because (when other things are equal) a "longer" view of our identity provides a more general rule of identity which is thereby better supported by applying to more instances. When other things are equal, to opt for a "shorter" view is to complicate the rules unnecessarily, so that they are not as well-supported. Once we have clearly in view what justifies applying the concept of identity over time (according to our account) there is a strong presumption in favor of "lengthening" identity. The fact that psychological connections are broken should not bother us in the least. This means only that there is apparent change; but we have rejected the Humean metaphysics which construes all such change on the model of destruction. The fact that we can see such changes as being governed by a more general tendency of change, such as a natural tendency to change oneself through rational reflection, provides reason to re-identify the same entity, the same person. And there is nothing trivial about this re-identification. The identity of each continuant in our metaphysics is a matter of how it brings about its own future. If its own internal tendency to create its future propels it through dramatic changes, the fact that these changes occur does not at all diminish the basis for the claim of identity.

I have said that our general metaphysics provides a presumption in favor of "longer" views of identity. Of course, this presumption can be defeated. In the sixth chapter we saw, for example, that the epistemically primary continuants which are countenanced by our metaphysics cannot persist by being uniquely copied. Since we are among these continuants, this means, unfortunately, that we cannot be resurrected by having God or advanced scientists make single replicas of ourselves. Although the view that we can persist through unique copying is "longer," it is defeated by other considerations. We also saw in that chapter that making a thing of the same kind from the same matter, such as a toy from the same building blocks, is not a way of recreating the same thing. Although this would "lengthen" the identity of the first object made from that matter, there would be insufficient reason to do so, since the states of the second thing would not really confirm the presence of states of the first thing. So there are various considerations which defeat a "longer" view. But when there are not such considerations, we should attempt to reach out with our identifications of continuants in general. What this means is that when considering what determines the identity of a thing, we should *generalize* as much as possible. If we thought of a rubber ball as something which is essentially spherical, then it would cease to exist when hitting the floor in a bounce and another rubber ball would come into existence when the spherical shape returned. But we can see its retention of shape as being a specific manifestation of a more general tendency to strive to be in that shape, a tendency which is also witnessed when the ball resists deformation and then brings itself back into the shape of a sphere. The fact that something strives to be in that shape is a more general fact than that it is in that shape, better supported by being observed in more instances. To see in what our identity consists, we should therefore ask how general a view of our identity is defensible.

In the first chapter I was critical of Locke's argument from the *de dicto* fact that, as self-aware, we have certain mental tendencies, to the *de re* claim that these determine our identity. I did not deny the *de re* claim but only insisted that it be better supported. And we saw that there are quite different ways of subscribing to the general idea of Locke's that our identity is "determined" by our self-awareness. What I want now to develop is one kind of Lockean view, supported by our general metaphysics. There is certainly something attractive in Locke's idea that the fact that I have that self-awareness which is expressed in I-thoughts is intimately involved in my identity over time. In the first chapter we were critical of this idea on the Kantian ground that the necessary appearance in memory of persistence over time does not provide a priori ensurance of actual persistence. But even when we keep this important objection in mind, there is still attraction to the Lockean idea. The reason, I think, is that our I-thoughts provide the most *basic way* of knowing of our identity. This is not to say that this access is incorrigible (Kant's example of consciousness being passed from one subject to another showed that it is not). The point is simply that I can think of myself only if I can have I-thoughts, but that while thinking of myself this way, I can coherently wonder about which of a quite broad range of conceptions of my identity is the true one. This is what gives rise to the whole problem of personal identity. Because I-thoughts are the most basic way of thinking of oneself, any account of personal identity must eventually relate a conception of our identity over time to ourselves as expressed in I-thoughts. If, then, there is some tendency to bring about one's own future states which is associated with the capacity for self-awareness, then we know that every self-aware creature, while self aware, will have this tendency, at least. To suppose without argument that such a tendency determines our identity would be to make that "slide" of which we have been critical. But, as a tendency to contribute to one's own future, it would be the kind of consideration that would make it a *candidate* in our general metaphysics for what is determinative of our identity. My strategy for defending a certain specific version of the general Lockean idea will be to indicate such a tendency and then see to what extent it can be "lengthened" or generalized.

What do we do, as self-aware beings, which explains how we contribute to our own future? In being self-aware we have direct knowledge that we possess certain characteristics. This knowledge is not of course like that of the feature-placing brute, who sees but does not know it sees. Self-awareness essentially involves making a judgment, in Harrison's sense, of being conscious of selecting a certain proposition as true. I know right now that I am seeing a computer, striking the keys and sitting up. It is not merely that my knowledge of these states reveals itself in my expectations, as my dog Argus's knowledge of where the food is shows up in his travellings. I am conscious of my selection of these propositions over their negations. What I want to emphasize is that this sort of selection is an activity of mine in which I am alone responsible for the way I become. Only I make my own judgments. As with the acorn which needs many surrounding elements to exercise its distinctive activity (of growth to an oak tree), I of course need an environment in which to exercise judgment. But when I do make a judgment, the fact that I come to be a certain way (accepting one proposition instead of its negation) is explainable only by reference to my own activity, the selection in question. The benefit of this knowledge is, of course, that it provides the materials for me to make inferences. I might infer from the fact that I see the computer that the power is on in the house or I might infer that I ought to change what I have typed. When discussing Harrison's account of judgment, we saw that a judger will make inferences since he will need to think of his judgments as non-arbitrary and hence inferable from facts which support these original judgments. Since these inferences will take the form of judgments, I want to say simply that self-awareness involves a tendency to make "judgments" and be understood to include in this the making of inferences. It is important to see also that the self-aware creature thus has a certain tendency to contribute to its own future states. When inferring, for example, that the power is on in the house from the fact that I see the computer, I come to think about the power only as a result of my own activity of making an inference. And even when I make the original direct judgment itself, I come to be a certain way only because of something I alone do. The reason for saying that the self-aware creature has a certain "tendency" (and not merely that these things happen to it) is that reference to the self-aware creature is essential in explaining how it becomes. In the same way we must suppose that the acorn has a tendency to grow into an oak tree. If it had no such tendency its growth would be the result of entirely external forces.

What this establishes is only the *de dicto* truth that self-awareness fundamentally involves the tendency to make judgments. Since this is a tendency to contribute to one's own future, it is, according to our metaphysics, a good candidate for what constitutes our identity. Although I believe that this tendency is, in a certain way, the one that is fundamental to being self-aware, I want to show that this will include other tendencies. The reason why self-awareness so clearly involves the tendency to make judgments (and inferences) is that this is evident when we consider the self-aware creature from the point of view in virtue of which it has this awareness. But as Kant showed, to have a defensible account of the identity of such creatures, we will have to know them as well objectively, as physical objects. As such, there will be many tendencies that they have, such as that of resisting pressure and of reflecting light. Since these tendencies pertain to them merely as material objects, however, they will be shared by those objects which constitute them, and thus do not promise to be helpful in determining the identity of the self-aware creatures. But the tendency to act from practical decisions would surely seem to belong only to the self-aware creature itself. Once we admit more than one object in the same place, the fact that a certain property is instantiated in a place does not determine its bearer, and it becomes philosophically challenging to show whether the same thing bears different properties found there. We need to know on which donkey to pin the tail. We saw that in Dretske's analysis of behavior, a thing behaves when the cause of a process is "within" the thing. With more than one thing in a place, this cannot be a literal matter of where in space it is. Now it seems clear that only the self-aware creature will be the one making the practical decisions, for these, it seems, are precisely what enable us to tell that a self-aware creature is physically present. The most obvious reason for thinking this, it seems, is that the practical decisions themselves issue from the presence of certain judgments. I decide to change what I have typed because I have judged that I ought to do this, since I have typed something wrong. This explains in what sense the tendency to make judgments is more fundamental than the tendency to make practical decisions, even though the creature who makes judgments will (as a knowable physical being) necessarily make practical decisions.

My main point in arguing that practical decisions issue from judgments about reasons is really to show that practical decisions are made by the same being who makes the judgments, the self-aware creature. I am sure no one will doubt this, but it seems desirable to see why this is so. The reason why I want to tie the practical decisions securely to just the self-aware being is simply that I want a more adequate and realistic characterization of the tendency to contribute to one's own future that is conferred by self-awareness. In being self-aware we not only make judgments and inferences but act in the physical world. We also resist pressure and reflect light but these are due to our physical nature and not our self-awareness. I will accordingly call the tendency to contribute to one's future that is associated with self-awareness the tendency to make "rational" decisions, understood as either decisions about what to think or about what to do, and I will leave quotes on "rational" to remind us that these may be woefully short of a more ideal form of rationality.

I have emphasized in this chapter that our metaphysics makes a strong, though defeasible, presumption in favor of "long" views of identity. I do not at this moment want to establish that the tendency to make "rational" decisions is what determines our identity. It is important to realize that this is not necessary to decide against Parfit's relatively "short" view of our identity. The question I want now to consider is whether the view that our identity is at least as "long" as it would be if the tendency to make "rational" decisions is what determines our identity is theoretically preferable to Parfit's "short" view. Maybe it is even "longer." We will consider that question later. Since we have seen that there is a strong presumption in favor of "long" views, the crucial question now is whether there is reason to defeat this presumption in the present case, by opting for the "shorter" view of Parfit. We have seen that there are some considerations that favor a "shorter" view. So the question now is whether such considerations can be mounted to say that our identity is non-trivially preserved only as long as deep affections and ideals are possessed, so that we should not say that it non-trivially extends as least as long as the tendency to make "rational" decisions is preserved.

It seems to me rather plain that no such considerations exist. Although dramatic changes in values are impressive to us, they are metaphysically not different from ordinary alterations. The point is basically the same one I made when arguing against the "succession of selves" view. The tendency to make "rational" decisions is exhibited not only in the pursuit of certain values, such as the promotion of Socialism, but is exhibited even in the change of values. This means that, however important a certain value is to a person, we *can* regard its possession as an *accident*. To say that we ought to favor "long" views of identity is equivalent to saying that we ought to regard properties as accidents unless there are special reasons not to. We ought to regard actually being in the shape of a sphere as an accident of a rubber ball, since this allows us to explain, in terms of an essential tendency to return to that shape, its spherical shape after repeated bounces. This is quite analogous to explaining the possession of different values at different times of life by an underlying tendency to make "rational" decisions, especially judgments. Even if Methuselah does change many times in personality and character, so long as we can make sense of these changes by seeing him throughout as a person who makes judgments, more or less reflectively, we ought to consider the various traits of personality and character spread out through his long life as accidents, the losses of which in no way erode the basis of his identity through time. I am not denying that there is such a general phenomenon as the erosion of the basis of identity, and soon I will give examples where I think this really occurs. But the point now is that when there is a tendency, such as the tendency to make "rational" decisions, that clearly and unproblematically explains the possession of certain properties, such as the attachment to Socialism, then we are in just that sort of situation in which, according to our whole metaphysics, we should count the properties as accidental ones. And this means that identity will be preserved non-trivially through their losses. The fundamental reason for doing this, to repeat, is that it allows us to apply rules of identity that have greater generality and thus reach out to more instances for more confirmation.

The completes my case against the "short" view of our identity described so well by Parfit. I admitted that the view does not seem implausible in the absence of an established metaphysics. And I believe that it is really rather obvious that the metaphysics we have established through transcendental argument counts against it. The hard part was establishing the general metaphysics. I emphasized that to decide against Parfit's "short" view we did not have to establish what determines our identity; we had to show only that there is reason not to "shorten" it from a "longer" view which counts the possession of values as accidental. But let us turn now to the question of what more we can establish with our metaphysics about the "length" of our identity.

I have argued that our identity is as least as "long" as the tendency to make "rational" decisions is preserved. This idea is, however, somewhat vague. It was clear enough what was meant when we considered changes with respect to what is important to us when this occurs through rational reflection. But what about an extraordinary case such as that described in the first chapter of complete and irreparable amnesia? If not only my memories but all my skills and traits of personality and character were expunged, but my brain were kept intact, and my body became that of an Afghan rebel, would he be me? We saw that Wiggins would say that he would be since he thinks that our identity is determined by the fact that we are members of a certain biological species; and we saw that Williams and Johnston hold similar views. Now the question is whether the idea that the "preservation of the tendency to make 'rational' decisions" should be interpreted so as to cover such complete breaks in psychology or whether it should mean that there must be a kind of psychological continuity, as seen, for example, in the actual connection between the elder Russian's political beliefs and the young Russian's reflections about Socialism and Fascism.

I think it is clear that our account favors the identification in question. For it is central to our account that what determines the identity of each of our continuants is that they are *responsible* for some kind effect on their own future. They are fundamentally the *sources* of the activity that is associated with their kind. This contrasts with a Lockean view, such as Parfit holds, in which personal identity is determined by a relation which obtains between the contents of the mental states themselves. On this view, what matters is not so much what *causes* the states, but how the states conform to this "surface" relation obtaining only between themselves. *Many* philosophers subscribe to this "surface" view of personal identity. It was, in fact, the way Locke looked at our identity. Recall his view that if the present mayor of Queenborough has apparent memories of Socrates's life, this makes him identical with Socrates. Our metaphysics rejects entirely any such view of identity for epistemically primary things in general, including ourselves. As I explained in the sixth chapter, although we have adopted in effect Locke's view of what determines the identity of material substances, we have rejected his view of personal identity because (in light of Kant's example of the billiard balls) we have required that our own identity be determined by our membership in a kind of material substance. This means that our identity is determined by an underlying real essence which explains our manifest properties. Mental states are merely manifestations of an underlying tendency to produce them, a tendency which is no doubt realized in a physical structure which can survive complete breaks in actual psychology. This is why I would be identical with the Afghan rebel.

I admit that this is counterintuitive, but the intuition that he is a different person from me can be variously explained. Aside from this, however, it is important to realize is that even if he is me, it does not follow that he is responsible for my misdeeds. When I argued for the connection between personal identity and responsibility I said that if I realize that someone is *distinct* from me there is no reason to feel responsible for his deeds. It does not follow that if I realize I am *identical* with someone I must acknowledge responsibility for what he does. The reason why I normally take responsibility for my future self is that my current decisions cause me to do what I will do, and I cannot consistently take responsibility for the current decision and deny that my future self, who will carry them out, is blameless. But the Afghan rebel is utterly beyond the influence of my current decisions, since these will be wiped out before my body is mentally revitalized in Afghanistan. There is accordingly no evident reason for my responsibility to extend to him, even if, as I maintain, he is identical with me. This may well explain the intuition that he is a different person.

I have not said that our general metaphysics has been developed enough to deal with all conceivable problems of continuant identity. But I would like to show that it offers a clear and even intuitive answer to one of the trickiest problems of personal identity. When discussing personal fission, effected by separating the two halves of the brain and housing each in different bodies, it seemed that the original person ceases to exist, since this person cannot be identical with either offshoot and it is arbitrary to identify the original with just one. Parfit imagines extending this case so that the two offshoots later fuse.[196] He imagines a case in which, by lifting his eyebrow, he undergoes fission (in order to work on a physics problem by different strategies), but then the two halves fuse as before when the person with either brain half lowers the eyebrow he controls. Parfit presents the case to illustrate the hopelessness of trying to give a definite, nonarbitrary answer to how many persons are involved, and thus to support his Humean view that persons are identified in relation to their

---

196. Parfit 1984, pp. 246–48.

mental states. Since I argued against this in Chapter 2, we should see how to settle the question of number. It seems that when we think that the original person undergoing fission ceases to exist this is because we think of the operation as permanent and irreversible. When this is denied, as in the present case, there is surely a strong intuition to re-identify the original person after the fusion. It may seem that I am committed to denying this, owing to my rejection of intermittent existence in Chapter Six. But I am not. What I want to argue for is a solution that Parfit does not consider. First, I claim that Parfit would continue to exist throughout the whole period. This is because personal persistence, as we have just seen, is not determined by "surface" relations between mental states but by the preservation of the source of these states. Now, Parfit's brain does continue to live throughout the fission and fusion, and so we can say that he does not cease to exist with the fission but continues to exist all along. But this does not force us to identify him with either or both of the persons who come into existence with the fission and go out of existence with the fusion. Although Parfit exists when the brain halves are separate, it is not he who is conscious then, but two distinct persons, each of whom has a different brain half. The reason for counting these as distinct persons is that each will have a point of view just like that discussed in the second chapter, a perspective of self-awareness that cannot be denied and cannot be identified with that of the other. Since it is arbitrary to identify either with Parfit, neither can be Parfit. Of course we do not have to overemphasize the difference between Parfit and these temporary persons. But neither is the idea that each offshoot would look forward to fusion with equanimity an entirely plausible one to me. Nevertheless, the point I wish to highlight is that our account allows us to see the persistence of a person throughout fission and fusion without admitting intermittent existence. And it does this because it claims that preservation of the source of self-awareness is enough to determine personal persistence.

In arguing for this general position, I have argued for another "lengthening" of our identity. The "preservation" of our tendency to make "rational" decisions should be understood to mean the preservation of the causal basis of this tendency which is no doubt realized in the brain. This basis is the fountain from which spring our mental states and the fountain can persist even with radical interruptions in its flow. It is clear enough that this basis is preserved in the case of the Afghan rebel who has my body and in the case of fission, where this is not permanent and irreparable. But there are other cases in which it is not obvious whether or not this basis is preserved. I will discuss two kinds of cases which may represent true cases in which the basis of identity is eroded so that the claim of identity in these cases is somewhat trivial.

Perhaps the most obvious kind of case is that in which, as a result of brain damage, a person suffers permanently a great diminishment of mental capacity, but yet is still capable of self-awareness. I am sure that the intuition of most people is that although the person still exists it is, to some extent, "as if" he or she has died. It is easy to see how our account vindicates this intuition. Since a tendency to form "rational" decisions will have been preserved, the retention of self-awareness shows that it really is the same person. But since the basis for this tendency will have been literally diminished, we can use the language of Parfit and Hume to say that the claim of identity, though true, is somewhat trivial.

In my second sort of case, we are to imagine that our bodies have undergone a radical transformation, as in some sort of science fiction fantasy. I will argue that in cases in which the transformation is significant, but not extreme, the claim of identity, though true, is somewhat trivial. To see why this is so, let us first attempt to imagine extreme bodily transformations, in which personal identity would appear be lost even if psychological continuity is somehow preserved. Consider, for example, the ridiculous science fiction transformation of a man into a giant fly who nonetheless somehow preserves the memories, beliefs, desires and so forth of the man. Needless to say, the strict Lockean must smile on this as a case of personal survival. It is equally clear that Wiggins would deny that identity is preserved, since a clear consequence of his view is that we cannot change in biological species: if our identity is determined by the fact that we are humans, an operation that would gradually turn us into members of another species would destroy our identity. Wiggins would emphasize (following Hegel) that the way in which our rationality is revealed is due largely to the kind of body that we have and hence the kind of biological species to which we belong.[197] Hegel complained that the idea that souls could migrate involved a "false abstraction." I take his point to be that minds as we know them must appear in the actions of a certain kind of body. To suppose that the same mind could appear in a very different body would be like supposing that the atomic structure of iron could be found throughout a bar of soap. But since that atomic structure just is the structure which (in normal circumstances) gives rise to the manifest properties of iron, it is absurd to suppose that (in these circumstances) it can give rise to the manifest properties of soap. Similarly, to suppose that a mind could occupy a very different kind of body would be to make the mistake of Cartesian dualism, of failing to see the necessary *connection* between the mind and its effects in a certain kind of body. We know a certain mind only if we know it as the basis of the behavior of a certain kind of body. This is really due to the Kantian point (discussed in the first chapter) that knowledge of one's mind in self-awareness must be supportable with an objective conception of oneself as a physical object, a body of a certain kind. To suppose that this same mind—the mind of the same person—could appear in an entirely different kind of body is to forget how we know in the first place about *which* mind (or person) it is that we are thinking. To revert to our previous language, this means that whether "the basis"—the *same* basis—of the tendency to form "rational" decisions is preserved depends on whether the same kind of body is preserved.

I have not agreed with Wiggins that we must belong to our biological species. I have instead tried to explain the rationale for this view, and what we have seen is that it depends on the idea that our persistence depends on retaining "the same kind of body." This does not seem to me to be nearly as clear as the idea of remaining of the same biological species. Even in the case of the man turning into a giant fly, it is an important part of the story that the mind of the fly-man is still able to work the body of the fly much like a human body, so that the case does not represent one of an "extremely" different body. It would seem that the extreme would be reached only when the mind occupied the new body with no capacity to animate it, since

---

197. Wiggins 1980, Ch. 6. See the quotation from Hegel on page 148.

it would have such different parts. But this, it seems, is incoherent, since we would have no basis for saying that it is really "occupying" the new body in question, *as* its mind. The upshot of these considerations, I suggest, is this. We are able to determine that our mind, or the basis of our tendency to form "rational" decisions, is "preserved" only so long as we can tell that "the same kind of body" is preserved. But we can imagine ever more significant transformations in our body that would diminish the basis for saying that it is the same body. When this happens, by the argument above—that this basis of our identity can be identified only via the kind of body we have—the claim that we continue to exist, though true, will be somewhat trivial. An interesting example to consider is a switch in one's sex (down to the chromosome). Surely, one would not be a distinct person, and yet we might well feel that the claim of identity is not as full-blooded as it is in normal persistence. The present argument perhaps lends credence to that feeling.

That popular example of the brain in the vat might seem to constitute a counterexample to the idea just defended—that it is essential to us to have a certain kind of body—for in such a state one's brain would be one's body. It might well be said in reply to this objection that it is the exception that proves the rule. For we recognize the brain only as the organ which mentally activates a certain kind of body. Cases in which there is less reason to say that it is the "same kind of body" would be those in which mental capacities would be differently manifested, not those in which drastic amputation has prevented any overt manifestation. Scientists have imagined forms of intelligent life in very different conditions accordingly developing very different sorts of bodies, for example, creatures in the form of jellyfish traveling through a chlorine atmosphere. What I think is correct in the position of Hegel and Wiggins is that if it were somehow possible to undergo a radical transformation into such a creature while still preserving self-awareness, the claim of identity, even if true, would be largely trivial, since the basis of this claim would have greatly eroded.

In the sixth chapter I argued that epistemically primary continuants must have criteria of identity over time which do not allow branching and I explained how our "Aristotelian" conception of them met this requirement. I want now to discuss some variations on the fission example to show how our account has some more intuitive results. Suppose that a person loses just one half of his brain while the other half remains intact with his body. It might seem that I am committed to denying that the original person is identical with the person with the remaining brain half. After all, it is something of an accident that the other half was destroyed and not merely separated, and if this happened there would presumably be branching, as in the example of the physics exam. So, it might be said, the relation of the original person to the person with the surviving brain half in the actual world would be just like the relation he would have had to each of the persons in the non-actual situation in which fission occurs. What this objection misses is the importance for personal identity of preserving the same kind of body. When all that happens is that the person loses one brain half, it is relatively clear that the same kind of body is preserved. Assuming that the remaining half would allow the person to animate the same parts of the body in the same ways, the relation of the original person to the resulting one is strikingly different from the one that would have obtained if fission had occurred. In fission, either the two brain halves would be cut off from acting on the body, so that there is just thinking (as in Parfit's physics exam) or they would animate different parts of the bodies. In the first case, their bodies would be nothing more than the brain halves themselves, and in the second, they would be something like Siamese twins. In neither case would there be the smooth retention of the same kind of body which, I submit, is what makes the loss of one brain half *within* the human body seem a relatively trivial affair. Suppose, by contrast, that one loses a brain half while only a brain in a vat. This hardly seems as sure a case of survival, and the reason, I suggest, is that it is not a clear case in which the same kind of body would be preserved.

Our allowance that certain changes would destroy or erode the basis of identity may seem to revive hope in the idea that Parfit's "short" view of the self is correct. If all this means is that there is an abstract possibility that I have been wrong, I am always willing to concede that. The point to bear in mind is that reasons have been offered for ruling out that definite possibility. Most generally, we have opposed the Humean metaphysical outlook that construes all change on the model of destruction. More specifically, we have seen (what is obvious) that even changes in deeply held values are explainable by the more general tendency to make presumably rational decisions. And our laboriously constructed metaphysics then favored opting for the more general tendency as what determines, non-trivially, identity even through these changes. Changes in values, however dramatic, are utterly *natural:* they are clear examples of changes engendered internally by consciously rational beings. By contrast, externally induced changes in biological species or sex may seem to alter the very physical foundation of conscious rationality in such a way as to call into question whether identity is really being preserved. Our own metaphysics provides a way of seeing how the two sorts of cases are relevantly different.

I have argued for the "shortening" of our identity in certain cases of brain damage and imagined cases of changes in biological species and sex. These are, I suggest, at least plausible examples in which the basis of identity would be eroded. What we have been considering more generally is how to interpret the idea that the tendency to make "rational" decisions is "preserved." Since this is the tendency to contribute to one's own future that is fundamentally associated with self-awareness, and since our general metaphysics favors "long" views, the "preservation" of this tendency is sufficient for personal identity. I want now to consider whether this is necessary for personal identity. If it is, then with the loss of this tendency the person ceases to exist. Our identity will be "shorter" than it would be if this tendency is an accident, manifesting some more general tendency.

To consider whether this is so, I want to use the fact that having the capacity for "rational" decisions is equivalent to being consciously rational. Since we saw that it was really the capacity for judgments that made possible practical decisions and that any judger, to be known as a physical object, would make such decisions, I want to explain the equivalence of having the capacity for "rational" decisions and conscious rationality by considering specifically how conscious rationality and the capacity for judgment are necessarily linked. As Harrison showed, in making a judgment the subject must think of himself as having reasons, at least available, in order for the consciousness of his selection of the proposition to appear non-arbitrary. This means that conscious rationality is necessary for judgment. Conversely, since to be consciously rational is to think of reasons as such, judgment is necessary for conscious rationality, since the thought of having reasons just is what makes us conscious of our judgments. Because of this equivalence, and the equivalence of the capacities for judgment and for "rational" decision, I will approach the question of whether the tendency to make "rational" decisions is accidental by considering what I think is the most plausible candidate for that of which conscious rationality would be a manifestation. Since "conscious rationality" is defined as the capacity to be aware of reasons as such, I suggest that the most plausible way of further generalizing our identity would be to see this awareness itself as merely accidental. I have previously described "primitive" rationality as merely having reasons, and when I discussed the creature, such as perhaps my dog, Argus, whose cognitions were confined to feature-placing, I explained how such a creature would be primitively rational. Conscious rationality results merely by adding the awareness of reasons to the having of reasons. Since considering this awareness as merely an accident of the associated primitively rational being appears to be the simplest way of generalizing conscious rationality, it appears also to be the most plausible. It is clear that it would also result in a "longer" view of our identity. If the awareness of reasons is merely accidental, then its loss does not destroy identity. It is reasonably clear from what we know empirically that there is a period in late pregnancy in which the fetus lacks self-awareness, and hence conscious rationality, but, in being sentient, is primitively rational. And there are also cases at the end of life, involving cerebral destruction, in which conscious but not primitive rationality is lost. If in becoming aware of reasons we do not come into existence but merely acquire a new accident, then we are identical with at least the sentient fetus from which we came and would be identical with the sentient body after cerebral destruction. Our identity would be "longer" than if we are essentially consciously rational.

In the last chapter I argued that bodies of sentient organisms, understood as things which are essentially striving to preserve a certain organic structure, are themselves sentient, and thus primitively rational. If conscious rationality is merely an accident, then we are identical with our bodies. Persons just are such bodies, so called when these bodies become aware of reasons as such. Shoemaker presented a now-famous example that seems to show decisively that we are not identical with our bodies.[198] If the brains of two persons were switched, it is difficult to avoid the conclusion that the people would have switched bodies, which means that they are not identical with their bodies. This is an example of what Wiggins would call "branching," which is surely sufficient to show numerical distinctness. And it seems clearly enough to involve bodies in our sense, of being things which are essentially striving to preserve a certain organic structure (by circulating blood, maintaining temperature and so forth). In preserving the structure of the human body it seems just as possible to switch brains as any other organ. But our attraction to the Lockean view certainly creates a strong intuition that we go with our brains. It must be admitted, however, that we do not know if such operations are physically possible, and some philosophers, especially Kathleen Wilkes, have chided others for drawing conclusions from merely imaginary cases not known to be physically possible.[199] I therefore want to raise the question of whether to show the distinctness of ourselves with our bodies it is *necessary* for such brain switches to be physically possible. I must say that even if this were shown to be physically possible, it is a strange way to argue for the distinctness of persons from their bodies. Surely there could be another species of rational life in which the central nervous system is spread so thoroughly throughout the body that brain transfers would be physically impossible. Would this mean that they would be identical with their bodies but we are not? It strikes me as philosophically counterintuitive to suppose that the answer would depend upon the biological species.

In arguing in the last chapter that sentience was insufficient to constitute the sentient creature as an entity distinct from its body, I argued that sentience appeared to be no more than a power which normally served the body's essential tendency to preserve the organic structure in question. Since the desires and perceptions and feelings of my dog, Argus, evidently function normally to preserve (or perpetuate) his bodily structure, there is no reason to think that they constitute him as an entity distinct from his body. Their presence does not

---

198. Shoemaker 1963, pp. 23–25.
199. Wilkes 1988.

seem to reveal an external force in potential opposition to the body. Now, it is certainly clear that self-awareness can aid in the preservation of the organic structure, and it hard not to think that this is why it was produced in evolution. But though it undoubtedly originated in the service of the body, it does not follow that it must have remained that way and could not have sublimated. I think that in light of what we have established so far, it is easy to see why we are distinct from our bodies, even if we cannot "branch" from them. The main clue comes from Plato's argument for the fact that the soul has parts: the very argument that we used repeatedly in the last chapter to decide whether or not a putative case of constitution was genuine. The argument for thinking that reason and appetite were distinct parts of the soul was that they are sometimes in opposition. I modified this idea to apply to cases of constitution. Since the behavior of the constituted object could not be simply inferred from that of the constituting object(s), the existence of the constituted object would have to be admitted. This was analogous to why we distinguish two billiard balls: when one billiard ball hits another we cannot explain the behavior of the other without mentioning the ball which hit it. By contrast, we can explain the freezing of water without mentioning the ice which is present, since the presence of the ice simply follows from what we say about the water. Now, it is really obvious that there are sometimes cases in which we are in this kind of "opposition" to our bodies, and these are exactly the kinds of cases that Plato had in mind when arguing that reason is distinct from appetite. As consciously rational, as capable of thinking of reasons as such, we are capable of holding up before us a range of different ideals, different reasons for acting, which need not serve the natural purpose of the body. An exclusive commitment to the health of the body is obviously not the only option for us. In his ethics, Kant makes much about the fact that our "natural purpose" is not to promote happiness (which he construes as the satisfaction of desires), but to obey the demands of rationality. This is certainly reminiscent of the view of Plato and Aristotle that our "function" is to reason. These views say in effect that we ought to aim for something different from what the body aims for. What is important for our present purpose is merely that we can, which is obvious enough. Whenever we do "oppose" the body by acting for an ideal other than that of bodily health, our presence cannot be simply inferred by describing what the body does (maintaining temperature, circulating blood, and so forth). The possibility of so acting, which is frequently empirically confirmed, shows that we are distinct from our bodies, in our sense, even if we cannot "branch" from them.

The fact, argued in the last chapter, that our bodies are sentient and thus primitively rational, and the fact, just argued, that our bodies are not consciously rational show that conscious rationality is not merely an accident; it shows that when awareness of reasons is obtained, something, the person, literally comes into existence. Now, as I mentioned above, it is reasonably clear from empirical evidence that there are times when there are human organisms which are sentient but not consciously rational. At such times, I am claiming, the sentient being is just the body, in our sense. But the body itself does not become aware of reasons, for this, as I have argued, cannot be attributed to the body. No doubt the body changes in some way that explains the fact that a person comes into existence. Similarly, when wooden planks become arranged in such a way that a ship is created, the fact that the planks have this arrangement explains why there exists something useful for sailing. But assuming (as I argued in the last chapter) that the ship is distinct from the planks, then it is the ship and not the planks which does the sailing. Similarly, when some watch parts are arranged to make a watch, it is the watch, and not the parts, which tell time, even though the parts are arranged in such a way which explains why there is a watch there. So, the body will no doubt have some property, such as a neural structure and activity, which explains why there is a person there who is aware of reasons as such, but since this awareness reveals the presence of something in potential opposition to the body, it cannot be attributed to the body.

I am committed to saying that when a person exists, there are two rational beings there: the person and the body. This may seem surprising, but I think it is harmless when we realize the vast gulf that exists between conscious and primitive rationality. What I am claiming is that the body is a brute, such as we have supposed my dog, Argus, to be. The body literally has perceptual experiences, feelings and desires. In having perceptual experiences it thereby has representations, assessable as true or false, and thus qualifies as primitively rational. But the contents of these are reportable (by us) with only feature-placing sentences, which have no internal logical structure, a fact which reflects the absence of the power of inference. The distance of ourselves from such creatures must be fully appreciated to get over the shock of thinking of our own bodies as primitively rational. Above all, we must keep in mind the lack of self-awareness. In the second chapter I supported the common intuition that my I-thoughts belong to just one thing. The fact that the body is only primitively rational is what saves us from the contradiction of supposing that my I-thoughts belong to both myself and my body. In the second chapter I defended the thesis of Strawson that the individuation of all things terminates in self-awareness, expressed in I-thoughts. I differentiate all other things *from* myself by descriptions which relate them uniquely to myself. It is not difficult to see, however, how I differentiate my body from myself. My body, though being like me in possessing my physical characteristics, my perceptual experiences and many of my feelings and desires, is different from me in lacking self-awareness, thereby lacking awareness of its reasons, and in being essentially constrained to strive to preserve its organic structure. Of course my body does not have all of my feelings and desires. The feeling of indignation or gratitude or the desire for justice obviously requires conscious rationality. But since feelings of pain or nausea and desires for water or air plainly serve our body, I claim that we ought to allow that the body shares these with us. They would be left if nothing else but our self-awareness (and all that necessarily attends it) were stripped away. I conclude that even though Descartes was right in thinking of us as distinct from our bodies, the Greeks were right in thinking of our bodies as sentient.

In showing why only I and not my body is consciously rational, I have shown in effect why I and not it make judgments, inferences, practical decisions and enjoy self-awareness. Burke, in arguing for only one thing to a place, realizes that there is a special problem for those of us who distinguish persons from their bodies.[200] He points out that on both reductionist and functionalist versions of materialism a mental event such a particular episode of thinking will be identical with

---

200. Burke 1980.

some physical event. But even though the person and the body will be distinct because of their different persistence conditions these differences seem to pertain to different times, such as their early or late histories, and not the present time in which both the person and the body share the physical event which is supposed to *be* the thought episode. How, then, he asks, can we avoid attributing the thought not only to the person but to the body? I admit that this is a serious problem, mainly because of the argument of the second chapter that shows that my I-thoughts can belong to only one thing. What we need to realize is that in my present solution it is argued that conscious rationality and all that that implies can be attributed to only something of a certain *kind*, associated with certain identity conditions. Even if an event occurs within a body which is identical with a certain thought episode, the thinking can be attributed to only a consciously rational being, whose identity is determined by a tendency to make "rational" decisions; and the body is simply not this kind of being. I am arguing therefore that any adequate materialist version of thinking must take account of the *kind of thing*, understood in terms of identity conditions, in which thinking takes place.

This completes my answer to Rawls. As we saw in the first chapter, he claimed that the philosophy of mind, which presumably addresses metaphysical issues, could show only that some form of psychological continuity underlies personal identity, so that it would be up to ethicists to choose the particular form of continuity that suited their ethical theory. Humeans would say that all forms of continuity would count, so that psychological disconnections would in general erode the basis of personal identity. But for Kantians, who see the person as implementing long-range plans, only the loss (or diminishment) of the capacity to reason would undermine personal identity. Hence, the difference in temporal "length." Ethics, according to Rawls, is "independent" in the sense that ethicists are free to choose which conception of the self they prefer. I charged that this claim of independence was sheer speculation, based merely on skepticism about what could be shown in metaphysics. I claim that by going back and demanding that our metaphysical views be rigorously supported, we have found good reason to support the commonly held "longer" view. In fact, I tried to establish a bit more than was necessary to refute

Parfit, but this only helps to show that even more can be done than Rawls thought was possible. What has interested me so much in Parfit's work is the dependence which he claims of ethics upon metaphysics. His general claim was not that from a metaphysics of personal identity we could derive ethical maxims, but that in *applying* our independently established ethics it matters what sorts of things we are, and this is an issue in metaphysics. Parfit attempted to establish a Humean view of the self that made the application of an ethics like Kant's look in practice more like a form of consequentialism such as Utilitarianism. By defending a "longer" view of the self I have argued for an application more in keeping with what Kant and common sense suppose. But on the general point, I have tried to show that Parfit, and not Rawls, is right: ethics *is* dependent on metaphysics.

My arguments for the practical importance of personal identity have resulted in a complex position which might well be summarized. In the third chapter I distinguished two kinds of concerns that the question of our identity seems to bear upon. There are many desires which are "self-involved" in the sense that their satisfaction requires the involvement of the same person who has them. The extent of one's persistence thereby marks the boundary beyond which there is no hope of satisfying them. There are also claims of desert which seem to depend upon whether it was the same person in the past who can claim compensation or who should face punishment. A view of identity which denies or denigrates the claim of identity with that past person would thereby seem to undermine the claim of desert. To support the common conviction that personal identity is relevant in such cases, I argued that the fact that only I can carry out my decisions is not trivial. This means that when someone is distinct from me, even if he is very much like me, neither of us is responsible for the other's deeds. But it does not mean that I am responsible for all that I may do. Normally I am responsible for my future self since he is the one whom I can animate by making practical decisions. Since after a complete break in psychology, none of my current plans could be carried out, there is no basis for holding him responsible for my current decisions. Some people claim that this break in psychology would not diminish the concern they have for their future self. I found that I do not feel the same, and I explained this, not by denying identity as a result of the loss of concern, but by requiring that in addition to identity, the preservation of my concern requires a psychological connection. The reason why I require identity for this concern is that I find that at least most of my self-involved desires have sprung up in the context of making plans in such a way that I need to conduct my life in certain ways to satisfy them—and only I can carry out my own plans. The argument against Parfit's metaphysics of the self was relevant to normal human life. I do not deny that there can be redeeming factors which justify withholding punishment even when there is the appropriate psychological relation to one's past self. My position is rather that the fact that one has undergone a dramatic change in values does not diminish the metaphysical claim of personal identity and so is itself no excuse. Parfit's "short" view is bound to appeal to those who think of themselves not so much as Kantian agents free to choose among very different ideals but as agents who find themselves situated with deep commitments. Whatever the merits of this may be, my position is that it should not be argued as a metaphysical issue of personal identity, since our account has shown that our identity is in fact rather well described by the Kantian view of the free agent. Those ethicists who favor the more general view of our identity which stresses our capacity for free choice will find repugnant the emphasis on being situated with certain definite commitments. For are we not *responsible* for these? How, then, could our *identity* be bound up with them? Would this not mean that we have no *choice* with respect to them? The "short" view would have diminished responsibility for our deepest commitments. Our metaphysics defends those who find that view repugnant.

Since our journey has taken many steps, it might be helpful to end with an overview. Our main concern has been to defend an account of personal identity, especially one which is sharp enough to decide between the "long" and "short" view of our identity which Rawls associated with Kant, on the one hand, and Hume and Parfit, on the other. Since any account of our identity will involve applying the concept of identity to ourselves, we wanted to know how to apply the concept more generally, to things of other kinds. This led us to construct a more general metaphysics within which we couched a view of our identity. Rather than adopting the popular "method of cases," however, we chose the transcendental method of starting from the austere assumption, as explained by Harrison, that we could make true judgments about the world. Providing such deep justification is not only philosophically desirable but enabled us to rebut the revisionist view of identity espoused by Parfit and Hume. This view is especially provocative because it appears to have important practical consequences with regard to what we can do and to what we can hope for. But this allegation of practical significance was called into question by a generalization of one of Parfit's own arguments. To show that our metaphysical investigation had more than theoretical importance, I argued in the second and third chapters that the boundary of our existence really does limit our responsibility and our hopes. The general metaphysics was developed and defended from the fourth through the eighth chapters. First I defended the reality of persistence by showing that continuants, including ourselves, are the epistemically primary objects of experience. This refuted the general Humean metaphysics which sees only flux: the metaphysics that not only Hume but also Parfit assumed in arguing for his "short" view of the self. The fifth chapter yielded a general rationale for thinking of continuants in the first place: references to them were necessary to apply the rules of confirmation that Harrison had shown were necessary for judgment. Hume had offered two psychological explanations for why we thought of continuants, one based on causation and one on similarity. Our argument in effect showed that causation but not sheer similarity was justificatory. The sixth chapter explained how our "Kantian" epistemology lead to an "Aristotelian" metaphysics. The identity of each of our continuants is determined by a tendency, distinctive of its kind, to contribute to its own future. Although we also found in this chapter that many issues of identity could be decided by the adoption of our metaphysics, we had as yet no way to determine if such a tendency of a thing was truly determinative of its identity. Since this issue is closely related to that of determining if a change is substantial or merely an alteration, the seventh chapter presented a conceptual framework for thinking of substantial change, and more generally of the constitution relation which obtains between a thing and its "matter." Explaining the constitution relation removed obstacles to its acceptance; the eighth chapter showed when we were justified in thinking that it really obtains. For this purpose, the general argument for why we are justified in thinking of continuants in the first place was applied to this special sort of case. We know that objects genuinely come into existence when thinking this enables us to apply a rule of confirmation that in turn enables us see a reason for a judgment that would otherwise be unknown. In Kantian jargon, it enables us to "synthesize the manifold" in a certain way, making a certain link, that could not be made without referring to an object of the kind in question. Since rules of confirmation can, however, be trumped by rules of greater generality, we should endeavor to "lengthen" accounts of identity, to generalize when we can our accounts of conditions of identity. It was precisely this principle which decided against the "short" view of our identity held by Parfit and Hume and in favor of the "long" view of identity supposed by Kant and common sense. A value, though felt to be important to us, is metaphysically possessed only accidentally, since changes with respect to them are clearly explained by the underlying tendency to form "rational" decisions. This tendency, in being mutually linked with the capacity for consciousness of reasons as such, could not be attributed to our bodies. And so we found, though our bodies are "primitively" rational in the sense of having reasons, they are distinct from us, as the "matter" which constitutes us. We come into existence when our bodies make possible the awareness of reasons and cease to exist when this capacity is lost. The "retention" of the tendency to form "rational" decisions can obtain even with radical breaks in psychology, but—against the view of strict Lockeans—it does require the "same kind of body." Impairment of the physical basis for making "rational" decisions and changes in the kind of body one has would erode the basis for making claims of identity, thus rendering them somewhat trivial even if true. But, contrary to what Hume and Parfit held, mere losses of psychological connections are not enough to erode this basis. In the course of normal human life it is, therefore, *not* as if we continually "die a bit." Even through dramatic changes in what is important to us we retain responsibility for our actions; and the prospect of such changes is no cause for despair.

References

Ameriks, Karl. 1982. *Kant's Theory of Mind: An Analysis of the Paralogisms of Pure Reason*. Oxford: Clarendon Press.

Aristotle. 1941a. "Categories." *The Basic Works of Aristotle*, ed. Richard McKeon. New York: Random House.

Aristotle. 1941b. "Metaphysics." *The Basic Works of Aristotle*, ed. Richard McKeon. New York: Random House.

Ayers, Michael. 1991. "Substance: Prolegomena to a Realistic Theory of Identity." *The Journal of Philosophy* 88.2.

Bennett, Jonathan. 1966. *Kant's Analytic*. Cambridge: Cambridge University Press.

Brennan, Andrew. 1988. *Conditions of Identity*. Oxford: Clarendon Press.

Burke, M. B. 1980. "Cohabitation, Stuff and Intermittent Existence." *Mind* 89.

Burke, Michael. 1980. "Dion and Theon: An Essentialist Solution to an Ancient Puzzle." *The Journal of Philosophy* 91.3.

Burke, Michael B. 1992. "Copper Statues and Pieces of Copper: A Challenge to the Standard Account." *Analysis* 52.1.

Burke, Michael. 1994. "On Preserving the Principle of One Object to a Place." *Philosophy and Phenomenological Research* 54.3.

Carnap, Rudolf. 1958. "Empiricism, Semantics and Ontology." *Meaning and Necessity*, second edition. Chicago: University of Chicago Press.

Chisholm, Roderick M. 1976. *Person and Object: A Metaphysical Study*. La Salle, Illinois: Open Court.

Chisholm, Roderick M. 1981. *The First Person: An Essay on Reference and Intentionality*. Minneapolis: University of Minnesota Press.

Daniels, Norman. 1979. "Moral Theory and the Plasticity of Persons." *The Monist* 62.3.

Doepke, Frederick. 1982. "Spatially Coinciding Objects." *Ratio* 24.

Doepke, Frederick. 1986. "The Trees of Constitution." *Philosophical Studies* 49.

Doepke, Frederick. "The Structures of Persons and Artifacts." *Ratio* 29.

Doepke, Frederick. 1989. "The Step to Individuation." *Synthese* 78.

Doepke, Frederick. 1990. "The Endorsements of Interpretation." *Philosophy of the Social Sciences* 20.

Dretske, Fred. 1988. *Explaining Behavior: Reasons in a World of Causes*. Cambridge, Massachusetts: MIT Press.

Dummett, Michael. 1978. "Truth." *Truth and Other Enigmas*. Cambridge, Massachusetts: Harvard University Press.

Dummett, Michael. 1981. *Frege: Philosophy of Language*. Cambridge, Massachusetts: Harvard University Press.

Evans, Gareth.1982. *Varieties of Reference*, ed. J. McDowell. Oxford: Clarendon Press.

Evans, Gareth. 1985. *Collected Papers*. Oxford: Clarendon Press.

Frege, Gottlob. 1966. "Begriffsschrift," Section 8. *Translations from the Philosophical Writings of Gottlob Frege*, eds. Peter Geach and Max Black. Oxford: Basil Blackwell.

Gewirth, Alan. 1978. *Reason and Morality*. Chicago: University of Chicago Press.

Griffin, Nicholas. 1977. *Relative Identity*. Oxford: Clarendon Press.

Guyer, Paul. 1987. *Kant and the Claims of Knowledge*. Cambridge: Cambridge University Press.

Haslanger, Sally. 1989. "Persistence, Change, and Explanation." *Philosophical Studies* 56.

Harrison, Ross. 1974. *On What There Must Be*. Oxford: Clarendon Press.

Hirsch, Eli. 1982. *The Concept of Identity*. New York: Oxford University Press.

Hirsch, Eli. 1991. "Divided Minds." *The Philosophical Review* C. 1.

Hume, David. 1968. *A Treatise of Human Nature*, ed. L. A. Selby-Bigge. Oxford: Clarendon Press.

Irwin, Terence. 1988. *Aristotle's First Principles*. Oxford: Clarendon Press.

Johnston, Mark. 1987. "Human Beings." *The Journal of Philosophy* 84.2.

Johnston, Mark. 1992. "Reasons and Reductionism." *The Philosophical Review* 101.3.

Korsgaard, Christine. 1989. "Personal Identity and the Unity of Agency: A Kantian Reply to Parfit." *Philosophy and Public Affairs* 18.2.

Kant, I. 1968. *Critique of Pure Reason*, trans. Norman Kemp Smith. New York: St. Martin's Press.

Kant, I. 1959. *Foundations of the Metaphysics of Morals*, trans. Lewis White Beck. Indianapolis: Library of Liberal Arts, Bobbs-Merrill.

Kolak, Daniel and Raymond Martin. 1987. "Personal Identity and Causality: Becoming Unglued." *American Philosophical Quarterly* 24.4.

Kripke, Saul A. 1972. *Naming and Necessity*. Cambridge, Massachusetts: Harvard University Press.

Kuhn, Thomas S. 1962. *The Structure of Scientific Revolutions*. Chicago: The University of Chicago Press.

Lewis, David. 1969. "Survival and Identity." *The Identities of Persons*, ed. A. O. Rorty. Berkeley: University of California Press.

Lewis, David. 1986. *On the Plurality of Worlds*. Oxford: Basil Blackwell.

Locke, John. 1975. *An Essay concerning Human Understanding*, ed. Peter H. Nidditch. Oxford: Clarendon Press.

McGinn, Colin. 1983. *The Subjective View*. Oxford:Clarendon Press.

Mellor, D. H. 1981. *Real Time*. Cambridge: Cambridge University Press.

Merricks, Trenton. 1994. "Endurance and Indiscernability." *The Journal of Philosophy* 91.4.

Mills, Eugene. 1993. "Dividing Without Reducing: Bodily Fission and Personal Identity." *Mind* 102.405.

Myro, George. 1986. "Time and Essence." *Midwest Studies in Philosophy*, Volume XI, eds. P. A. French, T. E. Uehling, Jr. and H. K. Wettwstein. Minneapolis: University of Minnesota Press.

Nagel, Thomas. 1986. *The View From Nowhere*. New York: Oxford University Press.

Noonan, Harold. 1989. *Personal Identity*. London: Routledge.

Nozick, Robert. 1981. *Philosophical Explanations*. Cambridge, Massachusetts: Harvard University Press.

Oderberg, David S. "Johnston on Human Beings." *The Journal of Philosophy* 86.3.

Parfit, Derek. 1976. "Lewis, Perry and What Matters." *The Identities of Persons*, ed. A. O. Rorty. Berkeley: University of California Press.

Parfit, Derek. 1984. *Reasons and Persons*. New York: Oxford University Press.

Perry, John, 1972. "Can the Self Divide?" *The Journal of Philosophy* 69.16.

Perry, John. 1975. "The Problem of Personal Identity." *Personal Identity*, ed. John Perry. Berkeley: University of California Press.

Perry, John, 1976. "The Importance of Being Identical." *The Identities of Persons*, ed. A. O. Rorty. Berkeley: University of California Press.

Plato. 1969. "Republic," 436a-439d, Plato, *The Collected Dialogues*, eds. Edith Hamilton and Huntington Cairns. Princeton: Princeton University Press.

Price, H. H. 1953. *Thinking and Experience*. London: Hutchinson.

Quine, W. V. 1960. *Word and Object*. Cambridge, Massachusetts: M.I.T. Press.

Quine, W. V. 1969. "Replies." *Words and Objections*, eds. D. Davidson and J. Hintikka. Dordrecht: Reidel.

Quine, W. V. 1973. *The Roots of Reference*. La Salle, Illinois: Open Court.

Quine, W. V. 1981. *Theories and Things*. Cambridge, Massachusetts: Harvard University Press.

Rawls, John. 1974. "The Independence of Moral Theory." Presidential Address, Eastern Meeting of the American Philosophical Association, December 28, 1974, printed in *Proceedings and Addresses of the American Philosophical Association* 47.

Reid, Thomas. 1975. *Essays on the Intellectual Powers of Man*, selection reprinted in *Personal Identity*, ed. John Perry. Berkeley: University of California Press.

Robinson, John. 1988. "Personal Identity and Survival." *The Journal of Philosophy* 85.6.

Rovane, Carol. 1990. "Branching Self-Consciousness." *The Philosophical Review* 99.3.

Rovane, Carol. 1993. "Self-Reference: The Radicalization of Locke." *The Journal of Philosophy* 90.3.

Russell, Bertrand. 1954. *The Analysis of Matter*. New York: Dover.

Russell 1956: Bertrand, "On the Nature of Acquaintance." *Logic and Knowledge*, ed. R. C. Marsh. London: Allen and Unwin.

Russell, Bertrand. 1958. *The ABC of Relativity*, revised edition. London: G. Allen & Unwin.

Russell, Bertrand. 1988. "Knowledge by Acquaintance and Knowledge by Description." *Propositions and Attitudes*, ed. Salmon and Soames. New York: Oxford University Press. Originally in *Proceedings of the Aristotelian Society* 11, 1910-1911.

Schwyzer, Hubert. 1990. *The Unity of Understanding, A Study in Kantian Problems*. Oxford: Clarendon Press.

Shoemaker, Sydney. 1963. *Self-Knowledge and Self-Identity*. Ithaca: Cornell University Press.

Shoemaker, Sydney. 1984. Identity, *Cause and Mind*. Cambridge: Cambridge University Press.

Shoemaker, Sydney and Richard Swinburne. 1984. *Personal Identity*. Oxford: Basil Blackwell.

Simons, Peter. 1987. *Parts: A Study in Ontology*. Oxford: Clarendon Press.

Smart, J. J. C. 1972. "Space-Time and Individuals." *Logic and Art*, eds. Richard Rudner and Israel Scheffler. Indianapolis: Bobbs-Merrill.

Stich, Stephen P. 1978. "Beliefs and Subdoxastic States." *Philosophy of Science* 45.4.

Strawson, P. F. 1959. *Individuals: An Essay in Descriptive Metaphysics*. Garden City, New York: Anchor Books, Doubleday & Company, Inc.

Strawson, P. F. 1966. *The Bounds of Sense*. London: Methuen & Co Ltd.

Stroud, Barry. 1977. *Hume*. London, Henley and Boston: Routledge & Kegan Paul.

Thompson, Manley. 1983. "Philosophical Approaches to Categories." *The Monist* 66.

Unger, Peter. 1990. Identity, *Consciousness and Value*. New York: Oxford University Press.

Van Inwagen, Peter. 1990. *Material Beings*. Ithaca: Cornell University Press.

Wheeler, Samuel C. III. 1986. "Persons and Their Microparticles." *Nous* 20.

White, Stephen. 1989. "Metapsychological Relativism and the Self." *The Journal of Philosophy* 86.6.

Wiggins, David. 1968. "On Being in the Same Place at the Same Time." *The Philosophical Review* 77.

Wiggins, David. 1976. "Locke, Butler and the Stream of Consciousness." *The Identities of Persons*, ed. A. Rorty. Berkeley: University of California Press.

Wiggins, David. 1980. *Sameness and Substance*. Cambridge, Massachusetts: Harvard University Press.

Wilkes, Kathleen. 1988. *Real People: Personal Identity Without Thought Experiments*. Oxford: Clarendon Press.

Williams, Bernard. 1973. *Problems of the Self*. Cambridge: Cambridge University Press.

Index